The Allocation of Resources

The Allocation of Resources

Theory and Policy

KENNETH D. GEORGE
Professor of Economics,
University College, Cardiff

and

JOHN SHOREY
Lecturer in Economics,
University College, Cardiff

London
GEORGE ALLEN & UNWIN
Boston   Sydney

First published in 1978

British Library Cataloguing in Publication Data

George, Kenneth Desmond
    The allocation of resources.
    1. Microeconomics
    I. Title II. Shorey, John
    330   HB171   77–30612

    ISBN 0–04–300073–8
    ISBN 0–04–300074–6 Pbk

Printed in Great Britain
in 10 on 11 pt Times
by Biddles Ltd, Guildford, Surrey

Preface

This book has grown out of a course of lectures given for second-and third-year students of economics and assumes that the reader has a reasonable knowledge of basic economics. We have attempted to highlight the main problems of resource allocation in present-day industrial economics. Consequently our approach is not a purely theoretical one, but one that attempts to apply economic analysis to practical problems. A rather wide range of microeconomic issues is covered, but if there is one theme that runs through the book it is that in the analysis of resource allocation problems both efficiency and equity considerations are important.

We should like to thank our colleagues Roy Thomas and Lynn Mainwaring for their comments on some of the chapters. We are greatly indebted to Caroline Joll, who read the whole manuscript in the most painstaking manner and whose valuable criticism led to substantial improvements in the exposition. The manuscript was typed with great skill by Tricia Buckingham, who also displayed an incredible amount of patience in the face of the most unreasonable demands made upon her by the authors.

Contents

10 *Contents*

Chapter 1

Introduction

This volume is concerned with the problem of resource allocation and its implication for public policy. The problem arises because resources are scarce, which makes it essential that they be both fully and efficiently employed. If they are not, the potential of the economic system to generate welfare cannot be fully realised.

The analysis of resource allocation is concerned with the questions of what goods are produced and in what quantities; what methods are used in production and with what factor inputs; and how goods are distributed between consumers. Economic analysis is also concerned with the efficiency with which resource allocation decisions are made. Indeed the starting point of the analysis is the proposition that the principle underlying economic management is the maximisation of total welfare. It follows that resources are efficiently allocated when it is impossible to find some change in output mix, production technology or distribution that will increase total welfare. The analysis of resource allocation is thus concerned with identifying the most efficient production and distribution pattern and with establishing the kinds of decisions that lead to the achievement of maximum efficiency or, at least, to an improvement in efficiency. In order to do this it is necessary to establish precisely what we mean by the concept of welfare, how individual welfare is to be measured and how individual welfares are to be aggregated into a measure of total welfare. It is then possible to answer such questions as: How should consumers allocate their incomes between the various goods and services available so as to maximise their welfare? How should firms combine factors of production so as to minimise costs? How much of each commodity should be produced? And how should output be allocated between consumers?

The issues raised above form the core of that part of economic analysis known as welfare economics. The standard apparatus used in this branch of theory is based on the Pareto value judgement that welfare is increased if one person is made better off and no one worse off. A position of optimality is thus attained when all such possibilities of increasing welfare have been exhausted. As a starting point to our analysis we shall, in Chapter 2, examine the assumptions underlying the analysis of Pareto optimality, the properties of this optimum position, and the conditions that are necessary for such an optimum to be realised. We shall see how a Pareto optimum position will be attained, given certain assumptions, both under universal perfect competition and in a planned economy. At this stage in our analysis we shall assume away the major problems that occur in the real world – problems arising, for instance, from economies of large scale production, and from the existence of social costs and benefits that are not taken into account in the decision making of firms and households. Chapter 3 examines the problem of assessing changes in welfare and discusses the usefulness of the Pareto criterion as a decision rule. There are, of course, difficulties involved in measuring the gains and losses arising from a reallocation of resources – difficulties, that is, of measuring changes in consumer's surplus and factor rents. Since almost any major change will result in some people gaining and others losing, the usefulness of the Pareto criterion is seen to be very limited. Although attempts have been made to devise criteria for assessment that are based only on considerations of efficiency, these attempts have been unsuccessful. When policy changes affect the distribution of income, value judgements relating to equity are bound to be involved in the assessment of change.

In view of the fact that equity as well as efficiency has to be taken into account in assessing the effects of a reallocation of resources, Chapter 4 deals with the distribution of income and wealth. The degree of inequality is examined in the light of official statistics. Particular attention is paid to the way in which positions of great wealth are attained, and to the causes of poverty in modern society. On the policy side three approaches are distinguished: the redistribution of factors, the redistribution of incomes, and government intervention in individual markets. All three approaches demonstrate the inter-relationship between equity and efficiency.

Apart from the fact that efficiency considerations alone cannot indicate the nature of a welfare optimum nor justify a change in the allocation of resources, there are also a whole host of problems or 'imperfections' in real market economies, which require serious modification of the view that the free market mechanism will result in an efficient allocation of resources. One such problem, that of factor indivisibilities, has received a great deal of attention in the literature relating to the pricing and investment policies of public utilities and other nationalised industries. Attention here has focused in particular upon marginal cost pricing, the case for which is based upon the fact that the equality of price and marginal cost will satisfy one of the marginal conditions for achieving a Pareto optimum position. Chapter 5 examines various issues in this area of economic analysis. These include the problem of defining and calculating marginal cost in practice, and of applying marginal cost pricing when capacity is not fully adjusted to demand, when there are peaks in demand and when costs are decreasing. One well-known problem with the decreasing costs situation is that the application of marginal cost pricing under such conditions results in a failure to cover total costs. A number of solutions have been proposed including price discrimination, multipart tariffs and government subsidies. There are problems with each of these solutions. All share the difficulty of measuring costs. In the case of price discrimination and multipart tariffs, there are also problems concerning the number of different prices that should be imposed and the frequency with which prices should be altered in response to changing demand and cost conditions. Where subsidies are involved, the problem of ensuring managerial efficiency may be particularly bothersome. It is important to stress, however, that the problem of managerial efficiency is by no means confined to public enterprises that are in receipt of subsidies, although it may well be more acute in this sector of the economy than in most others.

The whole issue of marginal cost pricing in the public sector raises a host of problems that come under the heading of second best. The basic point is that, if there are sectors of the economy within which the marginal requirements for optimality are not met and for some reason the constraints cannot be removed, then it does not follow that a policy of optimising in other sectors will lead to a more efficient allocation of resources. Given, for instance, the fact that the private manufacturing sector contains monopolistic industries with prices that are to varying degrees in excess of marginal costs and that are likely to remain so, should the government pursue marginal cost pricing policies in the public sector?

The problems arising from factor indivisibilities are not confined to the public sector. Chapter 6 examines the relationship between economies of scale, size and efficiency in the private sector of the economy. One important problem is that when account is taken of economies of scale a conflict may arise between the benefits of standardisation on the one hand and the demand for variety on the other. In some cases there will be a clear advantage in favour of standardisation, as in the case of the production of electrical fittings. In other cases economies of scale will be relatively unimportant and efficient production will be consistent with a large variety. In still other cases, however, there will be instances where the benefits of scale are large and where consumers can have either a restricted choice of commodities at a low price or a greater variety at a higher price. The varied tastes of consumers cannot be fully met, because some will prefer the more standardised system while others will prefer variety.

Economies of scale are not the only factors governing the size of firms. Other factors such as marketing and financial power are also relevant. However, whether it is economies of scale or other factors that explain the size of firms in individual markets, large firms possess market power that will tend to have an adverse effect on resource allocation. Another feature of modern day production is the dominance of very large diversified firms. The emergence of these firms means that administrative decisions taken within firms have increased in importance in comparison with the market mechanism as the means by which resources are allocated. The existence of large diversified firms, including the multinational companies, poses problems for efficient resource allocation that are, given the present state of knowledge, difficult to deal with.

A great part of the theory of resource allocation is a static theory that takes no account of the problems of adjustment. In Chapter 7 we look at some of these problems and in particular attempt to answer the following questions. First, how efficient is the market system in adjusting to short run changes in demand? Second, how efficient will the system be in making long run adjustments of capacity to changes in demand? Third, whatever the efficiency of the competitive system in allocating a given set of commodities on the basis of given techniques of production, how efficient is it in generating new techniques and new commodities through the process of invention and innovation? Fourth, how efficient is the market mechanism in effecting major structural changes in the economy in response to changes in competitive conditions?

The prices and marginal costs that are established in freely competitive markets reflect only private benefits and costs. If, however, in the process of production certain costs are imposed upon others and no compensation is paid, or certain benefits are conferred but no payment is received, then market prices will no longer be an accurate indicator of the value of goods to society. This important problem of externalities, and the closely related issue of the provision of public goods, is the subject matter of Chapter 8. All industrial economies generate various forms of pollution that are not adequately taken into account by the price mechanism. These include pollution of air and water, noise pollution and urban congestion. A number of possible policy approaches exist for dealing with such problems. For instance, the government could introduce a tax that brings prices more closely into line with social costs. Alternatively, quantitative regulations could be introduced to hold down the level of pollution to some predetermined level. These and other measures will be examined and their relative merits assessed.

A public good is an extreme form of externality. Examples include national defence, the police force and public parks. These goods either cannot be supplied on the basis of individual purchases in the market or, even if they could, would not be supplied in optimal quantities. Thus public goods have to be supplied communally and financed either by means of voluntary contributions or out of taxation.

Of course in many economies the number of goods and services supplied by the government and financed by taxation is not restricted to those that cannot be incorporated effectively into the market system. Considerable argument rages, for instance, over the provision of health and education services, not to mention certain manufacturing activities. The argument for these activities being in the public sector may rest on the existence of important externalities: on considerations of equity, on the view that in some cases the consumer is not the best judge of his own well-being, or on the inability of the market system to supply sufficient finance for the efficient provision of the commodity or service.

The problems of externalities and dynamic adjustment are relevant not only to individual industries. They may also apply to a group of industries and are at the heart of the regional problem. If the regional allocation of resources took place quickly and smoothly and on the basis of social costs and benefits, there would be no economic basis for a regional policy other than leaving things to the market. However, government intervention would be justified, even if a socially efficient allocation of resources would ultimately be achieved, if the adjustment of the economy to equilibrium was very slow. In practice, a further justification for intervention exists because the market does not lead to an efficient allocation of resources due to the divergence between private and social costs.

The final topic, discussed in Chapter 9, is cost–benefit analysis. This is a method of investment appraisal used in the public sector. It differs from investment appraisal in the private sector in that it deals with social rather than private costs and benefits. A private firm does not have to take into account the external costs that its investment inflicts upon others. These costs would, however, be included in a cost–benefit study. As another example, a private firm's investment might result in the employment of hitherto unemployed workers, who would otherwise have remained unemployed for the duration of the life of the project. In its profit and loss calculations the firm would include the cost of that labour valued at the wage paid. The social opportunity cost of this labour, however, would be lower than the wage, and it is this lower figure that would be relevant to cost–benefit analysis. Investment in the private and public sectors differs, therefore, not only in terms of the range of items included but also in the way that some of these items are valued.

Chapter 2

Optimal Allocation and Economic Welfare

2.1 INTRODUCTION

Every society possesses a limited and, at least in the short term, a fixed quantity of economic resources. These resources, or factors of production, as they are often called, are the inputs to the production process, from which a vast quantity of economic goods and services emerge, ultimately going to satisfy consumers' wants in one form or another. The total quantity of economic resources at any point in time is made up of a great variety of heterogeneous items, which can only loosely be ascribed to one or other of the four recognised categories: land, labour, capital and enterprise. At the same time the potential diversity of economic commodities is limited only by the ingenuity and the current technological know-how of the human mind.

One of the first propositions put before students of economics is that consumers' economic wants are insatiable. As a working generalisation it is assumed that every member of the community always prefers more to less commodities. In consequence there can never be enough goods in total to go round. This implies that the supply of factors of production can never be sufficient to meet the demand for them unless some kind of rationing device is employed. Economic resources can thus be said to be scarce, a proposition that provides us with one of the many alternative definitions of economics as a social science discipline. It is in part a study of how and to what effect society develops a system of production and distribution to cope with the problem of scarcity.

Students, who very early on have been introduced to Galbraithian ideas on the deliberate creation and manipulation of consumers' wants by producers, may find the notion of scarcity within developed economies somewhat difficult to accept. Are not many wants artificially manufactured by the considerable advertising machine, by the fashion cultivation of the mass media, by extensive recourse to built-in obsolescence and product differentiation, and by the ever easy exploitation of primitive fears about safety, health and status at the individual or national level? The answer must be that all these things do certainly play a part in exacerbating scarcity, especially in relation to certain commodities. However, though we cannot prove it conclusively, such factors alone cannot explain the existence of scarcity. It is unfortunately impossible to decide upon the degree to which such want creation is important, simply because it is so difficult to visualise the extent and structure of economic wants without such artifices and to foresee what, if anything, might take their place. We shall assume throughout this book that scarcity is a genuine economic problem for every society, however structured. The only support we can provide for this assumption is purely impressionistic. Consider any individual, with whatever political, social and economic persuasions and with a degree of susceptibility to advertising, fashion, status, tradition, etc. Imagine the list of goods and services that that person would, according to his or her particular preferences and priorities, wish to provide for each member of society. It would be very surprising if, in the vast majority of instances, the economic resources required to produce the contents of this list under present-day technical conditions did not greatly exceed the quantity available.

The problem of scarcity might be resolved or at least reduced in importance if certain wants could be deliberately ignored. In fact, however, scarcity cannot be sidestepped as easily as this, for we shall assume that one of the fundamental principles upon which our economic system is built states that all consumers shall have some direct influence upon the way in which resources are allocated. This principle of consumer sovereignty logically complements the basic objective assumed to govern the management of economic relationships in our society: that resources should be allocated so as to meet the economic wants of all its members, as consumers, as fully as possible.

Given, then, that economic resources are scarce, there arise the inevitable problems of choice. Decisions must be taken as to which alternative production processes are to be used in making each good, which goods are to be produced and in what quantities, and how a given quantity of final goods and services are to be allocated among consumers. Furthermore, since we aim to fulfil consumers' wants as fully as possible, it is essential that production and allocation be carried out as efficiently as possible. Let us, with the aid of a diagram, examine this problem of maximising economic efficiency a little further. Figure 2.1 shows a production possibility curve for a simple economy in which there is a fixed quantity of factors of production available for the production of two goods, x and y. This curve shows, for a given quantity of one good, the maximum amount of the other good that can be produced with the available factors of production and the current state of technology. Thus combinations such as *R* and *S* are just attainable. Combinations such as *N* are also attainable, since they lie within the production frontier, but combinations such as *P* are unattainable, since they require more resources than are available. The downward slope of the production possibility curve shows that there is an opportunity cost of producing an additional amount of either product. Suppose that there is a change in the pattern of production from *S* to *R*. This means an increase of *ab* in the production of *y*, the opportunity cost of which is a reduction of *cd* in the production of *x*.

Figure 2.1

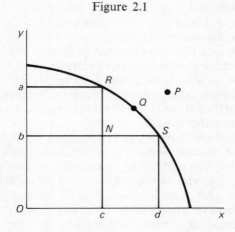

At point *N* the economy is within the production possibility curve, and it is possible, therefore, for more of both goods to be produced with the available resources. This would be the outcome if, for instance, there was a move from *N* to *Q*, and, assuming that more goods are preferred to less, such a move would increase welfare. The question arises, however, as to why the economy should be at point *N* in the first place. The answer may be that there are unemployed resources, or that resources are inefficiently used in production even though all resources are being employed. We shall concentrate on the second possibility, since the assumption of full employment will be made throughout. Inefficient production may arise because the factors of production are not, given their relative prices, being combined in the best possible manner. Alternatively, such inefficiency can come about because, although the most efficient production techniques are being used, there are problems of control in their day-to-day operation. So long as it is possible to increase the production of one good without producing less of another, merely by making better use of existing factors, production is technologically inefficient. This is always the case for any point inside the production possibility frontier. Only at points on the frontier, therefore, do we have efficient production.

In addition to the problem of efficient production, or technological efficiency, there is the problem of the efficient allocation of output between consumers. Given the distribution of income, a collection of goods will be efficiently allocated if it is impossible to increase total welfare, defined as a weighted sum of individual welfare, by reallocating goods between consumers.

Technological and allocative efficiency are still insufficient to define economic efficiency fully. For every technologically efficient combination of outputs along the transformation curve, such as *R* and *S* in Figure 2.1, there is an efficient allocation of the two goods. A choice has to be made between points such as *R* and *S*, and overall efficiency is attained at that combination of outputs which combines technological and allocative efficiency with the highest level of total consumer welfare. In order to identify that output combination a social welfare function has to be specified – that is, we have to define what we mean by individual welfare, and how individual welfares are to be weighted in the total. The social welfare function must also contain a statement about what constitutes a socially acceptable distribution of welfare. Which output combination is finally chosen will depend crucially upon this statement about distributive justice. Questions of the best output mix and considerations of equity are, therefore, inseparable.

In the next section the necessary conditions for an efficient allocation of resources to be realised are considered. Producing such a set of rules clearly necessitates *a priori* assumptions as to the form of the social welfare function. The rules that are set out are based upon the Paretian approach to economic welfare. Section 2.3 considers the attainment of Pareto efficiency in both market and planned economies. In section 2.4 are highlighted the limitations of the Pareto analysis, especially in its treatment of the distribution issue. In the final section our analysis is extended to include international trade and intertemporal allocative decisions.

2.2 THE PARETO OPTIMUM

The standard analysis used by economists for evaluating the efficiency of resource allocation is based upon the value judgement, associated with the Italian economist Vilfredo Pareto, that economic welfare is increased if one person is made better off and no-one is made worse off. Similarly, welfare is decreased if a change results in one person becoming worse off and no one better off. 'Better off' and 'worse off' mean increased or decreased utility associated with a change in the consumption of goods and services. Thus if one person's consumption increases and no-one else has to suffer a reduction, utility has increased. This in turn is assumed to be directly related to economic welfare, so that we may speak of an increase in the economic welfare of society. In an optimum position it is not possible to reorganise resources so as to make some person better off without making another worse off. An optimum position has the property that the collection of goods produced, valued at the equilibrium set of prices, has a higher value than that of any alternative collection that could be produced with the available resources.

Our analysis is based on the following assumptions:

1   An individual is considered to be the best judge of his own well-being, and thus a move from one position to another that he freely chooses to make will bring about an increase in his utility. Each individual's goal is to maximise utility. This ethical judgement attaches prime importance to individualism and underlies most of welfare economics.

2   An individual's utility depends only on the commodities that he consumes and on the factor services that he supplies. His utility is not in any way affected by the commodities consumed and factor services supplied by other people.

3   The costs of production of any one firm are dependent entirely on that firm's output and are in no way affected by activities external to the firm. This together with assumption (2) implies that there are no external economies or diseconomies in consumption or production. In other words, all benefits and costs are fully reflected in market prices.

4   All functions are continuous, are differentiable and have the 'right' shapes; i.e. indifference curves are convex and transformation curves are concave to the origin. Thus there are no problems caused by the presence of indivisibilities.

5   Complete information is available to individual decision-making units as to the choices open to them.

6   The supply of factors is fixed and independent of the distribution of income.

7   There is a given state of technical knowledge.

8   Full employment will be assumed throughout.

9   Initially we shall also be restricting our analysis to a closed economy and abstracting from the problem of time.

On the basis of these highly simplifying assumptions, the conditions required to achieve a Pareto optimum can now be examined. Since a Pareto improvement can result either from reallocating factors among goods, or from redistributing goods among consumers, or from changing the composition of the output mix, we shall present the conditions in the form of a series of marginal equalities under three main headings: the production optimum, the exchange optimum, and overall optimality.

2.21 *The Production Optimum*

The production optimum is concerned with the optimal use of resources in producing given outputs, and the optimum position is attained where it is impossible to increase the output of one commodity without decreasing that of another. What conditions need to be satisfied for this position to be reached?

Optimal Allocation between Products. First, for any two factors i and j used in the production of commodities x and y, the optimal allocation of the factors is where the ratio of the marginal physical products (MPP) of i and j in the production of x equals the corresponding ratio for y; that is,

$$\frac{\text{MPP}_i{}^x}{\text{MPP}_j{}^x} = \frac{\text{MPP}_i{}^y}{\text{MPP}_j{}^y}$$

This must be so whether the products are produced in different industries or are produced as different lines of activity within the firm. If this equality does not hold, production can be increased by a rearrangement of factors. For instance, if the marginal products of i and j in the production of x and y are as follows:

	x	y
MPP of i	10	4
MPP of j	4	2

a movement of 1 unit of i out of the production of y into that of x decreases the production of y by 4 units and increases that of x by 10 units, whereas a movement of 2 units of j out of the production of x into that of y decreases the output of x by 8 units and increases that of y by 4 units. The net result is an unchanged output of y but an increase in the output of x by 2 units. Whenever the ratio of the marginal products of two factors in alternative uses is unequal, it is always possible by switching factor inputs around to increase the output of one or both commodities.

The same result can be shown in terms of equality between marginal rates of technical substitution (MTS). The marginal condition for an optimal allocation of two factors i and j in the production of two products x and y then becomes

$$\text{MTS}_{ij}{}^x = \text{MTS}_{ij}{}^y$$

That is, the marginal rate of technical substitution between i and j in the production of x must be equal to that in the production of y. Figure 2.2 will help to explain why this must be so. The dimensions of the box measure the available quantities of the two factors i and j. The curve x_1 shows the different combinations of the two factors that are capable of producing a given quantity of x. Thus x_1 of x can be produced by using factor inputs in the combination i_2 and j_1, or the combination i_1 and j_2, or any other combination indicated by the co-ordinates of each point on curve x_1. Curve x_2 shows the different combinations of i and j that can produce another, greater, quantity of x, and so on. Analogous equiproduct

Figure 2.2

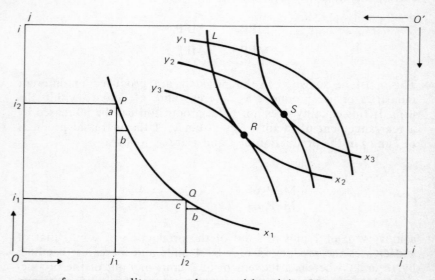

curves for commodity y are drawn with origin O', and the higher subscripts again denote higher output levels. The curves are downward sloping to show that if less of one factor is used, to maintain the same output more of the other will have to be used. The slope of the curves measures the marginal rate of technical substitution between the two factors, and is shown to be diminishing; that is, each curve is drawn convex to the origin, so that the slope of the curves decreases as we move from left to right. The economic meaning of this is seen by comparing points P and Q. At P the production of x_1 is achieved by using a lot of i and little j. If the input of j is increased by an amount equal to b, then the amount of i needed will be smaller by amount a. At point Q, however, if the amount of j used is increased by the same extent b, then the extent to which the use of i can be reduced will be much less than a and equal to c. As we move down the curve x_1, therefore, we find that each successive unit employed of factor j replaces decreasing amounts of factor i. In other words, the more intensively factor j is used in production, the more difficult it is to substitute it for the other factor. This results from the fact that the factors are not perfect substitutes. Thus we have a diminishing marginal rate of technical substitution of j for i. Similarly, as we move upwards along the curve we have a diminishing marginal rate of substitution of i for j.

Consider now point L in Figure 2.2. Clearly this cannot be an optimum position in the allocation of the two factors. At L it is possible to produce x_2 of x and y_1 of y, but a movement from L to point R would result in a larger output of y with unchanged production of x, and a movement to S would result in increased production of both commodities. At L the two factors are not being used optimally because at this point the marginal rates of technical substitution of the factors in the production of x and y, as shown by the slopes of curves x_2 and y_1, are not equal. As we have shown, it is possible to move from point L to other points such as R and S where the output of one or both of the products can be increased. Point R, however, is an optimal position, and so is point S, since here the marginal rates of technical substitution are equal, and from points such as these the output of one product can be increased only by reducing that of another. Transferred to a diagram in output space, points of tangency such as R and S provide us with the production possibility curve drawn in Figure 2.1. The problem of choosing between output combinations such as R and S will concern us later.

Optimal Allocation between Firms. In addition to the optimal allocation of factors between the production of different products there must also be an optimal allocation between firms. This brings us to another marginal rule which is that, for optimality, the marginal rate of product transformation (MRT) (that is, the amount of commodity y that has to be given up for one additional unit of x) must be the same for all firms in which both are produced; that is,

$$\mathrm{MRT}_{xy}{}^{A} \;=\; \mathrm{MRT}_{xy}{}^{B}$$

If this is not so, then a rearrangement of output between firms will increase total output. Suppose, for example, that the marginal rates of transformation in firms A and B are as follows:

$$\text{Firm } A: 3y \text{ for } 1x$$
$$\text{Firm } B: 2y \text{ for } 1x$$

By producing 1 unit less of x, firm A could produce an additional 3 units of y, whereas by producing 1 additional unit of x, firm B would sacrifice 2 units of y. The net result would be an unchanged total production of x and 1 additional unit of y.

The marginal rate of transformation of x into y is in fact equal to the ratio of their marginal costs. To see this, assume that the marginal cost of $x = £8$ and that of $y = £4$. Thus 1 extra unit of x would add £8 to costs, and to save this amount the production of y would have to fall by 2 units. The marginal rate of transformation, in other words, is 2:1, which is the same as the ratio of the marginal costs. This marginal rule for efficiency in production can therefore be stated in terms of the equality of marginal cost (MC) ratios:

$$\frac{\text{MC}_x{}^A}{\text{MC}_y{}^A} = \frac{\text{MC}_x{}^B}{\text{MC}_y{}^B}$$

That is, the ratio of the marginal costs of producing any two commodities x and y in firm A must be the same as the corresponding ratio in firm B.

2.22 *The Exchange Optimum*

Given the amounts of the various commodities produced, how are these commodities to be divided up among consumers? The exchange optimum is attained when it is impossible by means of exchange to make one person better off without making another worse off. This requires that for any two commodities and any two consumers the ratio of the marginal utilities (MU) of the two commodities must be the same. That is, for two consumers L and M and two commodities x and y we must have

$$\frac{\text{MU}_x{}^L}{\text{MU}_y{}^L} = \frac{\text{MU}_x{}^M}{\text{MU}_y{}^M}$$

Alternatively, the marginal condition may be stated in terms of the marginal rate of substitution between the two products. The optimal condition is then achieved when for any two consumers the marginal rates of substitution (MRS) between any two commodities are equal; that is

$$\mathrm{MRS}_{xy}{}^{L} \;=\; \mathrm{MRS}_{xy}{}^{M}$$

If this equality does not hold, then it is possible for at least one of the two consumers to benefit by exchange without making the other worse off. For instance, if consumer L is willing to exchange $1x$ for $1 \cdot 5y$, and if consumer M's rate of exchange is $1x$ for $1 \cdot 8y$, then both can gain by exchanging at the rate of $1x$ for $1 \cdot 7y$.

The marginal condition relating to the allocation of commodities among consumers can be represented geometrically in a similar way to the optimal allocation of factors. In Figure 2.3 the dimensions of the box represent the amount of the two commodities x and y to be allocated between the two consumers L and M. These

Figure 2.3

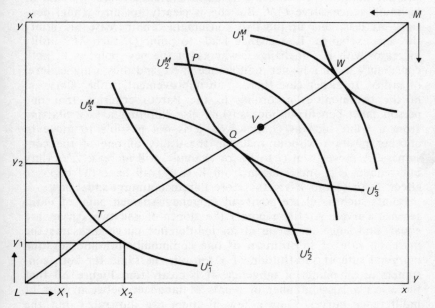

amounts correspond to a point such as Q on the production possibility frontier shown in Figure 2.1. The curves $U_1{}^{L}$, $U_2{}^{L}$, etc. represent the indifference map of consumer L, and the curves $U_1{}^{M}$, $U_2{}^{M}$, etc. represent the indifference map of consumer M. Each curve represents combinations of the two commodities that give the consumer the same level of satisfaction or utility and between which, therefore, he is indifferent. Thus looking at indifference curve $U_1{}^L$, consumer L is indifferent between the combinations of commodities x_1y_2 and x_2y_1, because both sets give him the same utility. The level of utility increases as the consumer gets on to a higher indifference curve. Consumer L therefore achieves higher levels of utility as he moves further away from the south-west corner of the box, and consumer M's utility increases as he moves further away from the north-east corner of the box.

The shape of each indifference curve shows that, if the consumer gets more of one commodity, then to maintain the same level of utility he must have less of the other. And each curve is drawn convex to the origin, indicating a diminishing marginal rate of substitution of x for y. In other words, as we move down the indifference curve $U_1{}^L$, say, with consumer L increasing his consumption of x, he is prepared to give up less and less y for each additional unit of x.

Now consider point P in Figure 2.3. With this allocation of the two commodities, consumer L is on indifference curve $U_3{}^L$ and M on indifference curve $U_2{}^M$. But this is clearly not an optimal position. At least one of the two consumers can increase his utility through exchange. If exchange leads to point Q, then M's utility increases with L's unchanged, whereas if the new point is V, both consumers attain a higher indifference curve and thus a higher level of utility. In either case there is an improvement in the allocation of the commodities according to the Pareto criterion that one person must benefit without anyone else suffering a loss. Starting from a point such as Q, however, it is not possible to move to another position without reducing the utility of one of the consumers. A move from Q to V, for example, will increase L's utility but reduce M's, and a move from V to Q will have the opposite effect. Both Q and V are therefore Pareto optimum situations.

Points such as Q are points of tangency between pairs of indifference curves. At these points the slopes of the two curves are equal, and since the slope of an indifference curve measures the marginal rate of substitution of one commodity for another, the marginal rate of substitution of x for y is the same for both consumers at all points of tangency. It is clear from Figure 2.3 that there are a large number of points of tangency between pairs of indifference curves. Only a few of them are illustrated, but the locus of all these points gives the 'contract curve'. All points on the contract curve are Pareto optimum points, differing from one another only in terms of the allocation of the commodities between the two consumers. The allocation of commodities may be as shown by point W, in which case consumer L gets the giant's share, or it may be as at point T, in which case M is well off and L is badly off. This raises considerations of equity, which will concern us later.

2.23 *Overall Optimality*

Given that the conditions necessary for the attainment of the production and exchange optima are met, one further condition is necessary for the attainment of overall Pareto optimality. This condition determines the relative quantities of the two commodities produced, and states that for resources to be optimally allocated between two commodities x and y the following equality must hold between the ratios of the marginal utilities and of the marginal costs of x and y:

$$\frac{MU_x}{MU_y} = \frac{MC_x}{MC_y}$$

Alternatively,

$$MRS_{xy} = MRT_{xy}$$

That is, the marginal rate of substitution between x and y in exchange must equal the marginal rate of transformation in production. Figure 2.4 shows one optimal position; the slope of the transformation curve at R is equal to the common slope of the indifference curves at T.

Figure 2.4 Figure 2.5

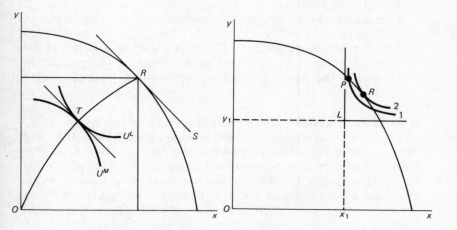

To see why this equality must hold, suppose that the $MRS_{xy} \neq MRT_{xy}$, that the former is $1y = 2x$ and the latter $1y = 4x$. If the production of y is reduced by 1 unit, this will allow the production of x to be increased by 4 units. Let the unit of y be taken from consumer M and replaced by 2 units of x. This will leave M as well off as he was before the change. However, there are now 2 additional units of x that are available to increase the utility of either or both consumers.

The same result is shown in a different way in Figure 2.5. The indifference map of one consumer, L, is superimposed on the diagram showing the production frontier, so that x_1 and y_1 represent the amounts of x and y respectively that are available to all other consumers. Movement along the part of the production frontier that lies 'within' the indifference map of consumer L thus affects only the combination of x and y available to L. Now consider point P. This is clearly not an optimal point, because without any loss of utility to other consumers the utility of consumer L can be increased by a movement along the production frontier from P to R, that is, by the production of more x and less y. Point R is an optimal position, since any movement away from this point will place consumer L on a lower indifference curve. At R the slopes of the indifference curve and of the transformation curve are equal; that is, the marginal rate of substitution equals the marginal rate of transformation.

To summarise, therefore, the following conditions must be met to attain a Pareto optimum:

1 The economy must be on the production frontier (efficiency in production).
2 Consumers must be on the contract curve (efficiency in exchange).
3 The common slope of the indifference curves at a point on the contract curve must be equal to the slope of the production frontier at the point representing the commodity bundle that is produced.

2.24 *Utility Possibility Curves and the Welfare Frontier*
The position of overall Pareto optimality is further illustrated using the concept of the utility possibility curve. It is convenient to describe this concept now, because further use will be made of it when we come to assess the welfare consequences of a change in the allocation of resources in the next chapter. The utility possibility curve is derived by transforming the contract curve, which is in terms of commodity bundles, into utility space. Take, for instance point R in Figure 2.4, which represents one combination of commodities x and y that lies on the production frontier. Starting from point R in the diagram, as we move along the contract curve towards point O, consumer M is moving on to higher and higher indifference curves and consumer L on to lower and lower indiffer-

ence curves; that is, *M*'s utility is increasing and *L*'s is decreasing. This information is shown by the utility possibility curve L_3M_1 in Figure 2.6. The point where this curve touches the vertical axis

Figure 2.6

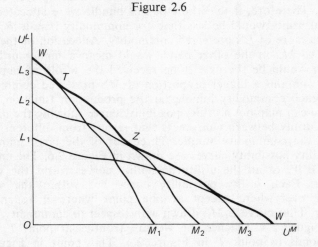

corresponds to point *R* in Figure 2.4. The total bundle of goods is allocated to *L*, and thus *L*'s utility level is at a maximum. As we move away from this point and allocate more and more of the commodity bundle to *M*, consumer *L*'s utility falls and *M*'s increases until we reach the point where the total bundle is allocated to *M*, and the utility possibility curve touches the horizontal axis. The utility possibility curve is negatively sloped, indicating that with a given bundle of commodities the utility of one consumer can only be increased at the expense of some other consumer. The height of the utility possibility curve has no economic meaning, since the utility of both consumers is measured with respect to an arbitrarily selected ordinal index of utility, so that where the curve touches the axes depends on the index of utility chosen.

Utility possibility curve L_3M_1 refers to one particular commodity bundle, *R*, in Figure 2.4. Clearly, there will be a different utility possibility curve associated with each point along the production frontier. Take, for instance, point *S* in Figure 2.4. For this commodity bundle the utility possibility curve will be L_2M_2. The reason that this curve cuts the other from below – starting at a lower point on the vertical axis and finishing at a point further along the horizontal axis – is found in the assumption that the two consumers have different tastes. In Figure 2.4 the indifference curves of consumers *L* and *M* have been drawn so as to indicate that *L* prefers commodity *y* to commodity *x*, whereas *M* has a preference for *x*, in the sense that at any efficient price ratio, such as the one at point T, the purchases of each consumer contain more of the preferred good. Now at point S, more of x and less of y is produced; that is, the commodity bundle contains less of L's preferred commodity. Therefore, if the whole of this bundle were allocated to L, his total utility would be less than for commodity bundle R, which contains more of L's preferred commodity. Allocation of the entire bundle to M, on the other hand, would mean a higher utility for M than would be the case if he received the whole of bundle R, since S contains a higher proportion of M's preferred commodity.

For each commodity bundle on the production function, therefore, we can map out a utility possibility curve showing the distribution of utility between consumers that results from different allocation of the commodity bundle. Three out of the large number of such utility possibility curves are drawn in Figure 2.6. The envelope curve, WW, of all the utility possibility curves forms the welfare frontier. Each utility possibility curve lies within the welfare frontier everywhere except at one point where it touches the frontier. Thus curve L_3M_1, drawn with respect to commodity bundle R in Figure 2.4, touches the welfare frontier at point T, which corresponds to point T in Figure 2.4. This point in Figure 2.6 represents the distribution of utilities for which commodity bundle R is optimal. Similarly, the utility possibility curve L_2M_2 is drawn with respect to commodity bundle S in Figure 2.4, and point Z on this curve represents the distribution of utilities for which commodity bundle S is Pareto optimal. For every distribution of utilities, therefore, there is a different Pareto optimum point.

We can summarise the analysis so far by saying that for maximum economic efficiency the economy must be at some point on the welfare frontier. On the welfare frontier all the marginal conditions are satisfied, and it is not possible to make any person better off without making someone else worse off. However, *any* point on the welfare frontier is Pareto optimal. The analysis therefore cannot tell us which particular point on the welfare frontier, and thus which particular distribution of utility, is superior to all others. This involves the question of distributive justice, and we shall return to it later.

2.3　THE ATTAINMENT OF OPTIMALITY

Having considered the conditions for Pareto optimality, we now turn to the question of what adjustment mechanisms exist that will bring about a Pareto optimal position. We shall see that, in principle, optimality can be achieved as a result of the operations of a freely competitive system or as the outcome of a decentralised planning process. In both cases we maintain the nine assumptions on which the analysis of the previous section was based. We turn first to the case of free competition.

2.31 *The Freely Competitive Economy*

It can be shown that a freely competitive system in which all consumers are utility maximisers and all firms are profit maximisers will, in long term equilibrium, fulfil the various marginal conditions outlined in section II. The necessary characteristics of the system are as follows. First, that there are a large number of buyers and sellers in each market, so that no single buyer or seller can influence the price of any product or factor. Furthermore, there is no collusion between buyers or sellers, and every decision maker in the system is therefore a price taker. Second, the prices that buyers and sellers face are those established at long term equilibrium. Third, there is freedom of entry and exit into and out of all markets. Fourth, every buyer and seller is informed of the price offers made by others.

The Attainment of Production Optimality. Let us first explain how such a competitive system will result in the attainment of the production optimum. Take, for instance, the requirement that, in the production of two commodities x and y, factors of production have to be combined so that their marginal rate of technical substitution is the same for both commodities. Let the amount of commodity x to be produced equal 100 units. Figure 2.7(a) shows the isoquant curve for $100x$, that is, the various combinations of the two factors that is just sufficient to produce this amount of x. The firm must find the least cost way of doing this.

Figure 2.7

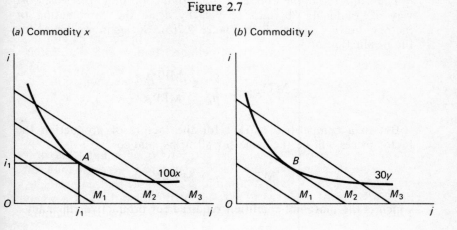

(*a*) Commodity *x*　　　　　　　　(*b*) Commodity *y*

The curves labelled M_1, M_2 and M_3 are isocost curves, that is, the combinations of the two factors i and j that, given the prices of the factors, can be purchased with a given sum of money. They are drawn as straight lines because of the assumption that the prices of the factors are the same whatever the quantities used by the firm. The relative prices of the factors are shown by the slope of the isocost line. As drawn, the price of i is twice that of j, so that a given sum of money will purchase twice as many units of j as of i. Clearly, the firm would not be able to produce $100x$ with a money expenditure of M_1. It is equally clear that it could do so with expenditure M_3, but that this would involve needless waste. The most efficient way of producing $100x$ is in fact by using combination $i_1 j_1$ of the two factors, which combination the firm can employ at a cost of M_2. This combination of factors occurs at point A where the isocost curve is tangential to the isoquant curve. The slope of the former measures the price ratio of the factors, and the slope of the latter gives the marginal rate of technical substitution. Thus we have

$$\mathrm{MTS}_{ij}{}^x = \frac{p_i}{p_j}$$

Alternatively, in terms of marginal physical products, the same result can be written as

$$\frac{\mathrm{MPP}_i{}^x}{\mathrm{MPP}_j{}^x} = \frac{p_i}{p_j}$$

The same reasoning applies to the production of y: the least cost way of producing 80 units of y is by using the combination of factors shown at point B in Figure 2.7(b). So again we have, for the production of y,

$$\mathrm{MTS}_{ij}{}^y = \frac{p_i}{p_j} = \frac{\mathrm{MPP}_i{}^y}{\mathrm{MPP}_j{}^y}$$

But in a competitive market for the factors of production the factor prices will be the same for all firms, and so

$$\mathrm{MTS}_{ij}{}^x = \mathrm{MTS}_{ij}{}^y$$

which is the marginal condition required for productive efficiency.

The Attainment of Exchange Optimality. A similar analysis shows how an exchange optimum will be attained. Consider any individual L, allocating his income between two commodities x and y in such a way as to maximise utility. L's preferences are shown by the indifference map in Figure 2.8(a). His income is indicated by the line y_6x_4 – his budget constraint. Thus if L spent all his income on commodity y, he could purchase y_6 units of y, and if he spent it all on commodity x, he would be able to buy x_4 units of x. Consumer L is able to purchase any combination of the two commodities indicated by points along the budget line. In other words, this line is a locus of all the combinations of x and y that can be purchased for the same amount of money, and since by assumption the prices of both commodities are fixed, the budget constraint will be a straight line. The slope of the budget line gives the ratio of the prices of the two commodities.

Figure 2.8

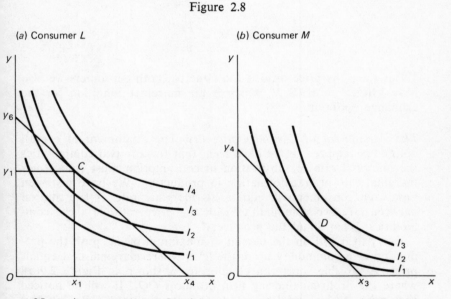

(a) Consumer L (b) Consumer M

Now since consumer L wishes to maximise utility he will want to be on the highest indifference curve possible, subject to the constraint imposed by his budget. This means he will choose point C and combination x_1y_1 of the two commodities. The point that maximises L's utility is the one where the budget line is tangential to indifference curve I_3. Therefore, at point C the slopes of the budget line and of the indifference curve are equal. The former measures the price (p) ratio of the two commodities, whereas the latter measures L's marginal rate of substitution between x and y. At C, therefore, we have, for consumer L,

$$\mathrm{MRS}_{xy}{}^{L} = \frac{p_x}{p_y}$$

Exactly the same reasoning applies to consumer M, whose preferences and budget line are shown in Figure 2.8(b). The preferences of M as shown by the shape of his indifference map are quite different from those of L. His income is also different and, as drawn, is clearly lower than L's income. The only thing that is common to both consumers is the slope of the budget line, because both face the same prices for the two commodities. By the same reasoning as before, consumer M will choose point D, which brings him on to the highest attainable indifference curve. And, as before, we have for M

$$\mathrm{MRS}_{xy}{}^{M} = \frac{p_x}{p_y}$$

But since the price ratio is the same for both consumers we also have $\mathrm{MRS}_{xy}{}^{L} = \mathrm{MRS}_{xy}{}^{M}$, which is the marginal condition for the exchange optimum.

The Attainment of Overall Optimality. The attainment of overall optimality requires, as we have seen, that for any two commodities the marginal rate of substitution in consumption must equal their marginal rate of transformation in production. We have just seen how each consumer will equate his marginal rate of substitution between any two commodities with the price ratio of these commodities. What about the producers?

Every firm will, in the pursuit of maximum profit, push the production of a commodity up to the level where marginal cost equals price. A possible short run equilibrium is shown in Figure 2.9(a), where the profit-maximising firm produces OQ_2. It will be noticed that price is also equal to marginal cost at output OQ_1, but this output would maximise losses rather than profits. This is one specific illustration of the fact that second-order as well as first-order conditions must be satisfied for optimality, or as we put, that all curves must have the 'right' shapes. In this case the first-order condition is that price equals marginal cost, and the second-order condition is that the marginal cost curve be positively sloped at the point of intersection with the demand curve.

Figure 2.9

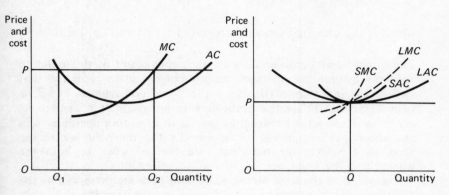

(*a*) Short run equilibrium

(*b*) Long run equilibrium

In the short-run profit-maximising position, however, there are opportunities for further expansion of the industry. The fact that price is greater than unit cost will mean that supernormal profits are being earned, and this will attract new entry. In long run equilibrium, all profitable opportunities for expanding production will have been exhausted and each firm will be in the position shown in Figure 2.9(*b*), with price equal to both short- and long-run marginal cost. This will be the case for the production of all commodities, so that for any two of them we have

$$\frac{\text{MC}_x}{\text{MC}_y} = \frac{p_x}{p_y}$$

In section II we noted that the ratio of marginal costs for any two commodities is equal to their marginal rate of transformation. This means that in a competitive market system

$$\text{MRT}_{xy} = \frac{p_x}{p_y}$$

However, the price ratio of the two commodities is the same as that faced by consumers, since by assumption the price of any commodity is the same for all producers and consumers. Thus we see that in maximising utility consumers equate their marginal rate of substitution of x for y to the price ratio, and that in maximising profits producers equate the marginal rate of transformation of x

for y to the price ratio. Since the latter is the same to both sides, we have

$$MRS_{xy} = MRT_{xy}$$

which is the marginal condition required for overall optimality.

The Supply and Value of Labour. It is convenient at this point to drop the assumption of fixed factor supplies and to recognise that one factor input in particular – the supply of labour – can be varied. We can relate the profit-maximising goals of a firm to its decisions in the labour market as well as to its output decisions, and also show that labour will be employed up to the point where the wage paid reflects the marginal valuation of work to both the worker and the employer.

The value to the firm of one extra unit of a factor service is the addition to total output that will result from employing that unit, times the price at which the output can be sold. That is, the marginal value product (MVP) equals the marginal physical product times the price of the product. Thus if 1 extra unit of factor services increases the output of good x by 5 units per period, and if each unit of output can be sold for £3, then the marginal value product is £15. If the factor service costs less than £15 to employ it will pay the firm to employ additional units. For profit maximisation, employment will be carried to the point where the marginal value product equals the factor price, that is, where

$$MVP_i = MPP_i^x \times p_x = p_i$$

On the supply side, the suppliers of factor services have to decide on the amount of work to offer, and they do this by weighing the advantages of income against the burden of work. An individual's choice can be illustrated with the aid of Figure 2.10, where income is measured on the vertical axis and time, which can be divided into work and leisure, on the horizontal axis. The straight line is the budget line, and points on it represent combinations of income and leisure that are available to the individual. The slope of the budget line represents the wage rate. The curve in the diagram is the worker's indifference curve between income and leisure, and the slope of this curve represents the marginal rate of substitution between time and money income. This shows us, in other words, the worker's subjective marginal valuation of his own work. At point G in the diagram, representing 10 hours of work, or 14 hours of leisure, per day, the worker's marginal valuation of leisure, as shown by the slope of the indifference curve, is greater than the

Figure 2.10

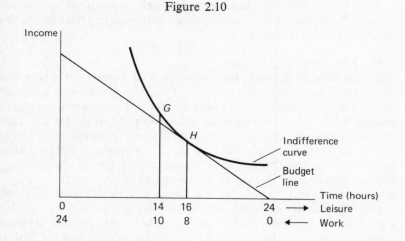

wage rate, as shown by the slope of the budget line. Thus he will choose more leisure and work shorter hours. The optimum point is at *H*, where the marginal valuation of work (MVW) equals the wage rate:

$$\mathrm{MVW}_i \;=\; p_i$$

Now we can see how a competitive system would be efficient both with regard to the allocation of work between households and between firms and with regard to the total amount of work offered. Once again the reason is found in the fact that the competitive system results in a common price, which all decision makers face. Each firm will, in order to maximise profits, employ factor *i* up to the point where its marginal value product equals its price. Since the price is common to all firms, the marginal value product of the factor will be the same in all uses. The same applies to workers. Each worker will offer an amount of effort at which the marginal valuation of work equals the wage rate, and since the latter is common to all the marginal valuation of work will be the same for all. As a result there will be an efficient allocation of the factor between activities and an efficient allocation of effort between workers. Finally, there will, because both firms and workers are confronted by the same wage rate, be equality between the marginal value product and the marginal valuation of work:

$$\mathrm{MVP}_i \;=\; p_i \;=\; MVW_i$$

and this secures an efficient supply of effort.

Thus we see that the working of the freely competitive system will in long term equilibrium result in all the marginal conditions for optimality being attained.

2.32   *The Planned Economy*

We turn now to consider how a position of Pareto optimality can be attained in a planned economy. The type of planned economy that we have in mind is one where the central government exercises general control by, for instance, setting output targets for the various industries and deciding upon the incomes of households. Other decisions, however, are delegated to the managers of state enterprises and to households. Thus managers are left to decide upon the combination of factors to be employed in the production of a given output, and households are allowed to decide how they will apportion their government-determined incomes among the various commodities available. Let us now see how this sort of arrangement will allow an optimal situation to be attained, looking first at the production optimum, then at the exchange optimum, and finally at the overall optimum.

The Attainment of Production Optimality. On the production side, the government will start by drawing up a provisional set of output targets for the various commodities that it believes will just be sufficient to make full use of the available resources. It will also attach prices to each of the factors of production that have to be used by managers in drawing up their production plans. The managers are instructed to draw up production plans that will produce the output targets at minimum cost on the basis of the factor prices determined by the government. When the factor requirements of each manager are submitted and added up, it will only be by an extreme stroke of good fortune that they will exactly exhaust the availability of the factors. A number of other alternatives are much more likely. First, the production plans might reveal that demand exceeds the supply of all factors. In this case the output targets were clearly set at too high a level and would have to be revised downwards. Second, it might transpire that there is a deficient demand for all factors in which case output targets would have to be revised upwards. Third, there might be an excess demand for one factor but an excess supply of another. In this case managers would have to be told to change their production plans so as to use less of one factor and more of another. They would be induced to do this by a revision of the prices attached to the factors. The price of the factor in short supply would be increased and that of the factor in abundant supply would be reduced. Managers would then have to submit a revised set of production plans on the basis of the new set of prices. In this fashion a set of production plans would eventually be produced that would make full use of all the available factors. Of course it must not be imagined that nothing will actually be produced until the central authority is absolutely certain that full factor utilisation has been achieved. Many of the shortages and surpluses will become apparent only when production plans have actually been implemented, which means that adjustments will have to be made in subsequent periods.

In addition to the full utilisation of all factor supplies, efficiency in production requires that the marginal rate of technical substitution between any two factors is the same in all the uses to which the factors are put. This will be assured in the planned economy for exactly the same reasons as outlined for the competitive system. As long as managers succeed in minimising the costs of production, the combination of factors used in each activity will be that at which the marginal rate of technical substitution is equal to the factor price ratio, and as long as the latter is the same in all uses, this will ensure that the marginal rates of technical substitution are also equal in all uses.

The Attainment of Exchange Optimality. The efficient distribution of the commodities must be undertaken in such a way that the marginal rate of substitution between any pair of commodities is the same for all consumers. How is this to be achieved? This time the government can be assumed to start by setting prices for the commodities. These prices, together with the weekly or monthly rate of production, will determine how much money income households must have per week or per month in order to be able to purchase all the goods. This amount of money income is distributed to households on the basis of what the government considers to be a just distribution. With given money incomes and given prices of commodities, each household will then allocate its expenditure so as to maximise utility. The analysis is exactly the same as that which applied to the competitive economy. Each consumer equates his marginal rate of substitution between two commodities to the price ratio of the commodities, and, since the latter is the same for all consumers, equality of the marginal rates of substitution of all consumers is ensured.

However, there is one snag. The output that has been produced may not be such as to enable all consumers simultaneously to fulfil their objective of maximising utility. For some commodities total demand may exceed supply, and for others there may be a deficiency of demand. If this is so, the government will have to set different prices, increasing the prices of those commodities for which there is excess demand and reducing the prices of those for which there is deficient demand. In this way an equilibrium will eventually be reached, where supply equals demand in all markets and where the marginal rate of substitution between any two commodities is the same for all consumers.

The Attainment of Overall Optimality. We started our analysis of the planned economy by assuming that the government establishes an output level for each commodity. There remains the question of establishing the optimum output mix – that is, the problem of overall optimality. This necessitates, as we have seen, charging prices for commodities equal to their marginal costs of production. In the competitive system this equality of price and marginal cost was ensured by the profit-maximising activities of firms. In the planned economy the marginal costs of production are calculated by managers, and prices are fixed on this basis by the central authority. We can thus visualise the government setting production targets for each commodity and prices for the factors of production designed to make full use of the available resources. Prices of commodities are set equal to the marginal costs of production, and on the basis of these prices and of planned production households are given incomes that are in total sufficient to purchase the output produced.

In practice, imbalances will inevitably appear, both in factor markets and in product markets. These imbalances can be corrected by price changes. Commodities for which there was excess demand would have their prices raised, and those for which there was deficient demand would have their prices lowered. But these price adjustments would mean that prices were no longer equal to marginal costs, so that output targets would have to be revised. By successive revisions of this kind, however, overall optimality would eventually be attained, in which all markets were cleared, the prices of commodities were equal to their marginal costs, and the prices of factors were equal to the value of their marginal products.

It is hardly necessary to emphasise the point that the adjustments required in reality to attain the optimum position would be enormously complicated, involving as they must a very large number of commodities and, when account is taken of variations in the skills of the workforce etc., a large number of factors as well. But it should not be thought that these problems are simple even in the competitive system. The adjustments that have to be made are the same in both types of economic system. Whether the freely competitive system is more or less efficient than the planned economy in effecting the adjustments necessary even to approximate to an optimal situation is another matter, which is beyond the scope of this book. Our task in later chapters will be to examine in detail the problems of a competitive economy.

2.4 THE SOCIAL OPTIMUM

We have demonstrated so far that, if the economy is at a position of Pareto optimality, the distribution of utility must be at some point on the welfare frontier. It has also been shown that in principle such a position can be attained either by the workings of a freely competitive market mechanism or by economic planning. Can we go beyond this, however, and indicate which of the points on the welfare frontier represents the point of maximum welfare from society's point of view? To do this would clearly involve making interpersonal comparisons of utility, for, as we have seen, a movement along the welfare frontier involves making one person better off at the expense of someone else's utility. To say that one point on the welfare frontier is better than another, therefore, involves having to say that society is better off when some people have more and others have less. The Pareto value judgement is of no assistance in solving this problem. We need something more specific – a social welfare function. If we assume that a social welfare function – reflecting the ideas of distributive justice held by society, or the government, or some independent tribunal, or even the authors – can be drawn up, then we may have a picture similar to that shown in Figure 2.11. The social welfare function is

Figure 2.11

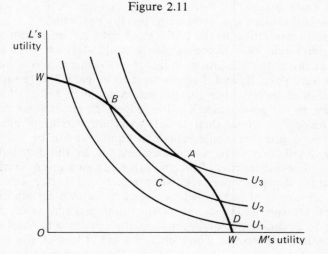

indicated by the set of contours U_1 to U_3, which ranks the different combinations of utility accruing to various members of society, any point on a higher contour being ranked higher than any point on a lower one. If the utility frontier is *WW* then although both *B* and *A* are points of Pareto optimality, point *A* is to be preferred because it lies on the highest attainable social welfare contour. Two other aspects should be emphasised.

First, it should be evident that long-term competitive equilibrium will coincide with the welfare maximum only by chance. The position of long run equilibrium is related to a given distribution of factors. Unless the pattern of demand remains unaltered in response to changes in factor distribution, changes in the latter will affect prices and so change the final equilibrium position. Therefore, in general, there is a different Pareto optimum position and income distribution for each pattern of factor distribution. In other words, competitive equilibrium can lead to any point on the welfare frontier, and only if the initial distribution of factor endowments is such as to lead to an equitable distribution of income will the competitive equilibrium coincide with the welfare optimum.

Second, it follows that, given the value judgements about the distribution of utility shown by the social welfare map in Figure 2.11, a point such as *C* – which is inside the welfare frontier and is therefore a point where at least one of the marginal conditions is violated – will be preferred to some points on the welfare frontier, such as *D*, because *C* lies on a higher welfare contour than *D*. In this case the relative inefficiency of *C* compared to *D* is outweighed by its more acceptable distribution of income. A Pareto-efficient change is therefore not necessarily socially desirable.

A possible solution to the problem of defining an overall welfare optimum would exist if the economy could start off with a clean sheet as far as the allocation of factor endowments was concerned. If this were possible, and if equity were to be judged in terms of the allocation of factors, then this allocation could be achieved according, say, to the government's value judgement about these matters, and competition could then be left to attain maximum efficiency. However, a problem would remain if equity was to be judged not by the distribution of factor endowments but by the distribution of income. The distribution of income arising from a given distribution of factors depends upon relative product and factor prices. An initial allocation of factors will be associated with a certain distribution of income. However, as competition proceeds and markets adjust to positions of equilibrium, relative prices and thus income distribution will change. Thus, only if it could foresee the outcome of competition would it be possible for the government to establish an equitable distribution of income by determining the initial allocation of factors.

Of course in practice the government does not start with a clean sheet. Income redistribution is brought about in part by various fiscal measures acting directly upon the distribution of income, most of which violate one or other of the marginal conditions for efficiency. An income tax, for instance, affects decisions on the work–leisure trade-off. Once more, therefore, we find that efficiency and equity considerations are inextricably bound together.

2.5 PARETO ANALYSIS, TRADE AND TIME

Finally in this chapter we consider briefly two important relaxations of our initial assumptions. We now introduce international trade and time into our discussion of Pareto efficiency in a market economy.

2.51 *Trade*

So far our analysis has been based on the assumption of a closed economy. International trade, however, may allow a country to attain a higher level of real income and utility. To show this we need to reintroduce the production possibility curve. In Figure 2.12, curve SS' is the production possibility curve of a country and shows,

Figure 2.12

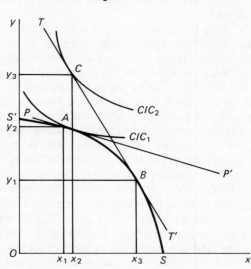

given the amount of one commodity, the maximum amount of the other that can be produced. Assume that without trade the Pareto optimum position for the economy is at point A, where society's marginal rate of substitution in consumption (the slope of the community indifference curve CIC_1) is equal to the marginal rate of transformation in domestic production (the slope of the production possibility curve). If trade is permitted and the world rate of exchange of good x for good y – that is, their relative prices in world markets – is given by the slope of the line TT', then the new production possibility curve is effectively SBT. Whereas before trade the country produced x_1 and y_2 of the two goods, it now produces x_3 and y_1. It now exports $x_3 - x_2$ of x, imports $y_3 - y_1$ of y, and consumes x_2 and y_3. At the new Pareto optimum position, point C, the marginal rate of substitution between the two commodities in consumption is equal to their marginal rate of transformation in production. Furthermore, this will apply to each trading nation, so that for any two countries 1 and 2, and any two goods x and y, we have

$$\mathrm{MRS}_{xy}{}^1 \;\; = \;\; \mathrm{MRS}_{xy}{}^2 \;\; = \;\; \mathrm{MRT}_{xy}{}^1 \;\; = \;\; \mathrm{MRT}_{xy}{}^2$$

A free market system ensures this result because all exporters and importers face the same prices. Starting from a disequilibrium position, relative prices would change until exports equalled imports for all countries. Utility maximisation and profit maximisation would ensure that market prices were everywhere equated with rates of substitution and transformation, thereby producing equality between the latter.

It should be noted, however, that trade need not result in an actual gain for all individuals. In the example given above, trade resulted in an increased consumption of both goods. However, it also raised the price of x relative to that of y. If commodity x is intensive in the use of factor i, then the owners of factor i will benefit. On the other hand, if factor j is used intensively in the production of y, the owners of factor j may suffer a loss. On the demand side, the rise in the relative price of x may make consumers who have a strong preference for x worse off. It may well be the case that the gains from trade far outweigh the losses to the owners of factor j and the consumers of good x, but unless the losers are actually compensated there are once more distributional as well as efficiency considerations to be taken into account.

In addition, of course, point C in Figure 2.12 is Pareto optimal only with respect to a particular community indifference map, which itself is associated with a given distribution of factors. There will be a separate Pareto optimum for each factor distribution. If the distribution at C is not socially desirable, free trade may lead to a lower level of welfare than some restricted volume of trade.

2.52　*Time*
The introduction of time into the analysis means that there is not only a choice between different combinations of goods today but

also a choice between more goods today and more goods tomorrow. Producers can increase their output in the future by devoting part of their resources today to the production of capital goods to be used in production in future periods along with other inputs. The rate of return measures the extent to which future output gains exceed the output foregone today. Consumers display time preference; that is, they normally prefer consumption sooner than later. They will thus trade consumer goods today only for larger quantities of consumer goods in the future. If, for example, a consumer is just willing to forego 100 units of output today for 110 units in one year's time, his marginal rate of time preference is said to be 10 per cent. The fact that he will consider trading future for present consumption at all makes it possible to release today's resources to produce tomorrow's capital goods and thus to exploit the rate of return on investment.

Assume that there is only one consumer, one producer and one good. In Figure 2.13(a) the indifference curves refer to consumer L's preferences between consumption of good x in period 1 and consumption in period 2. Given a constant stock of resources available from one period to the next, C_1 units of output could be produced in the first period and C_2 units in the second. If some of the resources available in period 1 are invested in capital goods that will provide output in period 2, the various possible inter-temporal combinations of outputs can be represented by the trans-

Figure 2.13

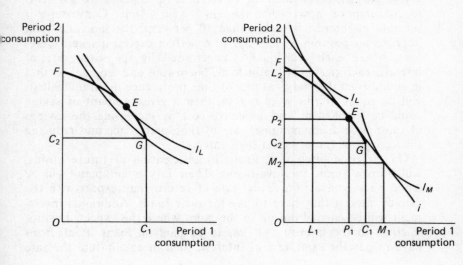

(a) One consumer   (b) Two consumer/producers

formation curve *FG*. The Pareto optimum situation is at *E*, where the output in period 2 is so increased that it just compensates the consumer for the loss of consumption in period 1. At the optimum point the marginal rate of transformation over time (the slope of *FG*) is equal to the marginal rate of time preference (the slope of the indifference curve). Generalising the argument to apply to more than one consumer and more than one good, the normal Paretian conditions again apply. The marginal rates of time preference (MRTP) of all consumers must be equal to each other, and equal also to each and every marginal rate of transformation between goods in period 1 and goods in period 2. Thus for any two individuals *L* and *M*, and any two goods *x* and *y*,

$$\text{MRTP}_{t_1 t_2}{}^L = \text{MRTP}_{t_1 t_2}{}^M \ldots = \text{MRT}_{t_1 t_2}{}^x = \text{MRT}_{t_1 t_2}{}^y$$

In a competitive market economy the above Pareto conditions will be fulfilled if the market interest rate on borrowing and lending is common to all borrowers and lenders and is allowed to move freely. Consumers and producers will adjust their consumption and investment activities and their borrowing/lending requirements until their rates of time preference and the rate of return on investment are brought into equality with the market interest rate. Any change in preferences or investment opportunities will precipitate interest rate changes to maintain this equality. Given that an individual's marginal rate of time preference is 10 per cent, if the rate of interest is less than this, then the individual will improve his position by increasing his borrowing. The cost of borrowing at, say, 8 per cent is less than the extra value he attaches (10 per cent) to consumption now rather than in a year's time. Conversely, if the rate of interest is higher than 10 per cent, the individual will improve his position by lending. In a perfect capital market, therefore, where each individual is confronted by the same rate of interest, each person will adjust his borrowing and lending, so that in equilibrium the marginal rate of time preference of all individuals will be equal. If this were not so, then a given amount of saving could be supplied at less subjective cost by increasing the savings of those with a low marginal rate of time preference and reducing the savings of those with a high rate.

On the production side, firms, in anticipation of future profits, will borrow funds for investment. Their investment plans will be based on a comparison of the rate of return they expect with the rate of interest they have to pay for their funds. Additional investment will be carried out up to the point where the expected return is equal to the interest that has to be paid on loans. If all firms have to pay the same rate of interest, then in equilibrium the rate of return expected by all firms will be the same. Since the rate of interest is the same for both borrowers and lenders, it follows that in equilibrium the rate of return on any marginal investment will be equal to the marginal rate of time preference of any consumer. If this were not so – if, say, the rate of return exceeded the marginal rate of time preference – then it would be possible to improve matters by devoting more resources to savings and investment and less to current consumption.

Figure 2.13(b) shows an equilibrium position for two individuals L and M who are both producers and consumers of good x. Both individuals have intertemporal production opportunities described by the curve FG. The resources available could support consumption of C_1 in period 1 and C_2 in period 2, if no investment borrowing or lending took place. However, if the market interest rate is represented by the slope of the line i, then L will maximise his welfare if he consumes L_1 in period 1 and L_2 in period 2. This means that, of the C_1 consumption opportunities he has in period 1, he devotes P_1C_1 to his own production activities and lends L_1P_1 at the market interest rate. His saving results in output C_2L_2 in period 2, of which C_2P_2 is the return to his own investment and P_2L_2 is the return on his loan. Consumer M maximises his welfare by consuming M_1 today and M_2 tomorrow. He devotes P_1C_1 to his own production and borrows P_1M_1, which is of course equal to L's lending of L_1P_1.

Finally, we should again draw attention to the importance of distribution. While the competitive process will guarantee the fulfilment of the Pareto conditions through time, the level of savings and investment will reflect the current distribution of resources between members of society. A change in income distribution will mean a new Pareto optimum position. Fulfilment of the Pareto conditions, therefore, does not mean that the level of saving and investment is socially optimal, for this cannot be determined without a consideration of distributive justice.

Chapter 3

Changes in Welfare

3.1 INTRODUCTION

A great deal of discussion has taken place in welfare economics concerning the circumstances in which an economist is able to recommend a particular policy measure. The assessment of any policy decision involves having to determine whether economic welfare will be higher or lower as a result of its implementation. In a system where individual preferences are all-important, this necessitates an evaluation of the effects of the decision upon individual utility levels and of the implication of these changes in individual utilities for the overall welfare of the community.

If all the changes in an economy were marginal, prices and marginal costs would accurately reflect gains and losses and the analysis of the attainment of efficiency in resource allocation would not have to proceed beyond that of the previous chapter. However, many changes in the deployment of resources have non-marginal effects. Market prices will not then provide all the information required for efficient decision making.

Take, for instance, the case shown in Figure 3.1, where, as a result of new investment, the cost of producing a good falls from C_1 to C_2 and price falls from P_1 to P_2, so that demand increases from q_1 to q_2. The gainers from the project receive extra output q_1q_2. Should this extra output be valued at the old or the new price? If

Figure 3.1

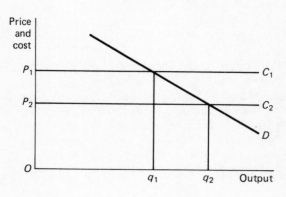

we were to use the new price P_2, many of the people who receive the extra output would in fact have been willing to pay more, whereas using the old price P_1 would lead us to overstate the gain, because the majority of the new consumers would not have been prepared to pay that much for the additional units of output. Market prices, therefore, are not an accurate way of valuing gains when non-marginal resource shifts take place.

The common approach to measuring gains and losses involves the concept of surplus, both consumer's surplus and factor rents. Consumer's surplus will exist if an individual has to pay a lower price for a commodity than he is prepared to pay for it. Similarly, a surplus or rent will accrue to the owner of a factor service if the market price for that service is higher than the minimum price that is necessary for the service to be offered. A position of Pareto optimality is therefore said to exist when it is impossible to introduce measures that result in an increase in one person's surplus without reducing that of someone else.

3.2 CONSUMER'S SURPLUS

3.21 *Marshallian Measures*

'The price which a person pays for a thing can never exceed, and seldom comes up to that which he would be willing to pay rather than go without it: so that the satisfaction which he gets from its purchase generally exceeds that which he gives up in paying away its price; and he thus derives from the purchase a surplus of satisfaction. The excess of the price which he would be willing to pay rather than go without the thing, over that which he actually does pay, is the economic measure of this surplus satisfaction. It may be called consumer's surplus.'

Alfred Marshall's definition of consumer's surplus is illustrated in Figure 3.2. The figure shows the value that an individual consumer attaches to each unit of the commodity as reflected in the price he is prepared to pay for it. Thus for the first unit consumed his marginal valuation is P_6, for the second unit it is P_5, and so on. In other words, if a firm could charge him a different price for each unit consumed, he would be prepared to pay a maximum of P_6 for the first unit and P_5 for the second. However, if the price that he pays for all units is equal to OP, he will purchase six units in all and on each one he will enjoy a surplus, the total money value of the surplus being equal to the shaded area in the figure.

Turning from individual to market demand, the demand schedule for any good x may be drawn as a smooth curve as in

Figure 3.3, with each point on the curve representing the market's marginal valuation of a given quantity of the commodity. Thus for output *OM* the marginal valuation is *MB*. Total consumer's surplus for this quantity of output is equal to the area of *APB*. If the price falls to *OF*, consumer's surplus increases by an amount equal to area *PBCF*. If good *x* were a new commodity that was introduced into the market and supplied free of charge, the addition to consumer's surplus would equal area *AOD*.

Figure 3.2

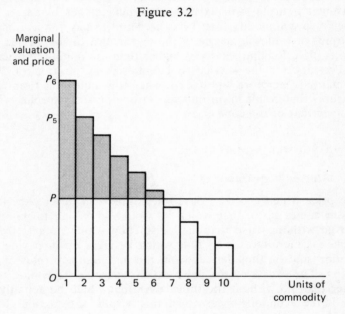

Figure 3.3

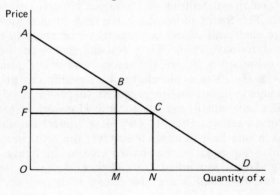

The aggregate demand curve is of course a *ceteris paribus* demand curve, the prices of other goods, income, tastes, population and the distribution of income all being held constant. Changes in these variables will shift the demand curve for the commodity in question, and thus alter the area under the demand curve that is used as the measure of consumers' surplus.

Certain important qualifications to the analysis are required if a fall in the price of commodity x affects the price of another commodity, y. Assume first of all that x and y are substitutes, and that x is produced under conditions of constant costs and y under conditions of increasing costs. If the price of x falls from P_2 to P_1, consumers' surplus is increased by the amount shown by the shaded area in Figure 3.4(a). The fall in the price of x will induce a left-

Figure 3.4

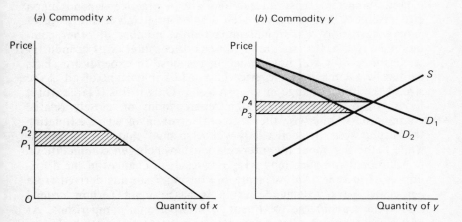

(a) Commodity x (b) Commodity y

ward shift in the demand curve for commodity y, so that the price of y will fall from P_4 to P_3, as shown in Figure 3.4(b). There is a further gain in consumers' surplus, therefore, equal to the shaded area in diagram (b). The increase in consumers' surplus on x represents the gain that results from a fall in the price of x, the price of y being P_3. The increase in consumers' surplus on y represents the gain resulting from the fall in the price of y with the price of x at P_1. The sum of the two shaded areas represents the maximum amount that consumers would be willing to pay in order to get the benefit of a reduction in the price of x. The dotted area in diagram (b) is *not* to be deducted in calculating the total gain in surplus, because it is already taken into account in the shaded area in diagram (a). At a price of y equal to P_4 the gain in surplus on x

includes the net gain in the utility of those consumers who have increased their consumption of x at the expense of y. The analysis would become still more complicated if x also had an upward sloping supply curve. In this case the fall in the price of y that was induced by a fall in the price of x would in turn affect the price of x, so that a further adjustment would have to be made in measuring the gains to consumers. However, so long as the equilibrium positions were stable, then successive repercussions would become smaller and smaller as the new set of equilibrium prices for x and y was approached.

If x and y were complements, a fall in the price of x would result in a rightward shift in the demand curve for y, and the price of y would increase. In this case there would be a loss of consumers' surplus in the consumption of y, which would have to be subtracted from the gain in surplus on x.

How important these interactions are in practice depends upon circumstances. For instance, even a substantial fall in the price of x may have only a marginal impact on a number of other commodities. Again, if there are conditions of constant costs in industry y, the price of y will not change in response to expenditure shifts caused by a change in the price of x. Most important of all is the size of the initial change in the price of x. Only if this is large will it be worthwhile checking for the repercussions on closely related commodities. Otherwise the degree of error involved in estimating the surplus area for good x only will be so small that it is not worthwhile bothering about the inter-relationships between commodities.

Additional complications arise as a result of changes in the distribution of income. Any measure of consumer surplus derived from aggregate market demand curves is based upon certain crucial assumptions about the treatment of interpersonal comparisons. At any given set of market prices the position of an individual consumer's demand curve for good A, and therefore the size of his consumer surplus, depends on the extent of his purchasing power. When we add up individual demand curves into an aggregate demand curve for good x, its shape, and therefore the size of total consumer surplus, will depend, given different tastes, upon the distribution of purchasing power among consumers. For every distribution there will be a different surplus area. Any measure of the total gains from an investment, for instance, derived from an empirically estimated market demand curve is necessarily specific to one particular income distribution – the current one. Even if we accept individual surplus changes as measures of individual utility changes, how we shall regard the total welfare gain thus derived depends in the end upon our attitude towards the existing distribution of purchasing power among consumers. Different measures of the gains available, and therefore different investment decisions, can arise from different views on distribution. Widespread use of aggregate consumer surplus measures must rely heavily, therefore, upon the assumption that the existing distribution of income is consistent with our welfare objectives.

More important in practice are the problems arising from changes in the level of income, population and tastes. For instance, in the estimation of the consumers' surplus derived from building a motorway, it would be misleading to base the estimate on the expected volume of traffic at the time when the motorway was completed. Allowance would also have to be made for the likely growth in the volume of traffic in the future.

3.22 *Hicksian Measures*

Apart from the *ceteris paribus* assumptions of the aggregate demand curve, there is one further problem with the measurement of consumers' surplus. This relates to the measurement of individual surplus. Essentially, what we are trying to do is to identify non-marginal changes in welfare and then to attach a monetary value to them. The problem is that with non-marginal changes the monetary value of a given change in welfare for a given consumer is not necessarily constant. A fall in the price of a commodity, for instance, will increase a consumer's real income, but what if he values the extra real income less highly? The changing marginal utility of money would mean the absence of a fixed measuring rod for converting utility changes into money terms. Merely to assume a constant marginal utility of income, as Marshall did, is not good enough, because it is only plausible for very small changes and therefore avoids the problem of non-marginal adjustments. Furthermore, if the marginal utility of income for an individual is not constant with respect to real income changes brought about by price changes, it is not constant either with respect to real income changes brought about by increases or decreases in money income. This makes it difficult to compare gains and losses over time. It also means that there can be no single fixed measuring rod for converting utility changes into money terms for all individuals.

These difficulties with the Marshallian analysis prompted Hicks to develop a different approach to the problem of measuring utility changes, based upon ordinal rather than cardinal measurement. This approach is illustrated in Figure 3.5, which shows part of the indifference map of an individual consumer. Assume that the consumer is initially at point A on indifference curve I_1 – the point where the indifference curve is tangential to the budget line y_2x_1. The price of x falls, so that the budget line becomes y_2x_4, and the consumer moves to point B, which is on a higher indifference curve, I_2. Because he has moved to a higher indifference curve the consumer's welfare has increased, and it is this gain, or increase in utility, that we want to measure in money terms. There are two ways to find the monetary value of this gain:

(*a*) *Measurement of the compensating variation.* We might ask: What is the maximum sum of money that could be taken away from the consumer when the price of x falls that would leave him exactly

Figure 3.5

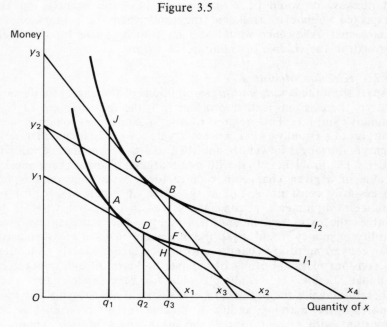

as well off as he was in his original position, the consumer being free to purchase as much of commodity x as he wants at the lower price? The answer is found by constructing a hypothetical budget line y_1x_2 parallel to the new budget line and tangential to indifference curve I_1. Thus if a sum of money equal to y_2y_1 is paid by the consumer when the price falls, this will leave him at point D on indifference curve I_1. He is now no better off and no worse off than he was before the price change. This sum y_2y_1 is the compensating variation in income for a price fall. It will be seen from Figure 3.5 that, even if the consumer has to pay a sum equal to the compensating variation, he will still increase his consumption of x. This is because x is now cheaper relative to other goods, and so there is a substitution effect that increases the demand for x from q_1 to q_2. In the case shown in Figure 3.5, however, if the consumer does not have to pay the compensating sum, he will further increase his consumption of x by the amount q_2q_3. This is the income effect of the price fall – with a lower price of x the consumer's real income is higher.

In this case the higher real income results in an increase in demand for the commodity. The income effect of a price change need not, however, be positive as in Figure 3.5. It may also have a negative or zero effect on the demand for the commodity. In the former case, B would lie to the left of D; in the latter, D would lie vertically below B. These two possibilities are illustrated in Figure 3.6(*a*) and (*b*).

Figure 3.6

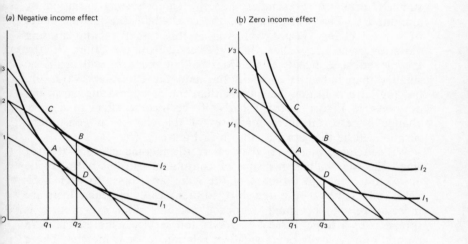

(*b*) *Measurement of the equivalent variation.* Instead of asking what maximum sum of money the consumer would have to pay following a price fall to leave him no better off than he was before, we could ask: What minimum sum of money will he have to receive, in lieu of the price fall, to enable him to enjoy the same increase in welfare? The answer to this question is obtained by constructing a hypothetical budget line y_3x_3 in Figure 3.5, parallel to the initial price line and tangential to indifference curve I_2. This shows that, if the consumer were to receive y_2y_3 instead of the fall in price, he would attain point C on indifference curve I_2 and so achieve the same increase in welfare. This sum is the equivalent variation of income for the price fall. The reader will see that for a price *rise* the compensating variation is y_2y_3 and the equivalent variation is y_2y_1.

(c) *Comparison of Marshallian and Hicksian measures.* How does all this relate to the Marshallian definition of consumer's surplus? In the case of a price fall the Marshallian definition relates to the larger quantity of x that is purchased after the price fall before deduction of the compensating income variation. In other words, it asks what maximum sum of money the consumer would be willing to pay to acquire the quantity q_3 at the lower price. The answer is *BF* in Figure 3.5, for, given that the consumer purchases q_3 units of x, the payment of this sum puts him back on the original indifference curve. Figure 3.5 shows the Marshallian measure of the change in consumer's surplus to be smaller than the compensating variation by amount *FH*. This will always be the case where the income effect of a price change is positive. And in this case the compensating variation will be smaller than the equivalent variation. If the income effect is negative, the Marshallian measure will again be smaller than both the compensating and the equivalent variation, but the latter will now be smaller than the compensating variation, as shown in Figure 3.6(a). Finally, if the income effect of a price change is zero, all three measures of the change in consumers' surplus will be the same, as shown in Figure 3.6(b).

We conclude, therefore, that where the income effect is zero or small the Marshallian measure of consumers' surplus will provide an accurate enough estimate of the gains and losses to each individual affected by a resource shift. In many cases income effects are indeed likely to be small, for each person's total expenditure is spread over a large variety of goods and services, the expenditure on any one typically being small in relation to total income. There are instances, however (housing, for example), where this is not so. In these cases the Marshallian measure would give a misleading measure of the change in surplus, too small for a price fall and too large for a price increase. In such cases we should on theoretical grounds make use of one of the Hicksian measures. The problem of deciding which measure to use will be discussed in Chapters 8 and 9.

3.3 FACTOR RENTS

Just as a consumer benefits by being able to purchase a commodity for less than the maximum amount that he would be willing to pay rather than to go without it, so the owner of a factor may benefit by being able to sell the factor for more than the minimum sum that he would be prepared to accept. This difference between what a factor earns in its existing occupation and the minimum sum of money necessary to keep it there, given all the alternative opportunities available, is factor rent. Changes in rent will occur as a result of changes in the prices of factors. We shall concentrate on the labour factor.

Assume to start with that each individual worker is free to select the number of hours that he wants to work at any wage rate. In Figure 3.7 the curve SS' traces out the minimum sum needed to

Figure 3.7

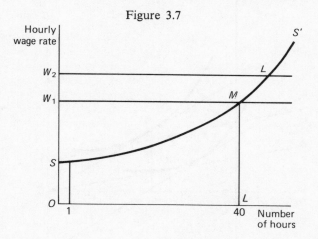

induce an individual to supply successive units of labour. For the first hour in the week this sum is OS; for the fortieth it is LM. With a wage rate of W_1, factor rent is equal to the area bounded by the wage level and the supply curve, that is, area W_1MS. If the wage rate increases to W_2, then rent increases by area W_1W_2LM. As in the case of the measurement of consumer's surplus, this approach uses observed market behaviour as a measure of surplus and is theoretically acceptable only when income effects are small.

A more general approach, however, is once again found in the use of indifference curve analysis. In Figure 3.8 the individual is initially in an equilibrium position at point A, where the price line OW_1, the slope of which represents the wage rate, is tangential to indifference curve I_1. The individual supplies L_1 labour and earns an income of AL_1. Let the wage rate increase to W_2. The new equilibrium position will be at B, where L_2 labour is supplied and BL_2 income is earned.

As in the case of the measurement of consumers' surplus, the gain in welfare resulting from the price change can be expressed as a compensating variation or an equivalent variation. To find the compensating variation we ask how much money has to be taken away from the individual, after the wage increase has occurred, in order to restore him to the level of welfare enjoyed on indifference curve I_1. This measure is OY_1, and it is given by the vertical distance between OW_2 and a price line drawn parallel to OW_2 and tangential to indifference curve I_1.

Figure 3.8

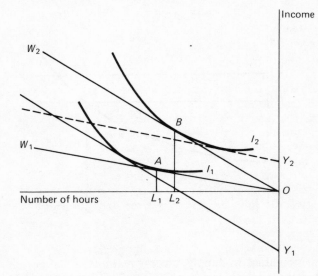

The equivalent variation measure of the gain in welfare is obtained by asking how much money would have to be given to the individual if he had to forgo the wage increase, to enable him to achieve the higher level of welfare on I_2. The sum that would have to be paid is OY_2, and it is given by the vertical distance between OW_1 and a price line constructed parallel to OW_1 and tangential to indifference curve I_2.

With a zero income effect, the compensating variation and equivalent variation measures are equal and both are equal to the area above the individual supply curve. In the case of the supply of a factor, however, the income effect cannot, as it can for the typical commodity, be assumed to be small. As we have seen, in the case of the typical commodity the consumer's expenditure on it forms only a small percentage of his total budget, so that a change in price will have only a small effect on real income. The income effect of a price change, therefore, will usually be small compared to the substitution effect. Furthermore, in most cases the income and substitution effects will work in the same direction – towards increasing demand when the price of the product falls, and vice versa. However, in the case of the supply of labour the income effect will normally be large. This is due to the fact that most workers derive the bulk of their income from the sale of one type of labour. A change in the wage paid for this labour will thus have a substantial effect on an individual's income and welfare. Not only is the income effect of a change in the wage rate likely to be large, but it will also, in most cases, work against the substitution effect. An increase in the wage rate means an increase in the price of leisure relative to goods. The substitution effect will therefore tend to result in a reduced demand for leisure time, that is, an increase in the supply of labour. The income effect of a wage increase, however, means that the individual is better off and can afford to increase his consumption, not only of goods and services, but also of leisure time. The income effect of a rise in the wage rate will thus tend to increase the demand for leisure and reduce the supply of labour. Where the income effect is stronger than the substitution effect, the net outcome will be that a higher wage rate results in a reduced supply of labour.

The importance of the income effect in determining the individual factor-supply schedule thus gives rise to problems when it comes to measuring factor rent. In most cases the income effect will result in a reduction in the supply of labour following a wage increase, so that the measure of the gain in factor rent as given by the area above the individual supply curve could be much smaller than the compensating variation measure.

In practice, however, the problem posed by the income effect is reduced by the fact that employees typically work a standard number of hours per week for a given wage. Because of this institutional constraint on the variability in the supply of labour, we can still make use of the area above the aggregate supply curve as a reasonable measure of factor rent for the case of the supply of a particular type of labour to an industry or firm. Each individual is offered a certain wage in return for so many hours of work, and so long as the individual receives some rent from the bargain he will offer his services. Thus in Figure 3.9 the first employee offers his services for a wage rate as low as T_1, and with the actual wage rate paid of WW' receives a rent of R_1. The second employee receives a rent of R_2, and so on. The sum of the R portion of the columns measures rent for the supply of this particular type of labour to the industry. An increase in the wage rate will clearly increase the rent received by existing employees. It will also increase the supply of labour to the industry, and there will be a rental element in the earnings of all but the last worker hired.

Figure 3.9

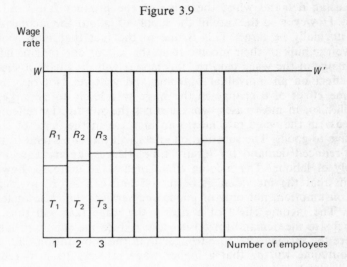

3.4   WELFARE STATEMENTS

So far we have been concerned with the problem of measuring the gains and losses arising from a.resource reallocation, using surplus measures of the changes in utility of individual consumers and factor owners. The various changes in individual utilities must, however, be brought together to produce a statement indicating what has happened to overall economic welfare, which is a weighted sum of individual utilities. How are we to deal with the diversity of movements in individual utilities when assessing the effects of a policy change? A number of criteria have been suggested, and our review of the three principal criteria will be aided by use of the concept of the utility possibility curve that was introduced in the previous chapter.

(a) *Pareto criterion.* The Pareto criterion states that we should recommend any policy change that makes some people better off and harms no-one. In Figure 3.10(a), point A represents the pair of utility levels for individuals L and M before the policy change. Other points along the utility possibility curve U_1U_1 represent alternative possible distributions within the existing policy framework. Let point B represent the position after the policy change. This is clearly a Pareto improvement, since both individuals are better off than they were at point A. Similarly a move from A to either C or D is also an improvement, since one individual is made better off and the other is no worse off. A move from A to E, however, is not a Pareto improvement. In this case M's utility increases but L's utility falls.

Figure 3.10

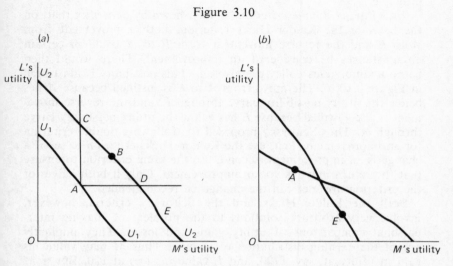

(*b*) *Kaldor–Hicks compensation principle.* In practice, however, there are very few policy options of any significance that do not involve someone suffering a loss of utility. The usefulness of the Pareto criterion is therefore very restricted. To tackle situations where some people gain but others lose, Kaldor and Hicks introduced the compensation principle. This states that if a policy change results in some people being made better off and some worse off, and if the gains of the former are sufficiently large to compensate the losers and still leave something over, then the change is deemed an improvement. In terms of Figure 3.10(*a*), the Kaldor–Hicks criterion states that a move from A to E will improve welfare, even though the change results in individual L becoming worse off. This is because, having attained point E, it is *possible* by a redistribution of income, using lump sum taxes or subsidies, to attain a point such as B where both individuals are better off. In terms of the geometry of the analysis, a change is an improvement so long as the initial point lies underneath the utility possibility curve that passes through the new utility combination. It should be noted that according to this compensation principle it is not necessary that compensation should *actually* be paid. If compensation were paid, then of course the Kaldor–Hicks principle would reduce to the Pareto criterion, since no one would be made worse off. It is also interesting to note that the Kaldor–Hicks criterion is a development of the Pareto criterion and gets its credibility from the 'general acceptability' of the Pareto value judgement. In fact, however, if compensation is not paid, it is a complete negation of the Pareto principle.

(c) *Scitovsky double criterion.* It was shown by Scitovsky that, on the basis of the Kaldor–Hicks criterion, both a movement from A to E and the reverse movement from E to A could in certain circumstances be considered an improvement. There would then be no unambiguous policy prescription. This possibility is illustrated in Figure 3.10(*b*). The move from A to E is justified because A lies below the utility possibility curve through E, and the reverse movement is also justified because E lies below the utility possibility curve through A. Thus Scitovsky proposed the following double criterion for an improvement: first, use the Kaldor–Hicks criterion to see if a change is an improvement, second, use the same criterion to ensure that the return move is *not* an improvement. Only if both halves of the criterion are met can the change be recommended.

Both the Kaldor–Hicks and the Scitovsky criteria, however, involve very arbitrary solutions to the problem of making interpersonal comparisons of utility gains and losses. They implicitly accept the existing distribution of income. Thus M may value his gain in utility at, say, £100, and L value his loss at £20. But if M is wealthy and L poor, £20 may mean a lot more to L than £100 does to M. Thus in the absence of compensation, a change may appear worthwhile that results in trivial utility gains to some and major losses to others. These criteria are, therefore, based upon the observed money valuations of individual gains and losses, which are in turn dependent on the distribution of income. Unless this distribution is accepted as just, a change that satisfies the Scitovsky criterion and where no compensation is paid may not be a good thing.

In making welfare judgements, therefore, if compensation is impossible we must combine the compensation principle with value judgements on distribution. This means in effect that we have to reintroduce the social welfare function, which embodies value judgements about the distribution of utilities. In Figure 3.11 the move from A to E is shown to be an improvement, since E lies on a higher contour of the social welfare function than A. However, had we drawn the function in such a way that E lay below contour 1, then the change from A to E would have reduced welfare.

We may summarise the discussion so far in the following way. A policy change for which the gains exceed the losses and where the losers are fully compensated will increase welfare and can be recommended. If a policy change results in a desirable redistribution of income and the gains outweigh the losses, then welfare will again have increased and the policy can be recommended. If a policy change results in gains exceeding losses but causes a redistribution of income that is considered undesirable then there is a conflict between efficiency and equity which will have to be dealt with in taking policy decisions.

Figure 3.11

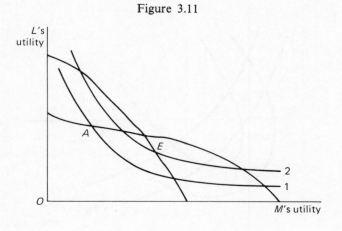

3.5 SOCIAL WELFARE FUNCTIONS

The conclusions above are based on the presumption of a social welfare function incorporating the Pareto value judgement that welfare is increased if one person is made better off and no one becomes worse off in terms of absolute levels of utility. It may be useful at this point to bring out clearly the nature of this ethical statement by contrasting it with a non-Pareto value judgement. Consider Figure 3.12. The Pareto assumption implies a welfare function as shown by the set of *SWP* curves. A non-Pareto assumption might produce a set like *SWR*. The latter includes curves indicating that, beyond a certain point, increasing the utility of one person while the utility of the other is constant actually reduces social welfare. Moving along the line *PP'* towards the right, the utility of *M* increases while that of *L* is unchanged. With the Pareto welfare function, overall welfare increases; with the other, social welfare first increases but then falls.

Increasing the utilities of some people while those of others remain unchanged can therefore reduce social welfare, if relative welfare levels are important. If certain groups become better off and leave others behind, this widens or creates divisions between groups in society. Even ignoring the possibility that individual utilities are themselves interdependent, such differences could be regarded as undesirable, at least beyond a certain point. A Paretian social welfare function ignores this possibility entirely.

Figure 3.12

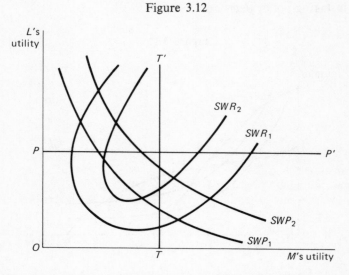

The emphasis on individualism, together with the need for a social welfare function incorporating value judgements relating to the distribution of income, brings us to the question of whether the social welfare function to be used in policy appraisal can be constructed from individual preferences. It has been demonstrated by Arrow, that, given the following conditions, such a construction is *not* always possible:

1   For every pair of alternatives *A* and *B* there must be a social preference or indifference.
2   The preferences of society must be consistent, so that, for instance, if *A* is preferred to *B* and *B* to *C*, then *A* must be preferred to *C*.
3   There must be a set of three alternatives that individuals are free to order.
4   The social choice between two alternatives *A* and *B* must depend only on individuals' ranking of *A* and *B*. Each individual's ranking of *A* and *B* must not be influenced by the presence of other alternatives *C*, *D*, etc. that may be in the set to be ordered; that is, each individual's ranking of *A* and *B* will be the same whether *A* and *B* are the only alternatives to be ordered or whether there are other alternatives *C*, *D*, etc. to be included in the ranking.

5 There must be a positive association between social and individual choices; that is, social choices must not change in the opposite direction from the choices of members of society.
6 Decisions must not be dictated by anyone outside the community or by any one person in the community. Social orderings of alternatives must be dependent on, and derived from, individual orderings.

The crux of Arrow's 'impossibility theorem' is that it is impossible to derive social choice from individual preferences without violating at least one of these conditions. One example illustrating the problem is the familiar paradox of voting.

Assume a society of three individuals, Jones, Davies and Smith, who have to decide between three alternative resource configurations *A*, *B* and *C*. Each individual expresses his personal preferences by ranking the three possibilities. One set of possible rankings is shown in panel (i) of Table 3.1. In this case the voting system produces an unambiguous result, the individual and overall social

Table 3.1

Order of preference	(i)			(ii)			(iii)		
	Jones	*Davies*	*Smith*	*Jones*	*Davies*	*Smith*	*Jones*	*Davies*	*Smith*
1	A	A	A	A	A	C	A	B	C
2	B	B	B	B	B	A	B	C	A
3	C	C	C	C	C	B	C	A	B

rankings being the same. A second possibility is shown in panel (ii). Here again *A* wins over *B*, *B* over *C* and *A* over *C*, but in this case the social ordering *A*, *B* and *C* is obtained not by unanimity but by a majority of two votes to one. If this pattern of voting repeated itself on all major policy issues, life could become pretty miserable for Smith! Panel (iii) shows a more complicated situation. In this case each individual's voting pattern is consistent, but the group's is not. A majority prefer *A* to *B*, and a majority prefer *B* to *C*, but a majority also prefer *C* to *A*! In this case, therefore, a straightforward majority-voting mechanism does not secure transitivity in social ordering. Furthermore, in the case shown, policy making is likely to exhibit instability, for, if each individual has one vote, then whichever policy is in force two individuals have the power to overthrow it in favour of another. For instance, if it so happens that *A* is in force, both Davies and Smith will vote to overthrow it because they prefer *C* to *A*. Where individual rankings are very different, therefore, simple majority voting does not provide clear guidelines for social choices.

To get out of the dilemma one or more of Arrow's conditions

must be dropped. The conditions that are particularly restrictive in Arrow's formulation are those which stipulate that social preferences must be derived entirely from individuals' ordinal preferences, no account being taken of the strength of those preferences. But clearly the strength or intensity of feelings of individuals is important. Jones may prefer alternative *A* to *B* very strongly, whereas Smith may have only a very slight preference for *B* over *A*. Clearly then there is a need for a mechanism whereby individuals can express their relative strength of preferences. In the market, strength of feeling is shown by the amount of money that a person is willing to pay to acquire a unit of a commodity. In other walks of life it is frequently expressed through the activities of pressure groups formed for the purpose of impressing upon the government the views of a group with an interest in a particular decision or set of policies. Thus, for instance, the announcement of plans to develop new limestone-quarrying activities or open-cast coal mining may cause action groups to be set up in the threatened area, which aim to stop the proposed development or at least limit its scope so as to preserve the attractiveness of the area as a place to live in. On the other hand there will be others with an interest in seeing that the proposed development is put into effect, stressing the growing shortage and increasing costs of limestone or coal and the need to increase supplies. If the intensity of feeling of the pressure groups is directly and closely related to the effort that they put into their lobbying activities, and if this in turn is related to the effectiveness of their action, then the decision that is ultimately arrived at is likely to be superior to the one that would be made were there no attempt made to communicate these intensities of feeling to the decision maker.

The leaves one further question to be answered, however, which is what weights to attach to individual preferences. Whether allowing decisions on resource allocation in the market to be governed by strength of preferences as revealed by purchasing power is acceptable, depends on how equitable is the distribution of income. Similarly, as indicated above, it is in the interests of efficiency that the policy maker be aware of the strengths of feeling from different quarters on particular issues. How the government weighs up the different viewpoints depends in principle upon its view of the current consensus. However, in practice it could also depend on the strength of the pressure groups involved – whether the pressure that they can bring to bear is very limited or whether it is so strong that they can dictate policies to the government by threatening, for example, to bring the economy to a standstill. The final distribution of resources will then depend in part upon the distribution of political power.

It is not possible to pinpoint one specific weighting system that the government should use or, indeed, one specific distribution of income, wealth or political power that is superior to all others. In any democratic system a range of possible weighting systems and distributions will in fact be tolerated. Individuals have their own vested interests, and their own different views on what is best for themselves and for society in general. Difficult conflicts of interest will inevitably arise throughout the system, but the system works because the policies adopted are sufficiently acceptable to the majority – or not sufficiently unacceptable to the minority. The social welfare function is therefore not a simple aggregation of individual utilities but a loose consensus among individuals and groups reached only by a process of interaction, of cross-fertilisation of ideas and attitudes, and of interdependence. The social choices that emerge from this consensus are liable to constant change as discussion, criticism and the assimilation of facts change the views that influence decision making.

Although it is not possible to define an ideal distribution, we would argue that a more equal distribution of income and wealth than now exists in most economies is desirable, and that the goal of greater equity in the distribution of income and wealth should be placed high up in the list of government policy priorities. This is not only because we regard a more equitable distribution as desirable in itself, but also because income, and particularly wealth, are related to the individual's freedom of choice, social status and political power. People with wealth have greater room for manoeuvre in their choice of jobs and social relationships, and also in their ability to exert pressure to change or modify government policies that threaten to reduce their welfare. The same is true of political power. In a society in which individual liberty is highly valued it is important to place the most stringent controls on institutions that exist to pursue the vested interests of particular groups in society. The government must be free to take all interests into account, and not only those groups with the greatest political muscle.

Chapter 4

The Distribution of Income and Wealth

4.1 INTRODUCTION

We saw in the previous chapters that the specification of a socially optimal allocation of resources requires an explicit statement of the social welfare function, such a function being defined in terms of the distribution of utilities between individuals. In practice, however, when it comes to examining problems of distribution we have to think not in terms of utilities but in terms of goods, or of the income from which goods can be purchased, or of the factors that generate purchasing power. This distinction between the distributions of utility and of income can be an important one. For instance, statistics on income distribution do not take into account the value of leisure to the individual, and it is possible that part of the difference in the income of two individuals is due to a difference in their valuation of work and leisure. The person with the lower income may attach greater value to leisure, and if this is so then differences in income will be greater than differences in utility. Nevertheless, the main focus of economists in this area has been on the distribution of income and wealth. Income may come from employment in the form of a salary or wage – the main source of income for most people – or it may come from property or wealth. But the advantages of wealth are greater than the stream of income that it generates. It is important in itself – partly because a person may augment his purchasing power over and above his current income by living off his capital, and partly because wealth may confer other benefits, such as power, prestige and independence.

If we could start an economy from scratch with an 'ideal' distribution of income and wealth, then, if all markets were highly competitive, and in the absence of externalities and dynamic problems, the free play of market forces would be an efficient way of allocating resources. The economy would attain a social optimum position with both efficiency and equity objectives achieved. However, even if we could start an economy in this way, in a dynamic world things would change. Changes in relative prices would alter the relationships between factor endowments, incomes and utility.

The incomes of farm workers, for instance, would decline relative to those of other people in the workforce as supply and demand conditions shifted to the disadvantage of food products and in favour of manufactured goods and services. Some people, through exceptional thrift, exceptional skills or exceptional luck, would accumulate fortunes, while others, less thrifty, less well endowed with ability or less fortunate, might sink into poverty. In addition, people's value judgements relating to matters of distribution might change. For all these reasons problems of distribution would emerge, and the government would have to adopt policies for dealing with them.

The world in which we live certainly did not evolve in this way – starting with an ideal distribution and evolving into one with socially unacceptable inequalities. Indeed, if anything the history of the last hundred years or so in Britain might be described as the reverse of this, with large inequalities becoming smaller, although not in a steady and continuing manner. However, major differences in income and particularly in wealth still exist. To some extent, of course, differences in income and wealth are essential for the efficient operation of the economic system. The problem is to decide at what point the degree of inequality becomes so large as to be deemed undesirable, and thus justifies the introduction of policies that make for greater equality even if this means some loss in efficiency. The question of whether existing differences are just or unjust is a matter for individual judgement, with each voting member of the population expressing his views at the ballot box.

Our first task, therefore, is to summarise the facts, such as they are, on economic inequality. Section 4.3 will then examine the main explanations given for inequality, and in section 4.4 we shall examine some of the alternative policies open to a government to correct inequalities.

4.2 THE DISTRIBUTION OF INCOME

Official figures on income distribution in Britain produced by the Central Statistical Office relate to the family unit – that is, in broad terms the husband, wife and dependent children. The income figures are based on information derived from income tax returns and include wages, salaries, interest, rent, dividends and fees, as well as transfer payments such as family allowances and pensions. A summary of these official estimates of income distribution is shown in Table 4.1. It can be seen from the table that in the early 1970s the top 5 per cent of income units accounted for about 17 per cent of pre-tax income, whereas the bottom 30 per cent accounted for about 11 per cent. After tax the inequality was, as one would expect, rather less, but not all that much less, with the top

5 per cent accounting for a slightly lower proportion and the bottom 30 per cent for a slightly higher proportion of total income.

Table 4.1   *The Distribution of income before and after tax in the United Kingdom, 1949 to 1973/4*

Income Group	Pre-tax				Post-tax			
	1949	*1959*	*1967*	*1973/4*	*1949*	*1959*	*1967*	*1973/4*
Top 5%	23·8	19·9	18·4	17·1	17·7	15·8	15·0	14·3
Next 5%	9·4	9·5	9·6	9·7	9·4	9·4	9·4	9·3
Next 60%	54·1	60·9	61·7	62·3	58·3	63·5	63·9	63·6
Bottom 30%	12·7	9·7	10·3	10·9	14·6	11·2	11·7	12·8

Source: Pre-1973/4 figures derived from Central Statistical Office, *National Income and Expenditure* (London: HMSO).
1973/4 figures derived from the Royal Commission on the Distribution of Income and Wealth, *Report No. 4* (London: HMSO, October 1976).

What about the changes in the distribution of income over time? The data in Table 4.1 shows that over the 1950s and 1960s there was a decline in the share of the top 5 per cent of income units, but also a decline in the share of the bottom 30 per cent. The income units who gained were those in the broad middle band. This pattern appeared in both the post-tax and pre-tax income distributions, and it points to two conclusions. First, it is not possible to say unambiguously that there was a reduction in inequality. Second, there seems to be no evidence that, over the period covered, government taxation policies became significantly more important in redistributing income. On the question of changes in the degree of inequality, the conclusion we draw depends on the weights we attach to the changing fortunes of different income groups. If our main concern is with fleecing the well-to-do then we may conclude that the picture showed some improvement. If, however, we attach a greater weight to the fact that the share of the bottom 30 per cent fell than to the redistribution away from the top 5 per cent, then we may conclude that inequality has increased.

The general pattern of income distribution shown in Table 4.1 is, of course, not unique to the United Kingdom. A similar picture emerges in other countries. Table 4.2 reproduces the results of an OECD study. Problems relating to differences in sources, the reliability of official data, the definition of income, the specification of the income unit, and so on make international comparisons a rather hazardous exercise. However, the statistics for each country taken on its own are surely reliable enough for us to conclude that there appears to be a large measure of inequality in the distribution of incomes in virtually all developed market economies.

Table 4.2 *The Distribution of Pre-tax Incomes by Household in Various Countries*

Country	Year	Top 10%	Next 60%	Bottom 30%
Australia	1966/7	23·8	63·6	12·8
Canada	1969	27·1	64·0	8·9
France	1970	31·0	60·5	8·5
Germany	1973	31·3	58·5	10·4
Japan	1969	28·6	58·0	13·4
Netherlands	1967	31·1	58·1	10·8
Norway	1970	24·5	65·7	9·8
Sweden	1972	24·4	63·9	11·3
UK	1973	24·7	64·8	10·5
USA	1972	28·4	63·5	8·0
Average		27·3	62·0	10·5
Dispersion (average for deciles)		0·20	0·06	0·10

Source: OECD, *Income Distribution in OECD Countries,* Occasional Paper (Paris: OECD, July 1976).

4.21 *Measuring the Degree of Inequality*

A common method of summarising information on income distribution is through the use of the Lorenz curve. It shows the share of income received by the bottom x per cent of income units. Two such curves are shown in Figure 4.1, relating to the official estimates of pre-tax income distribution in Britain in 1949 and 1973/4. This is simply a graphical way of showing the information given in Table 4.1, but it permits the introduction of a much fuller frequency distribution without any loss of simplicity. If income is equally distributed, so that, for example, every 10 per cent of income units receive 10 per cent of income, the Lorenz curve follows the diagonal. At the other extreme where one income unit accounts for all income, the Lorenz curve follows the horizontal and vertical axes.

Associated with the Lorenz curve is a summary measure of the concentration of income known as the Gini coefficient. It is equal to the area between the Lorenz curve and the diagonal, divided by the total area under the diagonal. Thus the value of the coefficient ranges from 0 when incomes are equal and the Lorenz curve follows the diagonal, to 1 when income is most concentrated and the Lorenz curve coincides with the axes. The lower the value of the coefficient, therefore, the less the degree of inequality. From

1949 to 1973/4 the coefficient in Britain fell from 0·41 to 0·37, suggesting a slight decline in the degree of concentration of pre-tax income. This merely indicates the dangers of using summary measures of income distribution. The fall in value of the Gini coefficient is due to the fact that the redistribution of income away from the top 5 per cent of income units just outweighed the fall in the share of the bottom 30 per cent. But as indicated above, if we attached greater weight to the losses of those on low incomes, then the Gini coefficients would appear as a misleading summary of what happened to the distribution of income. In Figure 4.1, if the entire Lorenz curve had shifted towards the diagonal from 1949 to 1973/4, then of course we could say unambiguously that the distribution became more equal in this period, but because the two curves intersect, we cannot come to any conclusion about the trend in income distribution without making value judgements about the relative importance of different income groups.

Figure 4.1

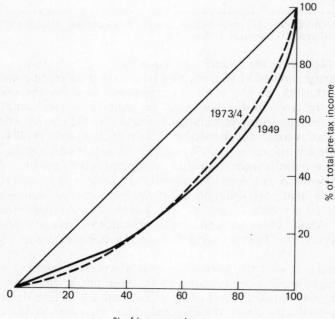

One further point about Lorenz curves is that they give no information on the levels of income. This is important not only in examining the distribution of income for a particular country over time, but also in comparing the income distributions of different countries in a particular year. Thus a comparison of two Lorenz curves might show that the share of the bottom 30 per cent of income units was lower in country *A* than in country *B*, but it might be the case that the average level of income was higher in *A* than in *B*, a fact that would be important in assessing the relative plight of the lower income classes in the two countries.

Turning then to the absolute level of incomes in Britain, the most striking feature is the wide range, with people at the top earning well in excess of £100,000 a year and, at the bottom, those self-employed people whose businesses have hit upon hard times and who in fact have negative incomes. The official figures for 1973/4 covered nearly 21 million income units with an average pre-tax annual income of £2 203. Out of this total approximately 2 000 units had an income of £50 000 and over, and more than 3 million units had an income of less than £1 000. The majority of people, of course, had an income somewhere in the middle ranges, over 16·5 million families having an annual income between £1 000 and £4 000. Although these figures are now out of date, if more up-to-date information were available it would almost certainly reveal a similar pattern – the majority of families in the middle income ranges, a relatively small number with very large incomes, and a substantial minority on very low incomes.

Before we turn to a closer examination of the extremes of the income distribution, something should be said about the deficiencies of the official data on which the above summary has been based.

First, there is a question mark to be set against the accuracy of the data. In Britain the information given above is drawn from income tax returns, and is thus affected by the incidence, and opportunities across income groups, of tax evasion.

Second, the official definition of income departs significantly from the one generally adopted by economists. From the economist's point of view, income in a given period is that sum of money a person could spend while maintaining the real value of his wealth intact. Included in this definition, but usually excluded in official estimates of income, are such important items as capital gains, fringe benefits and imputed rent. The inclusion of capital gains and fringe benefits would increase the share of people at the top end of the income scale, whereas an allowance for imputed rent would increase the share of people at both ends of the scale. Although reliable data on which to estimate the quantitative import-ance of these items is limited, it is likely that on balance their inclusion would result in an increase in the share of the top income groups.

Third, official estimates make no allowance for difference in needs. If those with low incomes tended to have fewer dependants than high income earners then the distribution of income according to need would be more equal than is indicated by the official data. The latter is in fact based on the family unit and thus makes no allowance for differences in the number of dependents supported by the income earner. Attempts have been made to allow for differences in the size of family and also for the composition of the family, so as to allow, for instance, for the lower needs of children than of adults. The result of these attempts is to effect a modest reduction in the dispersion of income.

Fourth, the use of annual income data is subject to certain criticisms. For instance, income in a particular year will include certain transitory components – the result perhaps of good and bad luck – which will not be repeated in subsequent years. If such transitory items could be taken out of the distribution, its dispersion would be reduced. Another important factor is that part of the dispersion in annual income is due to the systematic variation of income with different phases of the lifecycle, that is, to the fact that, typically, an individual will have a much lower income in his early adult years than in middle age, and a higher income in middle age than in retirement. If we are interested in differences in lifetime incomes, then annual data will exaggerate the extent to which income is concentrated. Some idea of the importance of this factor is obtained by comparing the distribution of income for the population as a whole with that within age groups. If lifecycle differences are very important, this will be reflected in a much lower dispersion of incomes within age groups. Although such a comparison does indeed show that income tends to be less concentrated within age groups than in the whole population, the difference is not all that great, indicating that lifecycle factors, although contributing part of the explanation of differences in annual income, by no means tell the whole story.

Fifth, our interest is basically with real rather than money incomes. Thus if we are concerned with a comparison of incomes in different parts of the country, account has to be taken of regional price differences. And if we are concerned with changes in distribution account has to be taken of changes in prices. One important aspect of the latter is that the rate of inflation is not the same for all goods and services, and this, combined with the fact that the composition of the household budget varies between families, means that inflation will have an unequal effect. For instance, pensioners and low wage families tend to spend a larger percentage of their income on food than other income units, so that during a period when food prices are increasing at an especially rapid rate, these groups will suffer more than others.

Sixth, the post-tax income statistics make no allowance for the impact of indirect taxes. This again is bound to affect the distribution of real purchasing power, because different income groups have different consumption patterns and some goods are subject to different tax rates than others. There can be no doubt that, in general, indirect taxes are regressive, bearing more heavily upon the lower than the higher income classes.

Seventh, the official statistics on income distribution do not allow for a whole range of goods and services that are provided free or at nominal cost by the State. These benefits, it can be argued, are fairly equally shared, and failure to make allowance for them will result in an overestimate of the concentration of purchasing power.

'. . . the more highly commercialised is a society and the more its every activity and manifestation is subject to economic transactions, the fewer become its free benefits with equal or random access, and the more the distribution of purchasing power becomes controlling for the distribution of goods and services. The hankering of some people, therefore, for a less commercial and less money-minded world turns out to be not merely a romantic notion but also a preference for a world in which some, perhaps many, of the good things of life were distributed independently of the distribution of income and wealth.' (T. Scitovsky)

In view of all the qualifications that have to be made to official data on income distribution, the general pattern summarised in Table 4.1 and the accompanying text has to be viewed with caution. This applies not only to the picture in any one year but also to changes in the distribution over time. However, attempts at quantifying the importance of individual qualifications have in general indicated a modest adjustment to the raw data. Furthermore, the adjustments have not all been in the same direction, so that some of the adjustments required would have been offset by others. In particular there can be no doubt about the existence of very high incomes at the top end of the scale and of the significant minority of poor people at the bottom, and it is to these groups that we now turn.

4.3 THE EXTREMES OF WEALTH AND POVERTY

4.31 *The Rich*
The people with the very highest incomes are men and women of property. It is important, therefore, to examine the distribution of wealth and to inquire into the main reasons for the fact that the

ownership of wealth is heavily concentrated in the hands of so few people.

Ideally, we should like to have information on the net wealth of every income unit – broadly speaking, the family unit. All assets and liabilities would be assessed, including, on the one hand, financial assets such as cash, money deposited in banks and building societies, shares, houses, cars and household goods; and on the other, mortgages, bank overdrafts, other debts, etc. We could then estimate the distribution of wealth among families. Unfortunately, in practice none of this is possible. The primary sources of data are the estates of the deceased, information on which is collected for the purpose of estate taxation. The overall wealth picture is derived by using the estates of the deceased as a random sample of the living population. The method used is to multiply the wealth of the deceased in a particular age and sex group by the reciprocal of the mortality rate for that group, corrected for social class.

This is clearly a rather crude method of estimating the distribution of wealth, but before turning to consider some of the main problems let us look at the picture shown by the official estimates. For 1974 the Inland Revenue estimates cover nearly 19 million individuals in Britain with total wealth holdings of £157 000 million. The top 10 per cent of wealth holders (roughly those with net wealth of £15 000 or more) owned nearly 50 per cent of total wealth; the top 7 per cent (those with net wealth of £20 000 or more) accounted for about 40 per cent; and the top 1·5 per cent (those with net wealth of £50 000 or more) accounted for over 20 per cent. The people at the very top (the 26 000 people with assets worth over £200 000 and accounting for only 0·14 per cent of recorded wealth owners) were estimated to hold 7·5 per cent of the total wealth. US official statistics on wealth are very limited, but what evidence there is suggests a similar picture. One study estimated that the top 1 per cent of the population owned 27 per cent of wealth in 1953, 26 per cent in 1962, and 24 per cent in 1969.

As indicated earlier there are a number of reasons why these estimates should be treated with caution. First, the assumption that the dead are a random sample of the living is obviously a very strong one, and the mortality rates used may also be inaccurate. Second, the estate duty statistics by no means cover all estates. The estates that are not included are those of people with little or no wealth. Their exclusion from the data clearly results in an underestimation of the concentration of wealth. The Inland Revenue has estimated the distribution of wealth in Britain making alternative assumptions about the circumstances of the individuals not covered by existing tax regulations. On the assumption that these people have an average wealth holding of £1 055, the share of the top 10 per cent works out at 61·5 per cent, whereas on the assumption that they have zero wealth it works out at 66 per cent. These figures, however, ignore the value of pension rights, and this brings us to a third problem. Decisions must be made about what items to include as personal wealth. One item that is not included in officially published data and whose inclusion would have a substantial effect on the results is the value of state pension rights. These are distributed more equally than other assets and so have an equalising effect on the distribution. Making an allowance for both occupational and state pension rights the Inland Revenue estimates for 1974 put the share of the top 10 per cent at 41 per cent. There is some dispute, however, as to whether pensions are properly regarded as part of personal wealth. The problem is that pensions are a form of wealth that is not realisable in the same way as bank deposits or stocks and shares. Fourth, the wealth in those estates that are covered is likely to be underestimated because many individuals will have taken steps to avoid estate duty. Fifth, there is the question of the most appropriate method of valuation. The estate duty method is based on what an asset would realise if sold. In many cases this realisation value of assets will be substantially less than their worth as a 'going concern'. For the latter the replacement value is the appropriate measure. A houseful of furniture, for example, will in general realise a much smaller sum on the secondhand market than its true worth to the householder. Similarly, the secondhand value of machinery may be substantially less than its value to the owner of a continuing business. Sixth, the estate duty figures relate, as we have noted, to individuals and not to families. Because the benefits of wealth will be largely shared by members of the family, the latter would be a more appropriate unit on which to collect data. A change from an individual to a family basis would result in a fall in the measured concentration of wealth, unless, that is, rich men have equally rich wives, in which case the existing estate duty data will, on this score, give a true picture. Finally, as in the case of incomes, there is the lifecycle factor. The distribution of wealth shown for any one year will undoubtedly show a somewhat greater dispersion than the lifetime distribution, since at any point in time there will be members of society who have little wealth simply because they haven't had time to accumulate it. An examination of the distribution of wealth within age groups will give some idea of the importance of the lifetime forces of accumulation. If they were an important factor, then we should expect to find the distribution of wealth within age groups to be much less unequal than for the population as a whole. Upon inspection, however, this is not found to be the case, the dispersion of wealth within age groups being of similar magnitude to the overall dispersion.

The concentration of wealth, therefore, is not simply a reflection of the larger wealth holdings of the senior members of the community, whose position everyone in time will automatically attain.

Clearly, if an attempt were made to adjust the official raw data so as to allow for these qualifications, the effect of some of the adjustments would be to increase the degree of concentration, while others would reduce it. For example, the inclusion of individuals who are missing from the estate duty figures would increase the concentration, whereas the inclusion of pension rights and the change from an individual to a family basis would reduce it. A somewhat different picture would thus emerge, depending on the position taken with regard to the problems that have been outlined. Atkinson's estimate for 1968 suggests that when adjustments are made to the raw official data, so as to take account of missing people and missing wealth (including state pension rights), the share of the top 1 per cent of individual wealth holders is likely to have been of the order of 20 per cent. Thus even when allowance is made for the various deficiencies embodied in the estate duty data, there is little reason to seriously doubt the general picture that they reveal – that of a considerable concentration of wealth in the hands of the relatively few.

But what about changes in the distribution of personal wealth over time? Although the concentration is substantial even today, it is not, so it would seem, anything like as concentrated as it was, say, fifty years ago. For instance, whereas the share of wealth held by the top 1 per cent may have been in the region of 30 per cent at the end of the 1960s, in the 1920s it was about double this figure. However, this picture is rather misleading. In part the sharp reduction must be due to the very big increase in estate duty and the incentive that this gave the top wealth owners to part with some of their wealth in the form of gifts during their lifetime. In addition it has become more common for property to be owned jointly by husband and wife. Both these factors would reduce the share of the top 1 per cent of wealth holders, but increase that of the next most wealthy group – say the next 4 or 5 per cent. This in fact is just what has occurred. From 1924 to 1968 the share of the top 1 per cent is estimated to have declined from 60 per cent to 30 per cent, but the next 4 per cent increased their share from 21 per cent to 25 per cent. In part, therefore, the long term decline in the concentration of wealth simply reflects a redistribution within wealthy families rather than an improvement in the relative position of poor families.

One of the most important factors tending towards a more equal distribution of wealth has been the increase in the number of people who are owner-occupiers, together with the increase in house prices.

The latter has ensured, for the majority of owner-occupiers, a substantial difference between the market value of their house and the outstanding mortgage, thus increasing their net worth. Another important factor is the movement in share prices. The great bulk of personally held shares are owned by the top 5 per cent of wealth owners. A sharp fall in share prices, such as occurred in 1974, would thus have the effect of reducing concentration. In fact a significant equalising tendency may have operated after 1973 not only because of the decline in share prices but also because of the greater downward pressure on house prices at the top end of the market. On the other hand, of course, it has to be recognised that such tendencies may be reversed in future by a boom in share prices and an above average increase in the price of expensive houses.

Finally in this section we turn our attention now to the important question of how positions of great wealth are attained. There are two main roads to the top: accumulation of self-made fortunes, and inheritance. Their relative significance is important in determining the extent and the direction of government redistributive policies. If the current wealth distribution is largely the product of individuals saving significant amounts out of large incomes, then the distribution and generation of earned income and the rate of return on accumulated wealth are the crucial policy variables. Membership of the top group will be relatively fluid over generations. If the distribution of wealth is primarily the product of inheritance, then of course the mechanism by which wealth is transmitted from generation to generation needs careful investigation. The wealth hierarchy will be rigid through time and over generations, and family membership of the top wealth groups will remain fairly constant. We shall examine each mechanism in turn.

Some inequality in the distribution of wealth will occur because of differences in earnings, and the fact that more can be saved out of higher incomes. We know, of course, that substantial differences in earnings do exist. They are due in part to differences between workers in personal characteristics, such as intelligence, educational attainment, experience and determination, and family background. In part they may be explained by the activities of trade unions and the government, and by elements of industrial structure such as the size distribution of firms. The role of custom and status is often important, as indeed are the forces of chance or luck. Whatever the explanation for earnings differentials it is clear that those at the top end of the scale are in a favourable position to accumulate wealth, especially if high earnings are combined with exceptional thrift. These two factors alone, however, are not sufficient to explain the actual distribution of wealth. Together they would certainly allow a person to accumulate a substantial fortune, but not until late in life, which would lead us to expect that the wealthy would be found primarily among society's highest age groups. However, there are many individuals who become rich before they reach middle age. For instance, in 1967 one-third of those in the United Kingdom with wealth in excess of £125 000 were under the age of 45.

A more important factor explaining the rapid accumulation of fortunes is an exceptionally high yield on wealth. This road to the top is therefore associated with the skills and luck of successful entrepreneurship. Those who have amassed fortunes by earning exceptionally high returns on their wealth have done so in a number of different ways. In some cases it has been due to the owner-ship of natural resources, such as land, which have greatly increased in value. The boom in the value of building land in the early 1970s resulted in fortunes for many landowners fortunate enough to benefit from planning regulations. Many have made their fortunes by correctly anticipating market changes, such as the change from counter service to self-service in the retail trade, the expansion of road transport for both passenger and goods, and the increased demand for holidays abroad. Early identification of such market trends has allowed people to gain an early foothold in an expanding sector of the economy and to benefit fully from the expansion. Others have made their fortunes by invention and the commercial exploitation of new products or processes. In all of this, of course, luck often plays an important part – the luck of having land, suit-able for building, in the right place; of making an important break-through in research that puts one ahead of competitors; of having good contacts, and so on.

The other important factor in explaining the existence of large fortunes is, of course, inheritance. The way in which inheritance affects the distribution of wealth from one generation to another depends on a number of factors. First, there are the laws and customs relating to inheritance. If they tend towards an equal division of estates among all children, there will be a strong ten-dency for the distribution of wealth to be equalised. If, on the other hand, the bulk of an estate is inherited by one child, large estates will be preserved. Second, there is the importance of family size. With equal division, the larger the number of children who exist to share the spoils the more quickly will large estates be dissipated. Third, the pattern of marriage is important. If wealthy men married poor women and vice versa, this would be a powerful force tending towards greater equality. However, if the wealthy tend to inter-marry the concentration of wealth will be preserved. Finally, we should mention the thriftiness of the children who inherit. If the children of the wealthy are thrifty, they may increase or at least preserve what they have inherited. On the other hand, if they turn out to be spendthrifts, the family fortune may quickly disappear.

Finally, what is the relative importance of entrepreneurship and inheritance in explaining today's top wealth holders? The answer to this question is not entirely clear-cut. Very few people actually go from rags to riches. Most of those who have made their own fortunes had the advantage of at least a modest inheritance. In a study by Harbury and McMahon it appears that, of the sons who left estates of £100 000 or more in 1965, 45 per cent had fathers who left more than that amount in real terms, 58 per cent had fathers who left over £50 000, and 33 per cent had fathers who left over £25 000. A later study by Harbury and Hitchens suggests that the importance of inheritance has declined in recent years. Of the sons who left estates of £100 000 or more in 1973, 35 per cent had fathers who left more than this in real terms, 48 per cent had fathers who left over £50 000, and 58 per cent had fathers who left over £25 000. However, these figures are likely to underestimate the benefits of inheritance, since they exclude wealth transmitted in the form of gifts during the father's lifetime, and it is quite possible that these could have amounted in many cases to more than the sum passed on after death. A growing tendency to make gifts *inter vivos* may also be a factor explaining the apparent decline in the importance of inheritance in recent years. In view of this and in view of the important headstart that even a modest inheritance affords, it is difficult to determine the extent to which fortunes are genuinely self-made. The evidence suggests that they form a substantial minority of cases, but that inheritance is still by far the most important single explanation of the inequality of wealth.

4.32 *The Poor*

Although there will always be some dispute over the question of how many of them there are, there can be no doubt that 'the poor' are still with us. Poverty is a relative concept. It relates to the deprivations suffered by a section of society in relation to what is regarded as necessary for normal living. This means inevitably that the definition of poverty involves judgements that will vary from person to person. Indeed, in the final analysis the judgement that has to be made is a political one.

In Britain successive governments have set minimum levels of money income for families of various sizes and composition. A person who is not working and whose income falls below the prescribed level is entitled to supplementary benefits. Most investigators in Britain have used the supplementary benefits scale as the official definition of what constitutes the minimum level of income, so that anyone below the scale is defined as 'poor'. On this basis it appears from an analysis of the family expenditure surveys that there are about 2 million people, or approximately 3·5 per cent of the population, living in poverty. Studies using Inland Revenue data, however, suggest that the figure may be as high as 5 million. Furthermore, the figures do not appear to have changed much since the early 1960s. There is no need to enter into a detailed critique of these estimates. It is sufficient to note that a substantial minority of the population are living in conditions of poverty, and on this everyone seems agreed.

What then are the causes of poverty? The proximate reasons are not difficult to establish. They are old age, large families, low earnings, unemployment and sickness. Two points are worth making about these various causes. First, their individual contributions to the total poverty picture have changed and are likely to continue to change over time. Unemployment in 1976 was a less important factor than in 1936, but a more important factor than it was in 1966. Old age has increased substantially in importance since the interwar years, reflecting the ageing of the population and a trend towards earlier retirement. Large families have over the same period declined substantially in importance, reflecting economic and social changes. Second, the factors listed above may interact in such a way as to sentence some families to a lifetime of poverty, or even generations of poverty within the same family. A person with a low income and several mouths to feed will find it difficult to save, and so may be entirely dependent on a state pension in old age. His children may leave school at the earliest opportunity in order to remove some of the financial burden, and even when in school may find their academic advancement impeded by the pressing need to find some sort of part-time work. They are more likely, therefore, than the children of well-endowed families to find themselves in low wage occupations with little prospect for advancement.

Why, it may be asked, have these causes of poverty persisted? After all, the period since the Second World War has, in general, been characterised by full employment and the existence of various welfare payments. As far as poverty due to low earnings is concerned, part of the problem no doubt has been the slow rate of structural change in the British economy. As far as the other causes are concerned, the main problem seems to be that the social insurance benefits paid by the government have been persistently below the government's own minimum standards.

Because of the persistence of poverty a variety of means-tested benefits have been introduced in an attempt to focus assistance on those in need. Thus there are supplementary benefits for those not at work, and family income supplements for those who are earning.

In addition, there are more specific means-tested benefits, such as rent and rate rebates, free school meals and free prescriptions. For various reasons, however, these means-tested benefits have failed to solve the problem. Many people who are eligible for assistance fail to apply for it partly because they do not realise that they are eligible, partly because of the rather complex form-filling exercise that has to be completed in order to prove eligibility, and partly because of pride and an unwillingness to reveal any dependence on state handouts. A further problem has been that the various means-tested benefits can reduce the incentive to work. A person may find that if he increased his earnings he would – as a result of paying income tax on the increased earnings and losing various means-tested benefits – be only a little better off. Such a person would, as a result of high effective marginal rates of tax, find himself in the 'poverty trap'.

4.4 POLICY

Now that we have outlined some of the main features of the distribution of income and wealth in Britain, what can we say about policy? In broad terms there are three different policy approaches available to the government: first, policies aimed at effecting a redistribution of productive resources, including wealth and human capital; second, fiscal measures to redistribute income; and third, direct interference in individual markets by way of manipulation of relative prices so as to confer benefit on certain sections of the community. Whatever the approach adopted, it is important to bear in mind not only the implications from the point of view of equity but also the consequences for efficiency. Thus, as we shall see, government intervention in individual markets may have adverse effects on the allocation of resources; and certain fiscal measures may change the balance between present and future consumption, while others may affect the incentives to work and thus the size of the national income.

4.41 *The Redistribution of Factors*
The basic justification for policies aimed at a redistribution of factors is founded on the principle of equal opportunity. At present it is manifest that individuals do not enter this world with equal opportunity. Some are born into wealthy families, into prosperous regions of the economy, and enjoy a good education. Others are born into poverty, into a depressed area of the economy, and receive an inferior education. There are a number of policies that the government could pursue that would help to correct this imbalance. The most obvious and direct approach is by means of fiscal measures

for the redistribution of wealth. One possibility here is to have an annual tax on wealth. Such a tax is certainly feasible since it already exists in a number of countries. However, it suffers from a number of disadvantages. First, the tax does not distinguish between inherited and self-made wealth. Second, an annual wealth tax would not be entirely appropriate if the lifecycle pattern of wealth holding varied between individuals. Third, there would be problems of valuation, and the administrative costs of collecting the tax are likely to be high. For instance, with an exemption limit as high as £50 000, about 200 000 tax returns a year would have to be dealt with at an administrative cost estimated at more than 10 per cent of the revenue. Finally, a wealth tax penalises savings and encourages the use of wealth to finance current consumption.

A more promising alternative would be an effective tax on the transfer of wealth. Up until 1974 the main tax on the transfer of wealth in Britain was the estate duty. It was a tax charged on the total amount of property, above the exemption limit, transferred at death. Although the nominal rates of duty were highly progressive, the effectiveness of the estate duty in redistributing wealth was blunted by two serious defects. First, it offered no incentive to the wealth holder to divide his property between a number of beneficiaries. Second, there were some gaping loopholes that made it easy to avoid paying the tax. The simplest means of avoidance was by passing on property in the form of gifts, for so long as these gifts were not made within seven years of death they escaped duty. Another way of reducing liability to tax was by the setting up of trusts, which enabled a distinction to be made between the legal owners of a property and the actual beneficiaries. In this way tax would be paid on the initial transfer of wealth to the trust but then the identity of the beneficiaries could change without any additional tax liability.

In 1975 the UK government introduced a capital transfer tax (CTT), which in effect added a gifts tax to the old system of death duties. CTT is a cumulative tax on all gratuitous transfers of capital whether they occur during a person's lifetime or at death. There is a higher rate of tax on gifts than on property transferred at death, but gifts of up to £1 000 per annum are exempt. CTT is not an accessions tax since it is paid by the person making the gift and not by the beneficiary. As a redistributive weapon CTT could of course be made more effective by bringing the rate of tax on property transferred at death into line with the rate on gifts between the living, and by lowering the exemption limit for gifts made in any one year. However, the tax suffers from the disadvantage that it does not give any incentive to people to split their wealth into small units and to transfer it to individuals who own little property.

An alternative that has been suggested is that there should be an accessions tax. This would be a tax imposed on the accumulated total of all wealth transfers *received* by an individual over his lifetime. A record would be kept of every gift or inheritance received by each individual, and a progressive tax levied on the total amount received, from whatever source. Thus, the first £10 000 received by an individual might be exempt, the second £10 000 taxed at a rate of 10 per cent, the next £5 000 taxed at 20 per cent, and so on. Such a tax would have the advantage of encouraging people to dispose of their wealth by splitting it up into several bequests rather than by leaving it to one beneficiary who would have to pay a high rate of tax. However, the tax would have disadvantages. The effectiveness of the strategy would be limited by the fact that in many cases the wealthy individual might not want to distribute his wealth beyond a small group of near relatives. In these cases in particular the tax would tend to discourage accumulation, although the precise magnitude of this effect would depend on the progressiveness of the tax. It would also involve substantial administration costs. On the other hand, the tax would most certainly be a potent weapon in redistributing wealth. In assessing the desirability of such a tax the redistributive effects, the extra administrative costs, and the effects in incentives to work and to accumulate, must all be weighed in the balance.

Apart from inequalities in the distribution of wealth there are also inequalities in the distribution of human and social capital. Another important reason for the unequal distribution of factors lies in the differences between individuals in the amount of education and training that they have received, and in the social capital that they enjoy. As far as education is concerned, the spread of state primary and secondary education has done much to equalise opportunity, but there remains a great deal to be done. There are still very substantial differences in the quality of education, and pressing problems exist especially in many inner city areas.

Apart from the problems of the inner city there are more broadly defined areas of the country that are disadvantaged, either because of rural depopulation or because of the decline of old industrial areas. Here again we find pockets of poverty, not only in terms of low money incomes, but also in terms of the poor quality of the social overhead capital. The solution to these problems requires long-term structural remedies as well as short-term fiscal measures. The long term remedies include a major extension of retraining facilities and a regional policy that provides new job opportunities in the depressed areas, both directly, by encouraging new investment, and indirectly, by improving the quality of education, communications and other social services. It is difficult to overemphasise the importance of these policies relating to the distribution of human and social capital, because they act upon the very forces that generate inequality.

4.42　Income Maintenance

Although longer term measures are an indispensable part of a sensible government policy aimed at redistributing income, there is the immediate and pressing problem of looking after today's poor. For this purpose some form of income maintenance scheme is necessary. Ideally, what we need is a scheme that will bring every individual above the poverty line and at the same time maintain incentives to earn and save.

(a) *Expanded national insurance.* We have noted that one of the main reasons for the persistence of poverty has been that national insurance benefits such as pensions and family allowances have been persistently below the level necessary to keep people out of poverty, as defined by the government. The national insurance system has also failed to give coverage to all income groups and has, for instance, neglected the welfare of groups such as single parent families. One possible solution, therefore, would be simply to make all national insurance benefits more generous, bringing them up to the predetermined poverty level and thus obviating the need for all means-tested benefits. As at present, the payments would be made to all, but the net benefits to those in the middle and upper income ranges would be reduced and, beyond some point on the income scale, eliminated by the 'clawing back' of benefits through the payment of income tax.

A major advantage of such a solution is that, with the exception of poverty that is due to low earnings, there are not likely to be any significant problems of coverage. Since payment of the benefits would be made to all regardless of income, no special machinery would be needed for dealing with the needs of the poor. The stigma of being identified via a means test as a member of the poor would be avoided. This important disadvantage of means-tested benefits, which is a major factor explaining the failure to obtain full coverage of those in need, would thus be absent.

Another point in favour of the scheme is that it would be unlikely to have a significant adverse effect on the incentive to earn more. A major feature of the scheme is that the withdrawal of benefits, through the payment of income tax as earnings increased, would be gradual. Those receiving benefits who were successful in increasing their earnings would not, therefore, be confronted with a very high effective marginal tax rate.

This same feature, however, would also give rise to a problem that would no doubt prove to be a major obstacle to extending the national insurance system, namely the cost involved. The gradual withdrawal of benefits would necessarily mean that many people who were above the official poverty line would in fact be net gainers. In itself this would be no bad thing, for in view of the impossibility of defining the poverty line with any precision there would inevitably be many people with incomes above the official line who were in poverty because of special circumstances. No doubt there would be others who would benefit without good cause, but this might be considered a small price to pay in order to increase the chances of complete coverage. Having said this, however, cost is clearly an important consideration, because the political feasibility of introducing any scheme hinges on it.

One further point in relation to the proposal to expand the existing social insurance system is that it would not cover poverty resulting from low earnings. For this purpose some other policy weapon would be required, such as a minimum wage policy – a possibility that is examined later in this chapter.

(b) *A social dividend.* More far reaching reforms of the social security system have, however, been proposed. The most radical of these is the idea of a social dividend, payable to all and exempt from taxation. The social dividend would replace all existing benefits, including tax allowances. The scheme is illustrated in Figure 4.2. *OS* represents the social dividend, the size of which depends on the size and composition of the family. A family with no other income would receive the full dividend, set at the level that the government regarded as the minimum needed to keep the family out of poverty. Families with any additional income would pay tax, and at an income level of *Y* the tax paid would be equal to the social dividend. At higher levels of income, families would be paying more in tax than they received by way of the dividend. It

Figure 4.2

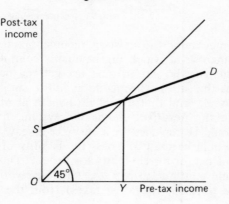

has been estimated that, if financed entirely by means of a proportional income tax, the rate of tax would have to be set at over
50 per cent. Any scheme involving a standard rate of tax at this
level is almost certainly doomed to failure. Those, such as Meade,
who have advocated this kind of approach have suggested various
ways of reducing the standard rate of tax, especially by introducing
an element of progressiveness into the tax system and by extending
the tax base to include, for example, the annual value of owner-
occupier houses. Even so, the introduction of a social dividend at
a level sufficient to bring everyone above the poverty line would
involve a substantial increase in taxation.

(*c*) *A negative income tax.* An alternative and less radical income
maintenance scheme is the introduction of a negative income tax
within the present tax structure and alongside at least some of the
present means-tested benefits. This, together with a concentration
of benefit on the low income group, would reduce the cost of the
scheme as compared to the alternatives so far discussed. One
version of a negative income tax proposal is shown in Figure 4.3.

Figure 4.3

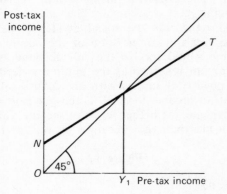

Post-tax income under the existing income tax is given by *OIT*.
The level of income at which tax payments commence is Y_1. This
means that people who pay income tax get the benefit of various
tax allowances that are not available in full to similar families with
incomes below Y_1, and that are of no benefit at all to the poorest
families. With the negative income tax system, however, the tax
allowances would be replaced by a cash credit payable to all. These
cash credits would be used to assess the liability of each individual
for payment of tax, or his eligibility for benefit. Those with incomes
above Y_1 would continue to pay tax, but those with lower incomes
would receive payment (negative taxes) from the government. In

order to maintain consistency with existing tax arrangements, the cash credit for a family with no earnings would be equal to *ON*. For such a scheme to operate everyone would, of course, have to complete a tax return.

As mentioned earlier, part of the attraction of such a scheme is that by concentrating benefits on the poorest families and by restricting the scale of benefits it would be less costly to introduce, and so would require a smaller increase in taxation than more ambitious schemes. At the same time, those in work and those out of work would both be covered. However, this type of solution, like all others, has its problems:

1 The restriction of benefits to the poor would inevitably mean that many families just above the poverty line would continue to suffer hardship.
2 The rapid curtailment of the negative tax benefits as income increased, together with the continued dependence of many families on means-tested benefits, would result in high effective marginal rates of tax on those close to the poverty line, which could have adverse effects on incentives to increase earnings.
3 Requiring everyone to file a tax return would cause a substantial increase in administrative costs, and this would have to be taken into account in evaluating the scheme.

The Effects of Policies on Incentives. At several points in the discussion we have drawn attention to the effect of particular policies on incentives. There are two aspects to this problem: the effect of high marginal rates of tax on the incentive to increase earnings, and the effect that the scale of benefits has on the incentive to seek employment.

Let us first of all consider the effect of taxation on the supply of effort. An income tax is equivalent to a subsidy on leisure, making leisure less expensive in relation to the price of goods. Because of this the substitution effect of the tax is to induce an increase in the demand for leisure and thus a reduction in hours worked. The income effect, however, will work towards a reduction in the demand for leisure and thus an increase in hours worked, as long as leisure is not regarded as an inferior good. And since in the case of the supply of labour the income effect will normally be large, economic analysis cannot predict with certainty what the net effect will be. In Figure 4.4 the wage rate is initially that shown by RW, and the individual is at point A where the wage rate is equal to his marginal rate of substitution between income and leisure. A proportional income tax is introduced, which changes the take-home wage rate to RW_1. As a result the individual reduces the number of hours he offers for work. Clearly, however, the indifference map could have been drawn in such a way as to show an increase or no change in working hours following the introduction of the tax. The effect of a tax, or of an increase in tax, on the supply of effort can only be determined by empirical work. The latter will seek to establish not only the direction of the effect but also its quantitative importance. As far as the latter is concerned, the effect of a tax is not likely, in the short run at least, to affect normal hours, since these are usually fixed by union–employer bargaining. Rather, the effect will be found in the willingness to work overtime, in absenteeism, and in the supply of effort within normal working hours.

Figure 4.4

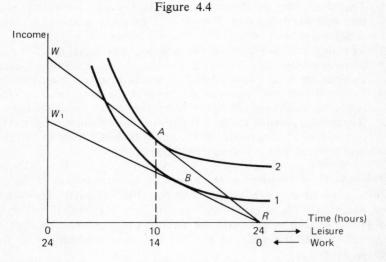

Turning now to the effect of the scale of benefits, it is clear that the higher the level of benefits in relation to wages the greater the danger that some people will refuse to work at all. There is a problem, therefore, of finding the right balance in social security payments – of being sufficiently generous to those in need while at the same time minimising the danger of being so generous as to swell to significant proportions the ranks of those who are unwilling to work. It was Beveridge's plan 'to abolish want by ensuring that every citizen willing to serve according to his powers has at all times an income sufficient to meet his responsibilities' (Lord Beveridge, *Social Insurance and Allied Services,* London: HMSO, 1942). There will always be a number of people who will abuse any system, and it is important not to allow such cases to divert attention away from the genuine difficulties faced by low income groups. At the same time, however, in the assessment of any particular scheme, consideration should be given to the possible effect of the scale of benefits on the willingness to work.

We cannot hope in such a brief sketch of an important topic to have done justice to the finer points in the debate that continues to rage in this field. What we do hope to have emphasised is the importance, in considering each possible solution, of examining a number of key questions, including costs, the effectiveness in alleviating poverty, administrative problems, and the effects on incentives. Alternative solutions may vary widely in their effects on incentives and in the administrative costs incurred in their implementation. They will also vary widely in terms of cost, but by and large low cost schemes can be bought only at the cost of falling well short of the goal of eliminating poverty. Any scheme that is to be effective in eliminating poverty, in the sense not only of maintaining adequate incomes but also of improving the quality of the social capital in depressed areas, will be costly and will involve a substantial redistribution of resources.

4.43 *Redistribution through the Market*
A third way in which the government can redistribute real income is by manipulating relative prices. The policies considered in the previous sections will, of course, have effects on efficiency – by affecting the incentive to work they will in turn affect the size of the national income, by affecting the incentive to save they will change the balance between present and future consumption, and by changing the distribution of income they will have repercussions on the allocation of resources between industries. The policies considered in this section, however, involve direct government involvement in individual markets, and the effects on efficiency are more readily observable.

There are innumerable ways in which the government can alter relative prices in order to benefit some groups in society. The following sections present a few of the main examples, and the analysis of each case serves to illustrate some of the consequences of government intervention.

Minimum Wage Legislation. In the previous section we drew attention to the possibility of extending the social insurance system as a means of eliminating poverty. Such a policy would not, however, solve the problem of poverty due to low wages. An additional policy weapon would be needed, one possibility being minimum wage legislation.

To examine the possible effects of such a policy, let us first assume that all labour markets are perfectly competitive and that differences in wages reflect differences in productivity. Let us

represent these differences by referring to the low paid as unskilled
workers and the highly paid as skilled workers. The initial demand
curves for these two groups of workers are shown as D_1 in Figure
4.5(*a*) and (*b*), and the initial wage rates as W_1. The introduction
of a minimum wage for unskilled workers of W_m will result in a fall
in the demand for the services of the unskilled, from OL to OM.
This fall in demand reflects the fact that at the higher wage

Figure 4.5

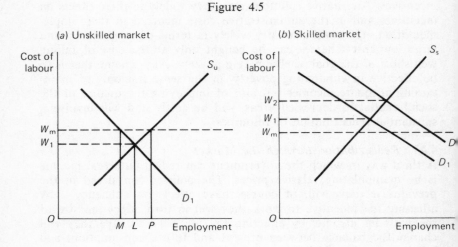

employers will find it profitable to substitute both skilled workers
and capital for the unskilled, the quantitative importance of this
being determined by the technical possibilities for such substitution.
The introduction of the minimum wage will shift the demand curve
for skilled workers to the right, to D_2, and the skilled wage will rise
to W_2. The net effect, therefore, will be that there is now unemployment among unskilled workers equal to MP, while the wage differential between skilled and unskilled workers will have shown little
change. Even if the employment of the unskilled is not reduced
directly, their higher wages will result in a relative cost increase in
those industries that employ a greater than average amount of
unskilled labour. The prices of the products of these industries will
therefore rise and the demand for them will fall, thus again causing
unemployment. By one mechanism or another, therefore, this
analysis suggests that minimum wage legislation that resulted in a
substantial rise in the wage of the unskilled worker would result
in unemployment.

Three other points may be made about the employment effect of
minimum wages. First, the effect in reducing employment may be

particularly important among part-time workers. To be effective, minimum wage legislation would have to relate to weekly earnings, and the result would be to make it unprofitable for firms to employ part-time labour. This factor would be particularly important in the distributive trades and some other service industries. Second, although the legislation may only apply to certain industries, the increase in wages may be much more widespread if higher paid workers attempt to restore differentials. Third, faced with excess supplies of labour, employers may be tempted to discriminate between workers on grounds such as sex or race.

It might be thought that a solution to the problem could be found in the introduction of legislation aimed at giving job security to the employee. This would make it difficult or costly, as a result of redundancy payments, for employers to dismiss labour, and might have the salutory effect of forcing firms to look more closely at their internal efficiency to see if higher wage costs could be absorbed by increased productivity. There may be some once-and-for-all benefit to be derived in this way, but it is important not to conceal the fact that, except in the very short term, it is not possible for the government or any other body to determine both the wage and the employment level. If an employer has to pay a higher wage rate than the one that would be established by market forces, some form of adjustment has to take place. If the firm cannot absorb the higher wage bill through increased efficiency, and is unable to dismiss labour, it will go bankrupt, and unemployment will increase in that way. Furthermore, once firms find that they have difficulty in dismissing labour during lean years they will become reluctant to recruit labour in good years. Instead they will rely more on overtime work from their existing workforce.

The argument so far has been based on the assumption of perfectly competitive labour markets. It may be argued that the predictions of the analysis are likely to be correct at least in terms of the qualitative effect on employment levels, since most industries that are characterised by low pay have a highly fragmented industrial structure. But this ignores the fact that unionisation is also usually very weak, so that the bargaining power of workers may still be far less than that of employers. If this is so, and if the bargaining power of employers succeeds in keeping wages below the level that would be achieved in a competitive situation, then higher wages need not cause unemployment. Figure 4.6 shows the case of a labour market where the buyer is a monopolist and the sellers are unorganised. The monopolist's demand curve for labour is D. The supply curve of labour, SS', shows for each quantity of labour the wage that the monopolist has to pay. The marginal cost of employing an additional unit of labour is, however, greater than the wage paid, because the increase in wages necessary to attract the additional unit has to be paid to the whole workforce. The profit-maximising firm will employ labour up to the point L, where the addition to costs from employing one more unit is equal to the addition to revenue, as shown by the demand curve, from employing that unit. The wage will be equal to W_m. Now, if the government fixes a minimum wage of OW, the firm's supply curve will become WBS', and not only will wages have increased but employment also will have increased to OL_1.

Figure 4.6

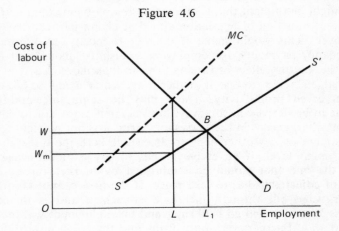

However, it is important not to lose sight of the possible adverse consequences of minimum wage legislation for the employment prospects of the unskilled. Over the longer term the most important contribution to solving the problem of low pay is likely to come in the form of increased resources devoted to training and retraining and, since the problem is in part a regional one, to the pursuit of an effective regional policy.

Rent Control. The purpose of this policy is to reduce the price of an item that is a very important part of the expenditure of low income families. The policy, however, results in great inefficiency in the housing market.

Figure 4.7 shows the demand and supply conditions for rented accommodation. The short-run supply curve, HS, is assumed to be completely inelastic. If rent legislation fixes the price below the equilibrium level P, at say Q, then an excess demand for rented accommodation will emerge, equal to HM. The result will be some form of rationing. Landlords will have to discriminate between different tenants and may do so on the basis of race, size of family or occupational status. Systems of payment based upon key money, insurance for breakages and so on are also likely to arise.

Figure 4.7

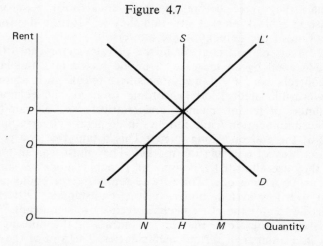

The policy is likely to have harmful consequences for the efficient use of the existing accommodation. Rent control reduces the incentive and ability to maintain property, and so the quality of accommodation in the controlled sector will decline. The policy also has to be accompanied by legislation to give security of tenure, otherwise, where the rental does not yield the landlord an adequate return, it would pay him to evict the tenant and put his property to other uses. Even if the rented stock of housing is initially used to full capacity, with the size of house or flat closely associated with the size of family, circumstances will of course change, so that small households may find themselves enjoying spacious accommodation, while large families are squeezed into small premises or have to wait longer for a suitable property to become available.

When adjustments take place on the supply side the position will become much worse. With prices fixed at *OQ* some landlords will make losses, and when the opportunity arises they will turn their accommodation over to alternative uses. Resident landlords may simply take the property off the market and use the accommodation themselves. Others will sell the properties in the home-ownership market. Many who would otherwise be prepared to let their houses will not do so. Old properties will not be replaced, and the construction of private properties for renting will diminish. Finally, resources in the construction industry will be diverted to sectors where controls do not apply. In terms of Figure 4.6 the supply of rented accommodation will fall from *OH* to *ON*, and the result will be an even greater level of excess demand. The frustrations and search costs imposed upon prospective tenants will be further increased, and people on low incomes may find themselves worse off than they were before the rent restrictions were imposed, because in a black market situation they will form a disproportionate section of the unlucky house hunters.

The effects of rent controls in the private sector can, of course, be made good by an increase in public sector housing. However, rent controls can have disadvantages here too. Even if accommodation were allocated strictly according to need, the economic circumstances of tenants change, and relatively well-off families may have accommodation while families in desperate poverty find themselves at the end of a long queue. This means that the poor have no quick way of entering the market. They must wait in the queue until they are allocated a house, and if public money is short their wait can be a long one. The private rented sector could provide a useful overflow system under such circumstances. Distortions in the private sector therefore become even more significant.

It is clear, therefore, that price controls in the housing market result in a number of serious inefficiencies. The aim of the controls has been to reduce the cost of living of those on low incomes. But from this point of view the policy has been a clumsy one. It has by no means been successful in concentrating help where it is most needed, and it has probably contributed significantly towards accentuating the problems of the housing market.

A possible alternative scheme for helping the poor is that of rent rebates. This policy would not have an adverse effect on the supply side of the market, and it would concentrate financial assistance where it was most needed. On the other hand, like all other means-tested benefits, its success would depend upon the extent to which those families that were eligible for rebates actually claimed them.

Whatever policy changes are made in the housing market, it is clear that existing subsidies could not simply be scrapped overnight. The costs of housing are an important part of the overall cost of living, and any substantial relaxation of controls could only take place in stages and as part of a fundamental reform of policy for dealing with poverty.

Farm Incomes. The incomes of farmers and farm workers have long been a concern of governments, and most attempts at dealing with the problems have resulted in some degree of inefficiency. Government involvement in this sector has aimed both at reducing the extent of short-run price fluctuations and at protecting the farm

sector from overseas competition and from long term changes in
the pattern of demand.

In a freely competitive market the prices of agricultural products
would fluctuate substantially. Fluctuation occurs as a result of
unplanned changes in production, due, for instance, to abnormally
good or bad weather conditions, combined with the fact that the
demand for most agricultural products is inelastic. In Figure 4.8,
with price at P_2 planned production is equal to Q_2. As a result

Figure 4.8

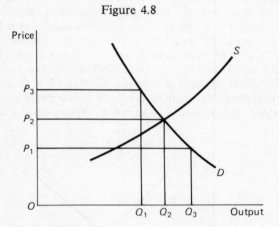

of a bumper harvest, however, actual production may be Q_3, and the
free market price will fall to P_1. The next year may see a much
smaller harvest and an output of Q_1, so that the price will rise to
P_3. If demand is inelastic, the result will be lower incomes for
farmers when the harvest is good and higher incomes when it is
poor.

A typical government response to these short term fluctuations is
to intervene and fix the price. If, however, the price is fixed above
P_2, there will be a tendency to overproduction. Warehouses will
fill up, and 'butter mountains' and 'milk lakes' will quickly form.
In order to restrict the supply coming on to the market these surpluses will either be destroyed – a clear waste of resources – or
dumped abroad – a clear gain to the consumers in these countries
at the expense of consumers at home. In an attempt to avoid even
larger surpluses the authorities may resort to such policies as quotas
for individual producers and cash payments for keeping resources
idle – policies that again involve obvious waste.

Fluctuations in domestic production may not generate such large
price changes when a country is engaged in international trade. The
shortage of domestic supplies as a result of a bad harvest may be

made good by increased imports, which will reduce the extent of the price increase. However, this need not be the case. A country that normally imports a certain proportion of its consumption of a particular product may be faced not only with a poor domestic harvest but also with reduced imports due to poor harvests overseas. Similarly, prices may be depressed as a result of good harvests in all major producing countries, and imports may simply result in even lower domestic prices.

Involvement in international trade may also result in longer term problems, if the domestic farm sector cannot compete with overseas producers and if the government decides to introduce protectionist policies. In France and Germany, for instance, large and generally inefficient farm sectors are protected from efficient producers such as Australia and New Zealand by tariffs on imported goods. The effect of such a policy is illustrated in Figure 4.9. The curve S_1 represents the supply curve of home producers for a particular output, say, wheat. The curve S_2 represents the world supply

Figure 4.9

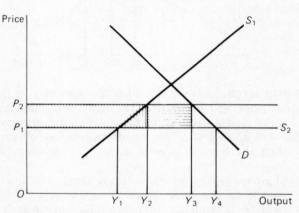

curve for wheat. The curve D represents domestic demand. Without government intervention, prices in the domestic market is P_1, with Y_1 produced at home and Y_1Y_4 imported. If the revenue so generated is not considered to provide an adequate income for farmers, the government may decide to intervene. It calculates that if prices were P_2 and domestic output Y_2, farmers would receive a satisfactory income. A tariff equal to P_1P_2 is therefore imposed upon the import of wheat. The market price is now P_2, imports are Y_2Y_3, and the government's revenue is equal to the horizontally shaded area. However, although farmers may be satisfied with the outcome, the consumer of course is worse off. He now has to pay higher prices for food products such as bread. Furthermore, it is clear that there is inefficiency in the home production of wheat, because that part of production equal to Y_1Y_2 depends upon government protection.

An alternative scheme would involve direct income supplements to farmers in the form of guaranteed prices. In terms of Figure 4.9, farmers are guaranteed a price of P_2 and therefore will plan to produce Y_2. No restrictions, however, are placed upon imports, so that market prices are equal to P_1. Since farmers receive only P_1 from the marketplace, the government must make up the difference in the form of a supplement equal to P_1P_2. The cost of the scheme equals the vertically shaded area. In this case the financial aid to farmers is raised by means of taxes that fall on the community as a whole rather than on consumers. Although everyone eats food, the importance of expenditure on food items as a proportion of total household expenditure varies substantially between income groups, being highest in general for those on low incomes. If farmers are to receive government aid, therefore, there is a strong argument in favour of administering it in such a way that the financial burden falls upon those who are best able to pay.

Another problem with agriculture in advanced economies stems from the low income elasticity of demand for many farm products. Productivity in agriculture has increased as a result of greater mechanisation, the application of fertilisers and better management. This increase in productivity, however, is not matched by increased demand as income levels rise, because in advanced economies the income elasticity of demand for agricultural products tends to be low compared to that for manufactured goods and services. As a result the agricultural sector will tend to generate persistent surpluses. In a freely competitive economy this will cause both agricultural prices and the profits of farmers to decline, and also the wages of farm labourers to decline relative to those in the manufacturing sector. This will in turn result in a reallocation of resources out of agriculture and into manufacturing. Farm incomes and wages will then come back into line with those of other sectors of the economy. If the government intervenes and, on grounds of equity, prevents the initial fall in farm incomes and wages by keeping agricultural prices at an artificially high level or by paying income supplements, the competitive adjustment mechanism will be impeded, and efficiency will be sacrificed.

All this is not to say, of course, that the government should stand aside and do nothing, leaving the market mechanism to effect the transfer of resources. Even if it were decided that the results brought about by the market mechanism should be accepted, it has to be recognised that the mechanism takes time to work, and its operation can be attended by considerable hardship. The movement of resources involves people and families, many of whom have a long tradition of working on the land and no alternative skills that would enable them to take up jobs in manufacturing. There are also those who would not leave the land at any price. For all these reasons there is a strong argument for government intervention. This intervention need not take the form of a manipulation of relative prices. For instance, generous assistance could be given to those who were prepared to move, in the form of cash payments and retraining facilities, while the problem of poor families remaining on the land could be dealt with by fiscal policies.

The government may, of course, decide to protect the income of farmers and the size of the farm sector over the long term. In this case the job of the economist is to point out the relative merits of different policies – to compare, for instance, the effects of a policy that manipulates market prices with one that supports farmers by means of a system of guaranteed prices. Here again both efficiency and equity considerations will have to be taken into account.

Food Subsidies. When the world prices of wheat and other food crops rise, this increases the production costs of food manufacturers and eventually results in higher prices for a wide range of food items, including such staple products as bread. To protect the poor against these price increases the government may decide to introduce subsidies. Producers will be paid a subsidy to offset their cost increases and thus prevent world price increases from being passed on to the domestic consumer. The attractiveness of such direct intervention is obvious from the point of view of the government. It appears that something is being done quickly, and is seen to be done, about controlling food price increases and their consequences for the poorer members of society. However, such policies have several important disadvantages.

In the first place, the price mechanism is a signalling device, there to warn consumers of increases in costs and to encourage them to economise in the use of goods whose prices have risen and to seek cheaper substitutes. Subsidies remove or weaken these signals. Second, subsidies can be very costly. In Figure 4.10 the supply curve has shifted from S_1 to S_2. Without intervention, prices would rise from P_1 to P_2, and the quantity consumed would fall from Q_1 to Q_2. If subsidies are introduced to keep the price at P_1, demand will remain at Q_1 and a subsidy equal to s will have to be paid to induce a sufficient volume of production. It should be noted that the subsidy required is larger than the price increase that would occur in the absence of government intervention. Third, the administration of the policy is likely to be costly and lead to inefficiency.

Figure 4.10

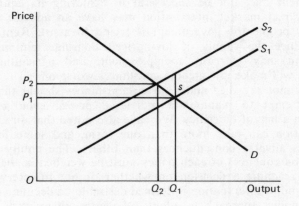

It may be difficult to determine the exact amount of the subsidy required to maintain existing prices, especially in view of the differences in efficiency that exist between producers. Problems will arise because of product differentiation. For instance, if a subsidy is to be paid to bakers so as to keep the price of a loaf of bread down by 1p, the authorities will have to define the size and type of loaf to which the policy applies. Producers will suffer if the government is slow to offset cost increases, and the regular payment of subsidies may foster inefficiency, which itself adds to cost pressures and higher prices. Fourth, once instituted, subsidies may be difficult to withdraw. If cost increases have continued for some time, and if through force of circumstances the government finds that subsidies have to be withdrawn then the consumer will have to face substantial price increases. Finally, subsidies, of course, benefit everybody and not just those in need. This makes such policies very costly. Even subsidies designed to keep down the price of a 25p loaf of bread by just 1p would mean an addition to government expenditure of several hundred million pounds.

In sum, there is little to be said in favour of policies that delay inevitable market adjustments, especially if the important goal of assisting those in need can be met more directly and more effectively by other policies.

The case studies presented above all have one important common message – that the primary role of prices is to bring about an efficient allocation of resources. If the government decides to intervene in individual markets, the stimulant to good resource management, which is an essential feature of the market mechanism, may be seriously weakened. In the long term, relative price changes resulting from government intervention will affect investment decisions and the speed and pattern of structural change. Furthermore, the government may not be successful in achieving its equity goals. Indeed direct market intervention may have an adverse effect on the very people the government is trying to assist. Rent controls may reduce the supply of low priced housing, minimum wage legislation may increase unemployment, and agricultural price supports will make low income consumers worse off.

We cannot say that under no circumstances should the government attempt to manipulate individual prices, even when this results in a loss of efficiency. We have also noted that direct market intervention can take more than one form, and some forms will have less adverse consequences than others. The equity and efficiency consequences of each policy must be weighed in the balance, both in reaching a decision on whether or not to intervene in a market and, if intervention is deemed desirable, in deciding on which specific policy approach to adopt. Of course, in practice, political constraints will have an important bearing on the choice of policies. However, the main point to be made in conclusion is that the possible adverse consequences of a policy that manipulates prices must continually be borne in mind, and the question must be asked as to whether the goal of a more equitable distribution of income could be achieved with greater certainty by more direct means, leaving the price mechanism as free as possible to perform its primary task.

Chapter 5

Public Utility Pricing and Investment

5.1 INTRODUCTION

It was pointed out in Chapter 2 that, to achieve a Pareto efficient allocation of resources in a market economy, prices everywhere have to equal marginal costs of production. From this it follows that the managers of state enterprises should be instructed to set prices equal to marginal cost. The prices that consumers have to pay will then measure the value of the resources used up in producing an extra unit of output. At these prices managers should be instructed to produce sufficient output and provide sufficient capacity to meet demand. Adherence to these 'rules' would result in a position such as that shown in Figure 5.1, with each enterprise producing that output which maximises net surplus – that is, total surplus minus total cost.

Figure 5.1

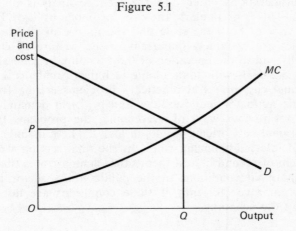

In this chapter we consider some of the problems involved in putting these rules into practice. Throughout we shall be concerned primarily with the activities of the so-called public utilities, that is, gas, electricity, telephones, railways and so on. The basic analysis is independent of the form of ownership, and so little attention will be paid to the degree to which the utilities are government owned. This may vary from complete public ownership and centrally supervised management, through loose government inspection of an otherwise autonomous management, to complete private ownership. This is not to say that the form of ownership and control is of no practical importance, and towards the end of the chapter some of the wider organisational problems of achieving efficiency will be briefly discussed. It should also be pointed out that some of the problems that will concern us have a much wider application than the public utility sector of the economy. Certainly they are frequently found in this sector in their most intractable form, but the difference between sectors is one of degree and not of kind.

Most of the analysis in this chapter is based on the assumptions of perfect competition in the rest of the economy and the absence of externalities. The assumption of perfect competition in the rest of the economy will be dropped in the final section of the chapter, with a more extensive analysis of monopoly in the private sector following in Chapter 6. The existence of externalities and the possibility that consumers may not always know best are complications that will be dealt with in detail in Chapter 7. During the course of the discussion we shall have cause from time to time to remind the reader of the importance of equity considerations. We have already seen in Chapters 2 and 3 how both efficiency and distributional considerations enter into the welfare analysis of resource allocation. This is particularly the case for public utilities. From the point of view of both the scale and the nature of their activities, the utilities are extremely important to the welfare of consumers individually and to the operation of the economy in general.

Section 5.2 deals with some of the technical problems in specifying marginal cost prices in practice – problems arising from such phenomena as factor indivisibilities and peaks in demand. Section 5.3 discusses various ways of overcoming the problems that arise when marginal cost pricing results in losses. These include two-part tariffs and internal-financing rules. In the final section we turn to the problem of second best, a theory that demonstrates that satisfying the marginal conditions in the public utility sector need not inevitably improve efficiency if these conditions are not satisfied throughout the economy.

5.2 TECHNICAL PROBLEMS IN MARGINAL COST PRICING

In practice, marginal cost pricing is not as easy to introduce into public-utility decision making as it first seems. There are a number of technical problems that have to be resolved, which can in fact produce some quite complex price structures. In this section we shall deal with five of these technical problems: those arising from the definition and calculation of marginal costs, from capacity considerations, from peaks in demand, from factor indivisibilities, and finally from economies of scale.

5.21 *Defining and Calculating Marginal Costs*
Do we set prices equal to short-run or long-run marginal costs? How do we measure marginal costs? In practice, what costs do we include, and in particular what do we do about joint costs? These are the questions that concern us to begin with.

Short- or Long-run Marginal Costs. Suppose that it is planned to introduce gas supplies into a region that has no existing power sources. It will be possible to choose between plants having different capacities and different initial capital outlays. Figure 5.2 shows the cost conditions for three such capacities, represented by short-run average-cost curves SAC_1, SAC_2 and SAC_3 and their respective short-run marginal-cost (SMC) curves. If there are an infinite number of technically feasible capacities (perfect divisibility), the long-run average-cost (LAC) curve can be drawn in the usual way enveloping the SAC curves. Figure 5.2 depicts a situation where there are neither economies nor diseconomies of scale, so that the

Figure 5.2

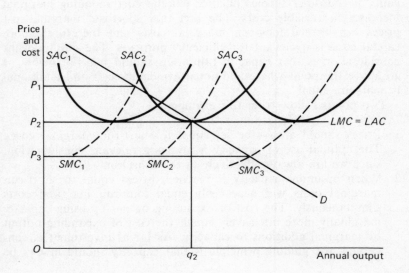

LAC curve appears as a horizontal line. The *LAC* curve is therefore identical with the long-run marginal-cost (*LMC*) curve, and they show the minimum unit costs possible for each output as every input is varied. Given that we are starting from scratch, our gas plant can be built at whatever scale current demand conditions justify. If the predicted demand for gas in the new area can be fully represented by the demand curve *D*, it is clear from the figure that the optimal output in this case is q_2. The optimum capacity is reached when the net benefits are maximised, that is, when the benefits from marginal output and marginal capacity changes equal the minimum resource costs of such changes. The benefits accrue as an increase in consumer surplus; the costs are measured by the *LMC* curve. Thus the optimal plant capacity is that represented by SAC_2. Once the plant is built, output should be priced at marginal cost. Since at output q_2 the long-run and short-run marginal costs are equal, the question of which marginal cost to use does not arise.

However, if a plant of suboptimal capacity such as SAC_1 were to be built, then long-run and short-run marginal costs would not be the same. In this case it can be demonstrated that Pareto efficiency requires that prices be set equal to short-run marginal costs. Given that a certain plant with average cost curve SAC_1 is in existence, the objective should clearly be to use that capacity as effectively as possible until such time as capacity changes can be made. Optimal utilisation of existing capacity is achieved by changing the input of the variable factor until the sum of benefits minus costs is maximised. In the short run then, optimal output is reached when prices equal short-run marginal costs, that is, when the marginal gains in consumer surplus balance out the corresponding marginal increases in variable costs. The fact that short-run marginal-cost prices can exceed long-run marginal costs and therefore ignore capital costs is irrelevant for efficiency purposes. The only relevant consideration is that capacity utilisation should not fall below or go above the point where additional avoidable costs and additional benefits are equal.

Two points follow from this example:

1 Prices should always be set equal to short-run marginal costs. The optimal use of capacity is always a relevant consideration, since we are always effectively in the short run.

2 When optimum capacity is reached, prices equal to short-run marginal costs will necessarily equal long-run marginal costs simultaneously. The cost of expanding output by using capacity marginally more intensively equals the cost of expanding output by marginal additions to capacity. As far as investment is concerned, the guiding principle is that capacity should always be

expanded if with the existing capacity $SMC > LMC$, and contracted if with the existing capacity $SMC < LMC$.

Given that short-run marginal-cost pricing is adopted, how are such costs to be defined? What is the relevant time period that we refer to as the short run? The problem lies in the fact that the period over which factors can be varied differs from one factor to another. One answer, therefore, is that the short run for any given production process should relate to the shortest time period over which at least one of its inputs is variable. Theoretically, the shorter the period, the greater the scope for marginal price adjustments, and thus for continuous optimum capacity utilisation.

In principle, therefore, short run changes in demand and cost conditions will require changes in prices, and over any substantial time period a large number of different changes will be required to keep capacity in optimum use. It is not feasible in practice, however, to charge instantaneous short-run marginal costs, and, since there are costs involved in administering a pricing system, it is also inefficient to attempt to do so. Furthermore, a great deal of short-run price fluctuation increases the uncertainty facing both the consumer and the producer and will increase the difficulties of making efficient decisions over the longer term. Thus, for instance, the more frequent the price changes for electricity and gas, the more difficult will it be for households to make rational decisions in choosing between electrical and gas appliances – commodities that will last for several years. The use of short-run marginal-cost pricing is subject to the qualification, therefore, that this should not produce so much price fluctuation that the costs of such a policy outweigh the benefits.

Difficulties in Measuring Marginal Costs. Some of the practical problems arising from attempts to calculate marginal costs arise from the novelty of the exercise and would be overcome by experience. It is worth saying a word or two, however, about two specific difficulties: the treatment of joint and common costs, and the treatment of capital costs.

Joint costs occur where the provision of one good or service necessarily means the provision of another good or service. Thus a train service from A to B necessitates a service from B to A. Common costs are costs that are common to a number of goods or services, although the supplying of one does not necessarily involve supplying the others. Thus the costs of the railway track between A and B are common to passenger and freight services, to services starting and ending at A or B, and to services using the line from A to B as part of a longer journey. Joint and common costs form a large proportion of the total costs of operating a railway system, and this clearly complicates pricing policy. How should these costs be allocated when calculating marginal cost?

First it should be noted that a certain amount of what at first sight may appear to be joint costs can often be ascribed unambiguously to particular production processes. Thus the additional capital costs of installing high quality, rather than standard quality, signalling equipment is relevant solely for the calculation of the long-run marginal cost of express passenger services. The additional running costs that may be incurred in using this equipment should similarly be assigned only to the short-run marginal cost of such services. However, when all such costs have been sifted out, any further allocation of joint costs is strictly impossible and arbitrary judgements are unwarranted. Optimum prices for the individual services should be set equal to the marginal separable costs of each service. As long as demand conditions remain constant such prices will, when capacity is optimal, produce a total revenue from all processes that is sufficient to cover total costs including joint costs. Losses will arise from joint cost situations only if the capacity is not of optimal scale.

So far we have glossed over a problem concerning capital costs. The capital stock of any production process provides a flow of services over a period of time. Figure 5.2, however, relates to output, prices and costs for a specific time period, such as one year. Each short-run cost curve therefore relates to cost changes as output varies in response to an increase or decrease in those factor inputs which are variable within a twelve-month period. It is necessary, therefore, to relate the costs of the capital stock to the same time period. To do this assume that the output of the plant is constant for every year of its life, that plant running costs are constant over the lifetime of the plant, and that no technical change occurs. For a given plant all capital costs are discounted forward to the base year when the equipment begins operation. This allows us to calculate the annual equivalent capital cost for the output of the plant. This is the constant annual sum of money for each year of the life of the capital stock that would, if discounted back to the base year, give a present value equal to base-year capital costs. Adding this figure to the annual operating costs gives the annual equivalent unit cost. In Figure 5.2 the curve SAC_1 represents the variation in annual equivalent costs per unit of output with the level of annual output. The curve SMC_1 represents the variation in annual marginal running costs with the level of annual output. In effect, Figure 5.2 is the same for every year of the capital stock's life. Therefore each pair of cost curves SAC_2/SMC_2 and SAC_3/SMC_3, etc. simply represents different initial outlays, and thus different annual equivalent capital costs. The *LAC* curve is derived as the envelope to the *SAC* curves. The *LMC* curve can be derived easily enough, as the change in annual equivalent costs when marginal changes in capacity and output are made.

In practice, estimating the *LMC* curve, even given our assumptions, requires the exact specification of both the life of the capital stock and the rate of discount used for estimating present value. The process is made more complex if different elements in the total capital stock have different life expectancies. The replacement value of each unit of stock that runs out during the set time period must be given a present value cost within the annual equivalent capital-cost calculation. The problem of specifying a time horizon is made less difficult, however, because the discounting process reduces the quantitative significance of all costs in far distant future periods. The second problem of choosing a discount rate is much more significant. It can have important implications for the value of the *LMC* curve and therefore for the choice of optimum capacity. The subject will be dealt with in depth, however, in Chapter 9.

5.22 *Capacity Considerations*

As concluded in the previous subsection, the optimum capacity for any productive activity is reached when prices set equal to short-run marginal costs also equal long-run marginal costs. In practice, changes in the capital stock take time, and sometimes, particularly where expensive equipment is involved, the time lag can be considerable. Consequently either capacity constraints or excess capacity can persist over long periods. Under such conditions average costs and marginal costs can possibly diverge to a marked degree. It is therefore important to decide upon the most efficient price strategy for these suboptimal situations.

A Capacity Constraint. Consider first a situation where capacity is below the optimum level. Figure 5.3 depicts a situation in which capacity limits are reached not gradually but abruptly, so that the SMC_1 curve is a reversed L-shape rather than a U-shape. The *SMC* curve is drawn in this way both to emphasise the capacity constraint and to simplify the analysis. Up to quantity q, marginal costs are constant and equal to *OC*. However, no additional amounts of the variable inputs will increase output beyond q, so that at this output the *SMC* curve becomes vertical. With demand curve *D*, price would be equal to *P*.

The interesting point about this example is that, although demand is certainly equated with supply, the consumer of the marginal unit is now actually paying more than the *money cost* of producing it (that is, $OP > OC$). Nevertheless, price *P* for output q is quite definitely the price/output combination that maximises total net benefits. The difficulty arises from the definition of short-run marginal costs. So far these have been interpreted simply in terms of the money costs of production. However this is not, in general, an accurate definition. To achieve Pareto efficiency, prices should be set equal to short-run marginal costs measured in terms of the

Figure 5.3

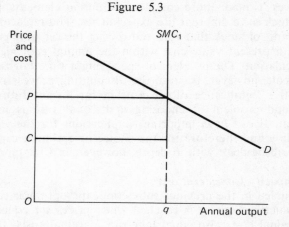

opportunity cost of the resources used. The latter is defined as the value of the resources in their next-best use. Thus if money costs of production are an accurate measure of the value of resources in their best alternative use, they will reflect the opportunity cost of employing the resources in their present use. This will often be the case. However, in the situation that we are now examining there is another way of looking at opportunity cost, which is that the opportunity cost of producing the Oqth unit for the marginal consumer is the benefit that would have been derived if that unit had instead been supplied to the consumer who is just excluded from the market. This is the marginal-user opportunity cost. Thus P is the short-run marginal cost in terms of user opportunity cost, though not in terms of production cost. Prices should be set according to whichever is highest – the marginal user opportunity cost or, assuming that they measure the opportunity cost of resources in terms of their value elsewhere, the money costs of production. In the case under consideration this means charging a market clearing price that rations the available output among consumers. It should be noted, however, that though there may be no objections on grounds of efficiency to setting prices above the marginal money costs of production, this may not be true on grounds of equity.

Excess Capacity. Let us now turn from situations where capacity constraints operate to one where there is excess capacity arising from a fall in demand. In Figure 5.4 current capacity is assumed to be such as to produce short-run average-cost curve SAC_4. Operating costs OC are assumed to be constant up to capacity output. At the output for which current capacity is optimal, short-run average cost equals running costs plus annual fixed capital charges, that is, $OC + CL$. The LAC/LMC curve is LL', assuming constant costs as capacity is extended. If demand were D_2, price P_2 would be appropriate and capacity would be optimal. However, if demand is in fact D_1, until capacity can be reduced so as to give curve SMC_2, the optimal price in the short run is P_1.

Figure 5.4

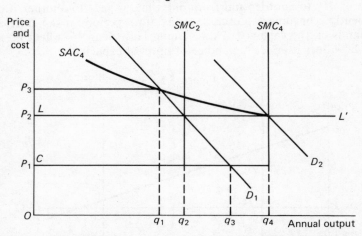

With excess capacity, price P_1 will not cover average total costs. A price set equal to P_3 would cover all costs, but then output $q_3 - q_1$ would be choked off by the price increase. This means that some consumers would be excluded from the market even though they were prepared to pay prices for additional amounts of the goods equal to or greater than the costs of producing that extra output. On efficiency grounds, moving from q_1 to q_3 would show a net benefit in welfare terms. The failure to cover costs results from the suboptimality of scale – an excess of capacity that, given time, will be corrected. It can nevertheless be a serious problem for those concerned with managing a production process operating under such conditions. The more important the fixed cost element in total costs, the greater is likely to be the size of the financial deficits. Changes in demand can be large, and the greater the excess capacity the greater the deficits. Furthermore, the more durable the assets involved the more persistent the problem. In general, capacity changes downwards will seldom be worthwhile until the time for replacement arrives. Unless there is significant alternative-use value in the equipment, scrapping operational equipment is only worthwhile if existing demand cannot cover its running costs. In Figure 5.4, therefore, equipment might be scrapped to reduce output to q_3, but that is all. The more durable the assets the less frequent is replacement and the longer is the period over which losses must be sustained.

5.23 *Peaks in Demand*
The analysis is now extended to take account of variations in demand conditions. For services such as electricity, gas and transport there are particularly strong variations in demand from one time of day to another and from one time of year to another. Consequently, consumers in the separate time periods make different demands on the capacity of the system. How does this affect prices, and how does it affect the choice of optimal capacity?

Figure 5.5

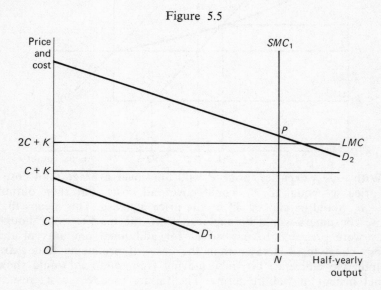

Figure 5.5 is drawn on the assumption that there are two periods of equal length – say half-yearly periods – with independent demand curves D_1 and D_2. Costs are assumed to be the same for both periods and comprise average variable costs OC, which are constant up to full capacity, and capital costs per unit, K, which have to be

incurred to produce units in addition to *ON*. Up to capacity, there-fore, the cost of an extra unit in either period is equal to *OC*. Beyond this it is $C + K$ for each period separately and $2C + K$ for the two periods combined. The long-run marginal-cost curve for the whole system is therefore *LMC*. Assuming a uniform charge for the units consumed within each period, Pareto efficiency requires that the prices charged should be *OC* in period 1 and *NP* in period 2. Existing capacity is clearly more than sufficient to meet the demands made by period 1, and price in this period covers only marginal running costs. 'Capacity demand' comes entirely from consumers in period 2, and to restrict demand to the available capacity they are charged a market-clearing price of *NP*. This is a case of a 'firm peak', that is, a situation where, though they pay prices equal to marginal operating costs, the consumers in one period make less than full use of existing capacity, and where only the consumers in the other period make a contribution towards the capital costs of the system.

Figure 5.6 shows a different situation where, with short run costs SMC_1 consumers in both periods make full use of the existing

Figure 5.6

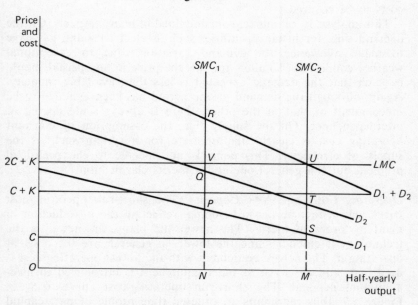

capacity. It is clear that demand in period 2 is greater than demand in period 1. Thus it might appear that once again all capacity charges should be borne by period 2 consumers, with period 1 paying for operating costs only – that is, prices of NQ and OC respectively should be charged. This, however, would not do. If these prices were charged, demand in period 2 at price NQ would be restricted to the available capacity output, while demand in period 1 at price OC would become much greater than the capacity currently available. In other words, this system of charging would in effect shift the peak demand from period 2 to period 1. This is the 'shifting peak' case, and the appropriate set of short run charges is NQ and NP. Demand in both periods will then be restricted to capacity, and both periods will be contributing to capacity costs.

In both the 'firm peak' and 'shifting peak' cases, if the combined short-run demand price is greater than the long-run marginal costs of extending the system – consisting of the operating costs of both periods plus the joint capital costs – the capacity of the system should be extended. In the case of the shifting peak (Figure 5.6), the long run optimum will be given by curve SMC_2 and output OM per period. At this point the combined charge MU, made up of MS and MT is just sufficient to cover long-run marginal costs, and total net benefits will be maximised. In addition, because of the assumption of constant costs this set of charges will enable total costs to be covered.

This analysis is, of course, oversimplified in many respects. On the demand side, for instance, utilities such as electricity and gas have to make allowance for demand variations due to exceptional weather conditions. To allow for this the price in any period should be such that the demand expected is less than available capacity. Again, although the demand in one period has been assumed to be independent of that in the other, there is always some degree of interdependence. On the supply side, the assumption of constant operating cost is clearly inappropriate for a system such as the supply of electricity. This point is not specific to the peak-load problem but is a general one and it merits clarification.

Operating Costs and New Capacity. The short-run operating-cost curve will in fact be upward sloping, reflecting the introduction of plant in 'order of merit'. The newer the plant, the newer is the technology it embodies and the lower, in general, are the costs of operating it. The newest equipment with the lowest operating cost is used first, and costs rise as older equipment is introduced to meet additional demand. The short-run operating-cost curve, C_1S_1 in Figure 5.7, thus represents an ordered time profile of past capital purchases. A similar effect would arise if the operating costs of older equipment were higher, not because of changes in technology but simply because of the effects of time and usage.

These factors also suggest that incremental capacity cost is not just a function of the capacity currently existing and the amount of new capacity being installed. It is also affected by the fact that, since the newest plant embodying the latest technology will have lower operating costs than existing plant, it will pay to run the new capacity as fully as possible. The operating costs of the system will therefore be lower, and this has to be deducted from the capital cost of the new plant. This is illustrated in Figure 5.7.

Figure 5.7

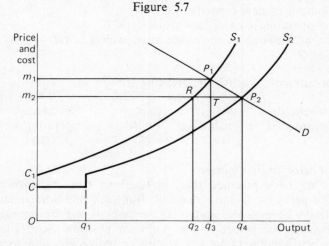

The initial position is given by demand curve D and system operating-cost curve C_1S_1. The marginal operating cost of the system is thus m_1, and a price of $P_1 = m_1$ is charged. If new capacity is introduced capable of producing Oq_1 units of output, at constant operating cost OC, this will be added to the bottom of the operating cost curve, and the whole curve will shift downwards to CS_2. Each unit of output will be produced at lower cost because equipment will be displaced upwards along the curve, each unit of equipment having a lower operating cost than the one formerly used to produce the same slice of output. The new capacity will allow some of the oldest equipment to be scrapped. The output attributable to the new plant, Oq_1, is equal to q_2q_4 – that is, to the fall in output due to the retirement of old plant, q_2q_3, plus the net increase in output, q_3q_4.

In evaluating the benefits and costs of the investment in new capacity, the saving in system operating costs, the scrap value of displaced equipment and the benefits to consumers of the extra output must all be set against the capital and running costs of the new plant. Let the output of the new capacity Oq_1 equal T units, the net increase in output q_3q_4 equal Q, and the fall in the output of the old plant q_2q_3 equal $T - Q$. Then the following items will have to be taken into account in investment appraisal:

1 The benefit to consumers from the extra output, which is approximately $\frac{1}{2}(P_1 + P_2)Q$, that is, area P_1TP_2.
2 The saving in system operating costs, which is approximately $\frac{1}{2}(m_1 + m_2)(T - Q)$, that is, area $q_2RP_1q_3$.
3 The scrap value of displaced equipment.
4 The capital cost, KT, where K is the annual capital cost per unit of output of new capacity.
5 The operating cost of new capacity, CT.
6 The net change in operating cost, which is $CT - \frac{1}{2}(m_1 + m_2)(T - Q)$.

The investment is worth undertaking if

Benefit to consumers		Scrap value		Capital cost		Net change in operating cost
(1)	+	(3)	>	(4)	+	(6)

5.24 *Factor Indivisibilities*

So far we have assumed that, in the long run, capacity can be adjusted perfectly to meet demand. But such fine adjustments will not always be possible, and in these cases it will be necessary to overshoot or fall short of the optimum position. Such situations arise when equipment is very lumpy or indivisible, and they pose further problems in defining marginal costs and in formulating investment decision rules.

In Figure 5.8 we revert, for simplicity of analysis, to the assumption of constant short-run marginal costs up to full capacity and also to the assumption that new and existing capital equipment are equally productive. If there were no problem of indivisibility of factor inputs, we could draw in the long-run marginal-cost curve LL', and with demand curve D a scale of operations could be built that would allow for full capacity use at output Oq. Suppose, however, that the choice of plant size is limited to three alternative capacities with short-run marginal costs as shown in the figure, which for ease of exposition we shall refer to as C_1, C_2 and C_3. With the demand conditions shown none of the three is optimal, in the sense of equating price to long-run marginal cost, for there is no scale of operations allowing for full capacity use at output Oq.

Thus if the optimum capacity is unavailable it is necessary to choose the best capacity from the three available. Following short-run pricing strategies, this implies a choice between capacity C_1 with price P_3, capacity C_2 with price P_2, and capacity C_3 with price

P_1. Using partial analysis, the choice can be made by considering the potential net benefits of moving from one scale to either of the other two. For example, during the planning stage assume that initially a decision is made in favour of scale C_1, because it is clear that the annual benefits (the area under the demand curve) exceed the annual running costs plus the equivalent capital cost of introducing that capacity. Would it be worthwhile changing the plans to adopt capacity C_2 instead? This decision involves comparing the extra benefits and costs associated with the additional capacity. The extra capacity would bring extra consumer benefits given by the surplus area ABq_2q_1. The extra costs, both capital and operating, are represented by area MNq_2q_1. Clearly, from the diagram, capacity C_2 is preferable to C_1. If we were to consider capacity C_3 instead of C_2, the additional costs would be $NTEFq_3q_2$ (capital expenditures would have to be made for the full capacity C_3, but the capacity would only be partly used, so that the running costs of output q_4q_3 would not be incurred). The benefits would be area BFq_3q_2, so that the move to capacity C_3 would be unwarranted.

Figure 5.8

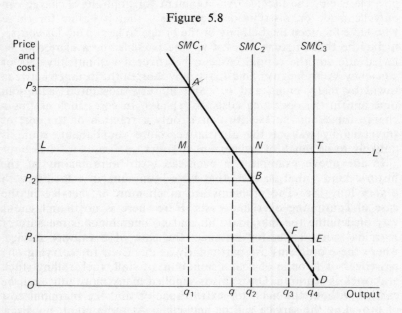

In Figure 5.8 the chosen capacity C_2 is fully utilised, but this need not necessarily be the case. If capacity C_2 did not exist, C_3 would be the optimum capacity. Thus an efficient investment decision, because of indivisibilities, can involve a conscious decision to produce either a shortage or an excess of capacity. Furthermore, such decisions can mean that the production process either earns supernormal profits (if capacity C_1 is the optimum) or runs a budget deficit (if C_3 proves to be the optimum). In this case, therefore, the deficits arise, not because of some temporary divergence between actual and optimal capacity, but because optimal capacity itself, as a result of indivisibilities, involves financial losses. The greater the extent of the indivisibilities, in general, the more likely and the more extensive are the deficits or surpluses.

Whenever indivisibilities of the above kind occur, certain ambiguities about the interpretation of marginal cost are likely to arise. Take first the extreme case of a bridge. A capital cost will, of course, have been involved in building the bridge, but once the facility has been constructed these costs are historic and do not, or should not on the grounds of efficiency, enter into the calculation of the optimum price. As long as there is no congestion the marginal cost of using the bridge will be virtually zero. There is therefore no point in charging for the use of the bridge if this would discourage its use, because welfare will be maximised by making the fullest possible use of the facility. An argument for imposing a charge can only be made on distributional grounds – that it is fair for those who have financed the building of the bridge to be repaid. Of course, it may be that in some cases it will be possible for a charge to be levied and for the capital costs to be covered without any loss of efficiency. A bridge over an estuary may shorten the distance between towns by many miles, and so result in very substantial savings in time and in the operating costs of vehicles. In cases such as this a charge for using the facility that is only a fraction of the cost of travelling by way of the alternative, more roundabout, route is unlikely to be much of a deterrent to users

In the above example the overhead costs were mainly of the historic kind – that is, costs that have been sunk in a facility with a very long life. The problems are much more intractable in the case of continuing overhead costs. Here there is no unambiguous way of defining the marginal unit and no unambiguous measure of marginal cost. Take, for instance, the case of a railway service, where these problems are particularly acute. Even for carrying one passenger or 1 tonne of coal a minimum of staff, fuel, rolling stock and track is required. Once this is supplied many more units can be carried without the need for extra capacity, and the marginal cost of providing the service will be negligible. At some point, however, an addition to output will require an increase in capacity – say an additional coach or even an additional train. The addition to total costs will then be very large.

This problem is similar to one that we have already encountered in this chapter; that is, it arises from the arbitrary limitation of the concept of marginal cost to those costs which are immediately escapable for the smallest unit of output. In other words, no greater significance should be attached to the passenger or tonne of coal as the unit on which to calculate cost than is attached to one of the units required in supplying the service. The decision not to carry an additional passenger may yield no saving in resources, but a decision not to run a particular service may result in large savings.

Even so, it is still the case that escapable costs will vary according to the way in which a service is defined. Take, for instance, a train service between *B* and *C* that is part of a line between *A* and *D*. A decision to take away the 10 o'clock train that leaves *B* for *C* will save little more than the fuel costs of the journey. Taking away all the services using one locomotive will in addition result in savings in manpower, in maintenance, in rolling stock and in the replacement of the locomotive. The abandonment of all services between *B* and *C* will lead to further savings of the kind already mentioned, plus the savings effected by not having to maintain the stations at *B* and *C*. Finally, if all services between *A* and *D* are withdrawn, the escapable costs are further extended to include the maintenance and replacement of track.

It is clear from this that escapable costs depend on the time period that is considered to be appropriate. The longer the period taken, the greater the number of replacement decisions that will have to be made, and the greater the escapable cost. With time, too, the problem of indivisibilities itself may be lessened. Timetables can be adjusted to take account of changes in the pattern of demand, and smaller coaches or buses may replace larger ones when replacement decisions are made. In this way capacity may correspond more closely to demand. However, the problem of indivisibilities will not disappear completely, and whenever it is important it calls for the application of a great deal of judgement and common sense in the application of marginal-cost pricing rules

5.25 *Decreasing Costs*

Up until now our analysis of marginal cost pricing has been conducted against a background of constant returns to scale. However, since economies of scale are often very important for public utilities, it is time to consider the implications of downward-sloping long-run marginal-cost curves for the implementation of efficient pricing and investment rules.

In Figure 5.9 the curve *LAC* represents average total costs per unit as a function of scale. From this the long-run marginal-cost curve, *LMC*, can be derived. Consider first the most efficient way of producing any output, such as *Oq*, within the range of increasing returns to scale. The optimal capacity is a plant with short-run average-cost curve SAC_2, which will be underutilised. If a smaller plant with cost curve SAC_1 had been built, the production of Oq would allow such a plant to be operated at full capacity, but it would clearly not be the cheapest way of producing that output. Because of economies of scale the larger plant, although it operates with some excess capacity, will have lower unit costs. The optimum position is one where there is both excess capacity and unexhausted economies of scale.

Figure 5.9

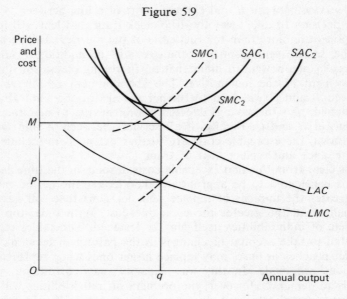

Economies of scale may be so important that the minimum efficient size of the firm is greater than the size of the market, so that, if all the benefits of scale are to be realised, there can only be one producer. It is also clear that, with decreasing costs, marginal cost pricing will result in financial losses. Some way has therefore to be found of financing the deficits.

5.3 PRACTICAL PROBLEMS IN PUBLIC UTILITY PRICING AND INVESTMENT

At several points in the preceding section it was shown that efficient pricing and investment strategies could result in financial deficits for the public utility concerned. With increasing returns to scale, for instance, marginal cost pricing results in losses.

At first sight it may seem that one possible solution to this problem is to raise all prices in such a way as to maintain a common ratio of price to marginal cost until all industries are able at least to break even. However, would allocative efficiency be preserved by creating a world of monopolies in which the degree of monopoly, as measured by the ratio of price to marginal cost, was everywhere the same? The answer is no, unless, that is, some very unlikely conditions were satisfied. These are that all commodities produced are for final consumption only, and that factor inputs are in perfectly inelastic supply. Suppose, for instance, that there are just two commodities, x and y, and one factor, labour, which costs £2 per hour. Assume, for simplicity, conditions of constant costs in the production of both commodities and let 1 unit of x require 1 hour of labour, and 1 unit of y require 2 hours. The marginal costs of production of x and y will therefore be £2 and £4 respectively, and with a common mark-up of 50 per cent prices will be £3 and £6. Now if 10 hours of labour are moved out of y into x, this will result in a loss of 5 units of y valued at just over £30, and a gain of 10 units of x valued at just under £30. The transfer of resources is therefore not justified, because, with the common price-marginal cost ratio, labour was optimally allocated in the first place.

Consider now the position if x not only enters directly into final consumption but also is used as an intermediate input in the production of y. Assume that in addition to 2 hours of labour the production of y requires 1 unit of x. The marginal cost of production of y will therefore be £7. With a mark-up of 50 per cent the price of y will be £10·50. In this case, however, because both commodities enter into final consumption, the proportionality rule will not ensure that the value of output is maximised. Thus in the production of y, 2 hours of labour produce goods valued at £10·50, whereas in the case of x, the same input of labour produces goods valued at only £6.

A further problem occurs if factor supplies are not perfectly inelastic, because proportional mark-ups would violate the marginal conditions in factor markets by affecting the work–leisure margin. Proportional mark-ups in the goods markets alone would leave the price of leisure too low. Therefore the wage, which is the price of leisure, must also be raised above the marginal cost of labour. If this cannot be done, the consumption of leisure will be too high and the supply of labour, and thus of goods, will be below the optimum level.

What other solutions are there to the problem of public utility losses associated with marginal cost pricing? One approach is the payment of subsidies by the government, and it is to the problems associated with such subsidies that we first of all turn.

5.31   *Subsidies*

The first problem connected with the payment of subsidies is that of equity and distribution. The people who finance the subsidies by paying taxes will not correspond exactly to those who receive the benefits from the commodity or service in question. Subsidies to public transport, for example, may be paid by many who prefer to use their own cars. Similarly, taxes to pay for hospitals will be paid by those who will not have cause to call upon these services. Some room for manoeuvre will sometimes be available for matching those who pay the taxes with those who receive the benefits of consumption. For instance, in the case of a local railway line the local authority could be asked to cover any deficit out of local resources. Even on grounds of efficiency, however, people who do not directly benefit from consumption should in fact pay something towards the finance of these services, the reason being the existence of 'option demand'. Even if an individual expects not to use the services of public transport and public health, they will still have some value to him as something on which he can always fall back if circumstances change. The market does not register option demand, and taxation is a method of making people pay for this benefit. Of course, we needn't rely on the principle of option demand to justify the financing of public utility deficits out of public funds. In practice a progressive tax system may well be acceptable as a way of covering deficits that are the inevitable outcome of efficient pricing decisions.

Another problem with subsidies is that increases in tax rates to pay subsidies to public enterprises may have adverse effects on the incentive to work and save. The likelihood of this effect being significant clearly depends on the size of the deficits that have to be financed. The larger the deficits, the greater the amount that has to be found in taxes and the stronger the possibility of a disincentive effect.

The third problem is the most important: that of ensuring the internal efficiency of public utilities. A preoccupation with marginal cost pricing and the problem of resource allocation may lead to neglect of the efficiency with which resources are used within firms, and it is quite possible that more may be lost through reduced managerial efficiency than will be gained by equating marginal cost and price.

The problem of internal efficiency is certainly not confined to the public sector. It is, as we shall see in Chapter 6, an important factor wherever monopoly power exists, but it will be particularly important in industries where losses are accepted as an inevitable outcome of pricing policy, and where the deficits are financed by state subsidy. What assurance is there in such circumstances that costs, and therefore losses, are minimised? Furthermore, continual government interference in the management of the enterprises concerned may only serve to make matters worse.

A fundamental problem here is whether the state can find a sufficient number of able managers who can be motivated by considerations other than profit making and who, without the barometer of a profit-and-loss account, will be continually on the lookout for ways of increasing efficiency. The outlook of employees is also crucial. To what extent does state ownership colour their attitudes towards efficiency and wage bargaining? Are there expectations that the 'bottomless public purse' will always come to the rescue to finance inflationary wage claims and financial deficits? And how will morale be affected by continuous loss making?

Whatever the answer to these questions, experience shows that maintaining internal efficiency is a major problem. What can be done about it?

First, a great deal can be gained by exposing public utilities and other state enterprises to competition. Even in the case of simple monopolies, competition is never entirely absent. It may exist in the form of imports, or as competition between industries – competition, for instance, between coal, gas, electricity and oil. The free play of such competition can do much to maintain efficiency. Further competitive advantages may be possible in some industries by the formation of smaller enterprises. It may well be that a national monopoly could be divided into two or more parts without loss of economies of scale. Even where some loss in terms of scale economies was involved, this might be outweighed by the greater efficiency induced by competition between two or more competing units.

Second, where competition does not supply the answer some form of efficiency audit will be required to check on the effectiveness of the enterprise in minimising costs and introducing innovations. It will also be helpful to have the interests of consumers safeguarded. Consumers may suffer not only in terms of higher prices and shortages of capacity but also with regard to the quality of the product or service. State support for consumer agencies and possibly consumer representation on the board will do something to protect the consumers' interests.

Third, where subsidies are paid it is best, where possible, to make them specific rather than general. This means that it is necessary to evaluate, as part of an efficiency audit perhaps, the major areas of activity of a state enterprise, to identify those which are socially desirable but which can only be supplied at a loss. A specific subsidy for each activity could then be paid. This, however, would not solve the problem. There might be difficulty in identifying the loss-making activities sufficiently narrowly to make the exercise worthwhile, and there would be further problems in fixing the precise amount of subsidy required. Furthermore, the subsidies would have to be adjusted to changes in supply-and-demand conditions, otherwise they would produce distortions in the allocation of resources. Nevertheless there is probably scope here for reducing the magnitude of the problem, even though it may not be the complete answer.

In view of the difficulties of combining a loss-making situation with internal efficiency there may be a strong argument in favour of departing from a marginal-cost pricing policy and instead setting prices equal to average total costs, so that the public enterprise at least breaks even. The misallocation arising from setting prices above marginal cost may not be great if the prices of substitutes in the private sector are also above marginal cost. Indeed, as we shall see when considering the problem of 'second best' in the last section of this chapter, elevating prices above marginal cost may in some circumstances improve allocation. Furthermore, the resource allocation effects will be small if the elasticity of demand is low. Another factor that has to be taken into account is that, if the payment of subsidies is avoided, this reduces the burden of taxation and thus weakens any tendency for high marginal-tax rates to reduce the incentives to work and to invest. It may well be, therefore, that, in certain cases at least, little if anything is to be lost on the allocative side by setting prices equal to average cost, whereas there may be much to be gained in terms of the greater check on internal efficiency.

The internal efficiency of state enterprises may also be promoted by setting them financial targets. Let us consider briefly two forms that such targets might take and that have in fact been used historically. These are self-finance targets and rate-of-return targets.

Theoretically, instructions to state enterprises to seek a certain level of self-financing of their investment expenditure have little to be said in their favour. Suppose that initially an enterprise fails to meet the self-finance target and also that prices cannot be increased. Then there must necessarily be a reduction in investment. However, investment projects should be evaluated by their prospective rate of return and not by the amount of self-finance available. Only by coincidence will the number of projects that are viable on rate-of-return calculations correspond to the number that can be financed internally. The amount of self-finance generated is a residual determined within correct price and investment strategies by the time profile of cash receipts. The alternative response that the enterprise may adopt in order to meet the target is to increase prices, but the extent to which this can be done depends on monopoly power, and the result is monopolistic price distortions. Setting a self-finance target also means, in effect, setting different rates of return on new investment for different industries depending on their capital intensity and rate of growth. Industries with high capital intensity and a fast rate of growth will be forced to look for higher returns than those with lower capital intensity and slower growth. Again this contradicts efficient investment policies, which should ensure as far as possible that closely competing industries such as coal, electricity and gas are looking for the same return on investment.

A target rate of return is a more sensible objective, but it is not without problems. First, a given overall profitability may be attainable at more than one level of output. Second, it will be necessary to isolate any uneconomic services that may be desired on social grounds, with the target return applying to the remaining, commercially viable, sections of the enterprise. Without this provision an overall financial rate-of-return target will only be obtainable by means of cross-subsidisation, with loss making activities being covered by profits made elsewhere in the organisation. Where loss making but socially desirable activities are present, it is better that they be supported by explicit subsidies rather than by cross-subsidisation. The latter imposes the burden of providing services below cost entirely on other users of the same agency. It will also lead to a misallocation of resources, since the higher prices necessary in the profitable parts of the undertaking will divert demand to competitors. This is an argument not against subsidies but against cross-subsidisation as a means of financing them. Third, there is the problem of valuing the capital of many state enterprises, such as the railways and coal. Fourth, there is the question of what rate of return to set. The rate of return looked for in the private sector of the economy has been suggested, but should it be the average for all private industry or that for industries producing close substitutes only? In both cases there is a general problem of allowing for differences in risk between the two sectors. There may also be more specific problems. For instance, in comparing coal with fuel oil it must be remembered that the latter is a joint product, the rate of return on which depends on how the oil companies allocate their costs. This in turn will be influenced by the price of coal and thus the rate of return in the coal-mining industry.

The problems associated with the subsidising of decreasing cost industries lead us to consider pricing systems that meet the marginal conditions for efficiency and also the condition that total revenue should equal total cost. The latter is argued for on the grounds that he who benefits should pay, and also as a check on internal efficiency. It is possible, in principle at least, to devise a scheme of charges that combines the principle of equity – that he who benefits should pay – with the principle of efficiency – that output should be carried to the point where marginal cost equals price. Two such schemes are price discrimination and multipart tariffs.

5.32   *Price Discrimination*

Price discrimination exists where relative prices do not accurately reflect relative costs. Thus it exists where different prices are charged for services or commodities whose costs are the same, or where price differences are greater than the corresponding cost differences. Price discrimination is also present where in spite of cost differences uniform prices are charged.

Three conditions are necessary for profitable price discrimination to be possible. The firm must have market power. It must be able to divide customers into groups with different elasticities of demand, or to sell the product in discrete quantities with different marginal valuations. It must not be possible for customers to buy in the cheap markets and resell in the expensive ones.

It is customary to distinguish between three types of price discrimination: first-, second- and third-degree. In the case of first-degree price discrimination the firm charges a different price for each unit of the commodity. For each unit the firm charges the customer his full marginal valuation of that unit. In this way the firm appropriates the whole of consumers' surplus. Second-degree price discrimination is a crude version of first-degree discrimination. In this case the demand curve will be stepped, with total output divided into a number of blocks, each block being sold for a different price. The case of third-degree discrimination is where there are two or more groups of consumers each with a continuous demand curve. This case is illustrated in Figure 5.10. Diagrams (a) and (b) show the demand (D) and marginal revenue (MR) curves in the two separate markets. Diagram (c) shows the combined marginal revenue curve, MR, and the firm's marginal cost curve, MC. The intersection of these curves determines the total output, OQ. This output is divided between the two markets in such a way that the marginal revenue from additional sales in each market is equalised. The prices charged are P_1 in the market with the more inelastic demand curve, and P_2 in the other market.

It is quite clear that price discrimination is a common practice. A few examples will suffice to illustrate its ubiquity. In private medical practice doctors may charge a rich man more than a poor man for the same professional services. Large buyers are often granted price discounts that exceed the cost savings associated with bulk supply. A firm may sell a particular commodity or service at a uniform price regardless of transport costs, thus absorbing freight charges and discriminating on a geographical basis. For instance, it costs the same to post a first-class letter from London to Edinburgh as it does to post it from one suburb of London to another.

Figure 5.10

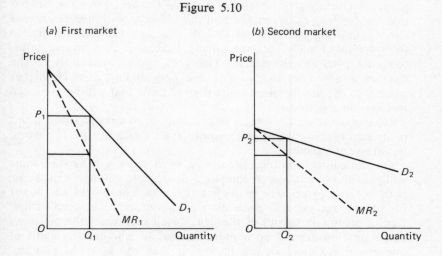

(a) First market

(b) Second market

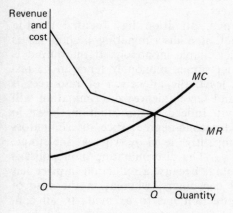

(c) Combined market

Again, many commodities, particularly those which are advertised nationally, can be bought at the same price in all parts of the country regardless of the distance from the factory. The dumping of surpluses also constitutes price discrimination. In the European Community, for instance, the agricultural policy has resulted in the accumulation of large surpluses of certain commodities, such as butter. In order to maintain prices at a high level within the Community, these surpluses have sometimes been disposed of by selling them off cheaply to countries in Eastern Europe. Price discrimination has for long been practised on the railways, with higher charges for transporting commodities that have a high value in relation to their weight. Finally, certain pricing strategies may involve intertemporal price discrimination. This may apply particularly to the case of a new commodity, with the firm adding a much higher margin to the first batch of units than to units that will be produced in later time periods.

How is the practice of price discrimination to be assessed in terms of its effects on welfare? Both equity and efficiency aspects have to be taken into account.

On the equity side the outcome in most cases will be that some will gain and others lose as compared to a simple monopoly situation, both because prices will be higher for some consumers and lower for others, and because price discrimination results in a redistribution of income in favour of the firm. In all such cases the merits of discrimination depend on a judgement as to whether the gains of one group are more or less important than the losses of another. As far as consumers are concerned, however, there is the possibility that all will gain. This possibility arises where marginal costs are falling, and where price discrimination results in such a large increase in output that prices will be lower, as compared to simple monopoly price, for all consumers.

Where efficiency is concerned, attention has focused on the question of whether the output of a discriminating monopolist is higher or lower than that under simple monopoly. If the output is higher, then, since output under simple monopoly tends to be restricted below the competitive level, the allocation of resources is likely to be improved. First- and second-degree discrimination will normally result in higher output. Indeed in the situation shown in Figure 5.11(a), both first- and second-degree price discriminators will carry output up to the competitive level q_c, whereas the simple monopolist restricts output to q_m. The discriminating monopolist is able to expand output to advantage because a reduction in price has to be made only to marginal consumers, whereas in the case of simple monopoly any price reduction has to be made to all consumers including the intramarginal customers who would have been prepared to pay more.

In the case of third-degree price discrimination the effect on output levels is not clear, since the comparison between discriminating and simple monopoly outputs depends on the shapes of the demand curves. Although anything is possible, it is generally thought that the most likely outcome is that the output of the discriminating monopolist will again be greater.

Figure 5.11

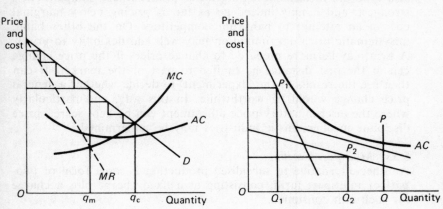

(*a*) Greater production with discrimination   (*b*) No product without discrimination

Finally, on the question of efficiency there is the possibility that some commodities would not be produced at all without price discrimination. This case is illustrated in Figure 5.11(*b*). The average total cost curve, *AC*, lies at all points above the demand schedules, so that there is no single price that will allow the enterprise to cover costs. However, by charging a high price P_1 in one market and a lower price P_2 in the other, an average price of P is achieved that is higher than the average cost of the total output produced. In cases such as these it is generally argued that price discrimination is, on grounds of efficiency at least, a good thing.

The argument that price discrimination, when it increases output levels, is desirable on grounds of efficiency, may be persuasive in a generally competitive world with isolated pockets of monopoly power, where monopolised industries are competing with substitutes that are produced under competitive conditions. The position is not so clear cut, however, where monopolised industries are in close competition. If close competitors do not operate similar pricing strategies, the allocation of resources may be adversely affected.

This brings us back to the question of the relationship between price discrimination and competition. Although the static analysis of price discrimination associates it with monopoly, looked at in a dynamic context the practice may in fact be pro-competitive in its effects. Whether this is so hinges largely on the question of whether price discrimination is practised in a systematic or unsystematic fashion. If the former, then the results are likely to be anticompetitive; if the latter, they may well be pro-competitive. Systematic price discrimination may, for instance, reinforce a monopoly situation by creating strong links with distributive outlets, thus raising entry barriers to potential competitors. It may also take the form of accepting lower profits where competition is strongest, and it may indeed go as far as pricing below marginal cost in an attempt to bankrupt competitors. On the other hand, unsystematic price discrimination may well add flexibility to prices. A firm may be more prepared to change prices if the price change can in the first instance be limited to part of the market. It can then use the results of the 'experiment' to decide whether a general price change would be worthwhile. In this way, and particularly where the discriminatory price adjustment can be kept secret, price discipline in oligopolistic industries may be undermined.

5.33   *Multipart Tariffs*

Another alternative to subsidised production is some form of two-part or multipart tariff, consisting of a fixed charge plus a charge for each unit consumed.

A problem with the simplest form of two-part tariff is that it may violate the Pareto-efficient conditions, because the imposition of the fixed charge will increase average costs to the consumer. Consumers near the margin who would buy the good at marginal cost prices alone are discouraged, and a loss of consumer surplus occurs. How important a loss this will be clearly depends on the size of the fixed charge. The problem is illustrated in Figure 5.12, where a public utility is assumed to be in equilibrium with output q_3 and price equal to marginal cost, OC. A loss equal to area $MVTC$ is incurred. If the deficit is recouped by a fixed charge, the charge will be area $MVTC$ divided by the number of customers. For some customers who consume units within the range of q_2q_3 the fixed charge will be enough to discourage demand. Clearly the fixed charge has to be set at zero or near-zero level on such units of output if the Pareto efficiency conditions are to be met. A simple two-part tariff cannot do this. One possibility is to introduce elements of price discrimination into the system. If, for example, the n consumers of units q_1 were each charged OP per unit consumed plus a fixed tariff of $QUWC/n$ (note that $QUWC = MVTC$), while the consumers of units q_1q_3 were charged operating costs only, then total costs would be covered and the efficiency criteria complied with. Such a policy would, of course, have consequences on the equity side, which would also have to be taken into account.

Where there are peaks in demand, efficient pricing procedures call, as we saw in an earlier section of this chapter, for different charges at peak and off-peak periods, with consumers of peak period units paying a higher charge than consumers of off-peak units. Theoretically, and ignoring the costs of administering a sophisticated price system, there may have to be a large number of different charges reflecting differences in capacity utilisation.

Figure 5.12

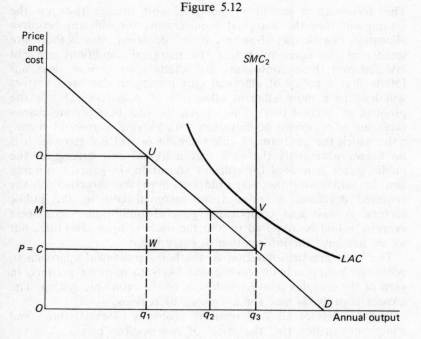

However, whether the price structure is based upon a multipart tariff or price discrimination, an over-riding consideration in practice will be the cost of its administration. In the case of electricity charges, for example, there is a cost involved in attempts to add additional refinements to the system of charges, including the increased cost of metering. Similarly, in the case of traffic congestion in towns, attempts to introduce charges related to the degree of congestion, which would have to vary by time of day as well as by type of vehicle, would run into the same difficulties of administration costs. In practice the important thing is to see whether there is a system of charges that, allowing for the administration costs involved, is likely to improve matters.

Finally, where neither price discrimination nor multipart tariffs can be introduced the authorities have to choose between a policy of marginal cost pricing plus financial losses, and average cost pricing or some form of target-return pricing policy. As indicated earlier in this chapter, the choice of policy must be based on considerations of both allocative and internal efficiency as well as equity.

5.4   SECOND BEST

The argument in favour of marginal cost pricing rests on the assumption that the marginal requirements for efficient resource allocation can be met elsewhere in the economy. But if there are sectors of the economy where the marginal conditions are not satisfied and these constraints are unalterable, then it does not follow that a policy of marginal cost pricing in the 'free' sectors will lead to a more efficient allocation of resources. This is the problem of 'second best'. Thus, given the fact that private manufacturing is composed of industries with varying degrees of monopoly, which the government either cannot or will not remove, it is no longer necessarily the case that marginal cost pricing in the public sector is needed for efficient allocation. In general, nothing can be said about the magnitude or even the direction of the required deviation of price from marginal cost in the public sectors. A vast and complicated general-equilibrium second-best exercise would be required to find the optimal price structure, but we do not have the information to carry it out.

The basic practical question is whether a piecemeal approach to economic policy is both feasible and likely to improve matters, in view of the complex interdependencies of the economic system. The answer is probably yes, for a number of reasons.

Suppose first of all, and ignoring problems of externalities and complementarities, that the prices of commodities produced in the private sector are equal to or greater than marginal cost. Then it seems plausible that, if there are any goods or services produced in the public sector at prices less than marginal cost, these prices should be increased until they are at least equal to the marginal cost of supply. It would probably be safe to go a step further and, in the case of price setting in each industry in the public sector, attach greater weight to the price–cost margin in closely competing industries in the private sector. Thus if, for instance, the general range of price–cost margins in the private sector was 0–20 per cent, but in the case of a particular nationalised industry all the closely competing industries in the private sector had margins above 15 per cent, then it would be sensible to set the margin in the nationalised industry towards the top rather than the bottom end of the range.

Second, there may be cases where one is justified in optimising within one sector while largely neglecting what happens in the rest of the economy. The energy and transport sectors are two likely candidates. Suppose that price–cost relationships are substantially out of line in the energy sector. Coal, oil, electricity and gas are close substitutes in many uses, so that a non-optimal pricing structure within the sector will result in substantial misallocation. If, on the other hand, the demand for energy as a whole is inelastic, then a move towards a more rational price structure within the energy sector will have substantial benefits in terms of a more efficient allocation of resources between different types of fuel, without having much impact on the allocation of resources between the fuel sector and the rest of the economy.

Third, we must recognise that there may be circumstances when setting prices below marginal cost will be justified. One such case is where a close substitute generates large external diseconomies. If for some reason nothing can be done about these externalities, then there can be a case for setting the price of the substitute below marginal cost so as to divert resources away from the industry that is generating the externalities. Thus the use of private motor cars in towns generates external diseconomies. As we shall argue in Chapter 7, there are two ways of tackling the problem directly: a congestion tax, and quantitative controls upon the use of cars. However, if either of these policies is for any reason unacceptable, there is a case for subsidising public transport, so that prices can be lowered and demand diverted away from the private sector.

Another case where there may be an argument for setting price below marginal cost is where close complements are sold at prices well in excess of marginal cost. Thus if household electric appliances are produced under highly monopolised conditions with prices well above marginal cost, lowering the price of electricity below marginal cost will increase the demand for electric appliances and induce the monopoly appliance producers to increase supply. But electricity has, as we have seen, close substitutes as well as close complements, and this complicates matters. Considering just electricity and gas, and electrical and gas appliances, then, if initially the price–marginal-cost distortion is large for electricity and electrical appliances and small for gas and gas appliances, resource allocation is likely to be improved if the price of electricity is lowered towards marginal cost.

Second-best theory is important in demonstrating that we cannot charge blindly into the prescription of optimising policies in one sector regardless of repercussions elsewhere. The consequences of second best for defining the optimum allocation of resources are grim, but in practice this does not mean that nothing useful can be done. When it comes to policy the job of the economist is to find ways of *improving* matters, rather than to strive to attain the unattainable optimum position.

Chapter 6

Factor Indivisibilities, Size and Efficiency in the Private Sector

6.1 INTRODUCTION

In our analysis of public utility pricing and investment in the previous chapter, we mentioned the possibility that economies of scale may well be so important in certain industries that it may be most efficient to have only one supplier of the good or service in question. Apart from these extreme cases, however, economies of scale will be sufficiently important over a wide range of industries to severely limit the number of firms consistent with technological efficiency. This will in turn encourage large production units, impair the operation of competitive market processes and therefore, possibly, make allocative efficiency unattainable. In the next section of this chapter the sources and significance of economies of scale are discussed. In section 6.3 a look is taken at the major problems that such economies are likely to cause: alienation among workers; the conflict between standardisation and variety in consumer choice; and finally monopoly power. The growth of large-scale production units cannot, however, be attributed entirely to the pursuit of economies of scale by business interests. In practice such units emerge as part of a deliberate attempt to secure the pecuniary and non-pecuniary benefits that arise from sheer size and market dominance. In section 6.4 the nature of some of these 'benefits' and their wider welfare implications are considered. We shall focus our attention in particular upon three areas of business behaviour: marketing and advertising; diversification; and multinational activities. In the concluding section an attempt is made to identify some of the issues for public policy that arise from our analysis.

6.2 THE NATURE AND IMPORTANCE OF ECONOMIES OF SCALE

On the production side of a firm's activities the main sources of economies of scale are specialisation and the division of labour. The advantages to be secured in this way have been well known since they were expounded by Adam Smith in the *Wealth of Nations.* They are the increased skill that a person gains in working continuously at one task, a saving of time that is gained by specialisation and that is otherwise lost in passing from one job to another, and the introduction of specialised machinery to perform repetitive tasks. The realisation of these benefits is clearly related to the size of the production unit. Thus, in the case of labour, greater division of labour is possible in large plants than in small, and, even more important perhaps, larger plants can make fuller use of specialised inputs. Economy of operation in using highly skilled workers and machines whose minimum size is capable of producing a large output depends on the ability to spread the costs incurred over as many units of output as possible, and for this the large plant has an obvious advantage over the small one.

Another advantage of large machines and equipment applies in particular to industries such as petroleum refining, chemicals, electricity generation and shipping. In such industries there are economies of increased dimensions. It is possible to design plant to handle a small as well as a large output, but very often the larger unit has the advantage. First, there may be a technical advantage in building a large unit. If, for instance, the dimensions of a unit to be used for handling hot material are doubled, the volume of the unit will increase eight-fold but the area only four-fold. Since heat loss is related to surface area there is an advantage in building the larger unit. Second, the construction costs of building larger units are likely to increase less than proportionately to output. Again this is due to the fact that construction costs are more closely related to surface area than to volume. Above a certain size the construction of larger units may involve the use of more costly material, more costly welding techniques and more costly handling equipment, but certainly over a wide range the larger unit is likely to be economical in terms of the unit capacity cost of investment. Third, the larger plant may have lower unit operating costs than the smaller one. For instance, doubling the size of an oil tanker will not double the size of the crew. There are limits, of course, to the sizes to which plants can be extended to take advantage of these economies. There is no point, for instance, in building a ship so large that it cannot enter any port.

Both the economies of specialisation and of increased dimensions may be seen as examples of factor indivisibilities. If labour and capital were perfectly divisible, there would be no advantage to be gained from these sources. Where indivisibilities are present, smaller capacities may be technically possible but will suffer the penalty of higher unit costs.

A further example of production economies of scale arises from the economies of massed reserves. If a firm has to have 'stand-by' equipment so as to maintain production in the event of a breakdown, then if the firm is only large enough to employ one machine it may be forced to double its capacity. If, however, it is large enough to employ several machines, one machine in reserve may still be enough to cover the possibility of machine failure. A large firm therefore needs to hold a smaller proportion of equipment in reserve. Similarly, in the holding of stocks a larger firm needs to hold smaller stocks of final product in relation to sales in order to meet any sudden increase in demand or unexpected breakdown in production. Again, if there were no indivisibilities in inputs or outputs, such economies would not exist.

From this brief description of some of the main production economies of scale it will be clear that scale has many dimensions: the size of plant, the rate of output per week or per year, and the total output over the lifetime of the product. Some economies will be associated with one dimension of scale, and some with another. Thus there are economies that will be related to the size of the plant irrespective of the degree of specialisation within the plant, for example the economies arising from the use of large machines and the economies of massed reserves. Other economies will be product-specific economies, related to the number of products produced within a plant. Here the important factors are the rate of output per unit of time and the length of time over which the product is to be produced. The former determines the benefits derived from the division of labour, while both determine the extent to which high capital costs can be spread so as to reduce unit fixed costs. The benefits of standardisation may therefore be attained both by reducing the number of varieties, so increasing the rate of output of remaining products, and by extending the interval between changes in the design of the product.

In addition to plant scale economies there are economies that are related to the size of firm. These are the economies of multiplant operation. Some are real economies in that they save resources that are released for other uses and so benefit the economy as a whole. Others are pecuniary economies, which benefit the firm only at the expense of someone else. These firm-specific economies may be found in all the major functions undertaken by the firm.

First, there are management economies. The large firm is able to benefit from the full time employment of specialists who could not be fully used by its small competitors. In other words there are benefits to be derived from the division of labour in management as well as on the shop floor, and the large firm has fuller access to these economies than the small one.

Second, there are marketing economies. On the purchasing side there are possible economies to be obtained in bulk ordering. These may include an element of real economies in so far as it is cheaper for the supplier to service a large order than a series of small ones, but a substantial proportion of the savings under this heading is likely to be pecuniary in nature; that is, they will be due to the bargaining position of large firms, which enables them to squeeze better terms out of their suppliers.

Third, there are economies in research and development. There are several advantages that the large firm may have in this field, and these will be explored in Chapter 7.

Fourth, there are capital-raising economies. In some activities the amount of capital involved may be so large that only the large firm will be able to raise the sums required. Large firms are also able to raise new money – whether in the form of debt or equity capital – on more favourable terms. This is partly because the fixed transaction costs involved in raising new money are spread over a larger sum, partly because the larger firm is better known to investors, and partly because the profitability performance of large firms shows, in general, greater stability than that of small ones, so that the lender is exposed to less risk.

The important practical questions arising out of this discussion are: What is the minimum size that firms have to attain in order to exhaust all the important economies of scale, and how large would such firms be in relation to the size of the market? Attempts at measuring economies of scale have in the main concentrated on technical economies. Silberston's study of economies of scale in 25 UK manufacturing industries found considerable variation in the importance of economies of scale across industries. In the production of aircraft, diesel engines and certain types of machine tools, for instance, it was estimated that the minimum efficient scale of production of a single product was greater than the entire UK market. For four other products – newspapers, dyes, turbo-alternators and computers – the minimum efficient size was the same as the UK market. At the other end of the scale it was calculated that plants producing footwear and engineering castings needed to account for only 0·2 per cent of UK output to achieve all the technical economies of scale. For 21 out of 30 cases, however, the minimum efficient size for a product or group of products produced in a single plant was estimated to be 20 per cent or more of the UK market. In other words, for these 21 cases the UK market could support a maximum of only 5 plants of optimal size.

A few comments on the estimation of economies of scale are in order. First, to the extent that studies such as those referred to above exclude economies of multiplant operations, they underestimate the importance of scale economies. It is generally thought, however, that in manufacturing industry multiplant economies are relatively unimportant as compared with technical economies, especially if the purely pecuniary economies that benefit the firm but not the economy at large are ignored.

Second, the relevant market is not always the national market. In some cases it will be wider and may indeed embrace the whole world. In others it will be narrower and embrace only a region of a country. Transportation costs will clearly be important in determining the relevant market. One of the important factors determining transportation costs is the nature of the product. Products that are bulky and have a low unit value – such as cement and sand – will have a restricted geographical market because of the sharp increase in transportation costs that will occur as more distant customers are reached. On the other hand, transportation costs will be of little relevance in limiting the geographical extent of the market for compact high-value products, such as photographic film and transistors.

Third, economies of scale are estimated on the assumption of 'ideal conditions'. It is assumed that, if plants of minimum efficient scale were built, management would in fact be able to realise all the technical benefits of such plants – that these benefits would not be dissipated by such factors as technical failure, labour unrest and incompetent management. Estimates of scale economies may also reveal very little about the efficiency of large plants actually in existence. Large plants may have been built up over a considerable period of time and thus embody a substantial proportion of outmoded equipment. A large plant may also produce a wide variety of products and fail to benefit from economies of specialisation and long production runs. For these and many other reasons potential economies of scale may not be fully exploited.

Nevertheless, when full allowance is made for such qualifications there can be little doubt that economies of scale are an extremely important factor in industrial organisation.

6.3 PROBLEMS ARISING FROM ECONOMIES OF SCALE

The importance of economies of scale gives rise to a number of problems relating to resource allocation and other aspects of efficiency. Three of these problems are alienation, the conflict between variety and standardisation, and market power. They will be discussed briefly in turn.

6.31 *Alienation*
Adam Smith's observations on the advantages of economies of scale

are well known, but he was also aware of the dangers. Consider, for example, the following quotation from the *Wealth of Nations*:

'The man whose whole life is spent in performing a few simple operations . . . has no occasion to exert his understanding or to exercise his invention in finding out expedients for remaining difficulties which never occur. He naturally loses, therefore, the habit of such exertion and generally becomes as stupid and ignorant as it is possible for a human creature to become.'

Or, as Karl Marx put it in the *Communist Manifesto*:

'Owing to the extensive use of machinery and to the division of labour, the work of the proletarians has lost all individual character and consequently all charm for workmen. He becomes an appendage of the machine. . . . Modern industry has converted the little workshop of the patriarchal master into the great factory. Masses of labourers, crowded into the factory are organised like soldiers . . . they are daily and hourly enslaved by the machine, by the onlooker and, above all, by the individual bourgeois manufacturer himself'.

Of course, Marx saw alienation as the result not merely of working in large units but specifically of working under a capitalist system of organisation with its emphasis on profits and private property. More recent analysis, however, tends to treat the concept of alienation as relevant to work in any industrial society.

The worst consequences of the division of labour and large scale industry as seen by Adam Smith and Karl Marx have been avoided by the spread of education, the increase in leisure hours and the mechanisation of many onerous jobs. However, many problems still remain. The size of plant plays an important part in determining the nature of the employees' work situation and in shaping their attitudes towards their jobs, their fellow workers and their management. Sociologists have analysed the work unit as a social group and attach considerable significance to the effects of isolation and alienation in determining workers' behaviour. The sheer size of the labour force in large plants dwarfs the individual's contribution, encouraging feelings of insignificance and detachment. The bigger the plant the greater the extent of impersonal bureaucratisation, which both inhibits the individual worker's attraction to the organisation and alienates him from the whole ethos of the work unit. Complex job definition – the creation of technically separate departments and the resulting reduction in personal interaction between employees – inhibits contact among workers, among managers and between the two groups. It also considerably increases the number of possible focal points for conflict. Furthermore, the larger the plant, the longer is the length of the hierarchical chain and the further workers are removed from the decision takers. The greater, therefore, is the likelihood of distorted or inadequate information and of commands passing along the chain resulting in the kind of inefficiency and increased costs now described as the consequences of 'control loss'.

If the nature of technology in large plants is such as to make for difficult relations between management and workers, it is also likely to foster antagonism between workers. Mass production methods tend to encourage the use of piecework and bonus schemes. These introduce problems of status and differentials into the work relationship and incite rivalry and recrimination between workers.

The nature of the technology employed by large plants also tends to assign workers to limited, sterile and repetitive tasks in surroundings marred by dirt, noise and overwhelming physical size. Increasing 'functional specialisation' narrows the work content and the responsibility attached to a particular job, depriving the worker of non-material rewards and job satisfaction, such as pride in workmanship and recognition of achievement. This inevitably further encourages workers' disillusionment with the entire *modus operandi* of the production activity and, equally inevitably, guarantees that such dissatisfaction will be expressed in conflict of various kinds. To the extent that work no longer fulfils the inner potential of workers, challenges his talents and brings psychological benefits, it encourages self-estrangement and detachment from the job. Work inevitably becomes instrumental rather than an end in itself.

Finally, the larger the size of the plant the greater the number of jobs likely to be performed. This may lead to a proliferation of trade unions and makes the process of reconciling differences of interest within the work unit that much more unmanageable. There is a further aspect to this. A large plant with an extensive hierarchy of control not only keeps workers divorced from decision making but also tends to have the same effect upon low level management. Since, in so many cases, the latter are the people with whom workers settle grievances, their frustrations and disorientation will inevitably result in significant costs for the plant.

If our analysis of alienation is correct, against the direct economic advantages of economies of scale we must set several potentially important indirect economic and non-economic disadvantages. The economic problems arise in this context from the reduced productivity and increased industrial conflict that may accompany large scale production. Alienated workers will not work as hard, as carefully or as long as committed workers. The very existence of extensive piecework, quality control and overtime schemes in large plants is symptomatic of the difficulties management has in securing the potential advantages of large scale operations.

Large scale units face many problems in labour/management relations. A liberal pluralistic view of industrial relations in general would recognise the existence of marked underlying differences of interest within industry, but would argue that the majority of actual disputes can be settled without resort to non-institutionalised forms of conflict. The presence of alienated workers and the low quality of workplace relationships in large plants is, however, much more conducive to conflict. The reduced costs of production made possible by economies of scale must therefore be set against the increased costs brought about by higher wages, more frequent strikes and absenteeism, higher labour turnover, and so on. Not only will the incidence of conflict tend to be higher in large plants; it will also be more costly each time it occurs. There are two reasons for this. First, reliance upon continuous flow methods of production and heavily capital-intensive techniques increases the mutual interdependence of work units within the plant. An expression of conflict in one area unavoidably has repercussions throughout the remainder of the plant. A fall in output, a stoppage of work, a deterioration in quality or a loss of power in one department means a loss of efficiency in another. Second, reliance upon specialisation between plants where each plant accounts for a large proportion of the total output of a product means that any production failure within one plant can have serious consequences for the whole industry. The implication is that all the potential benefits of economies of scale will not be realised because of the loss of internal efficiency within large production units.

Perhaps more important than the indirect economic costs of large scale are the social and individual problems that large scale produces. Even if on the grounds of efficiency, therefore, the balance of advantage lies with large plants, there may still be strong grounds for limiting the size of plants and foregoing the benefits of economies of scale whenever it is feasible to do so. Working hours still account for the greater part of man's active life, and job satisfaction is in itself a crucially important aspect of human welfare. The analysis of alienation suggests that such satisfaction is in general much less likely to be achieved in large plants than in small ones.

6.32 *Standardisation versus Variety*
The existence of economies of scale means that there may well be a conflict between the objective of achieving low costs through

standardisation and the objective of satisfying the consumer's demand for variety. The extent of this conflict will depend upon the exact circumstances surrounding the production of each commodity. We may, however, identify three categories of product.

First, there are the products, such as electrical fittings and bicycle spare parts, where there is a clear advantage in favour of standardisation. The economies of scale are significant, and in general the advantages of variety are very limited.

Second, there are the products where there is a clear advantage in favour of variety and where economies of scale, although present, are not particularly important quantitatively. This may be because all economies are exhausted at a firm size that is still relatively small in relation to the size of the market, as in the case of footwear, or because, although the minimum optimal size of firm may account for a significant share of the market, the cost disadvantage of operating at suboptimal sizes is not very large. In such cases, suboptimal-sized firms may be able to survive quite comfortably, especially if protected by product differentiation, and the conflict between standardisation and variety will be trivial. To the extent that consumers display strong preferences for variety the opportunity costs of meeting that demand will not be excessive.

Third, there will be products, such as motor cars, for which both the economies of scale available and the demand for variety are important.

The third group of products sets a problem of alternatives. Consumers can have *either* a very restricted choice of product at a low price, *or* a greater variety at a significantly higher price. The dilemma of choosing between these alternatives is compounded by the fact that consumers' tastes are so varied. Some will prefer the more standardised set of products, while others will prefer greater variety. Whatever combination of products is actually produced, the preferences of all consumers cannot be met simultaneously. Nor, except by chance, will the set of products actually produced in the market satisfy the conditions of Pareto optimality.

This can be illustrated by assessing the effects of adding one additional variety to a given set of products in a particular sector of the economy. The additional product will have a non-marginal impact on the sales of other products and thus will affect the extent to which economies of scale can be realised. More fully, the addition of one more product will have the following repercussions: First, the new product will be closer to the preferences of some consumers than those products already in existence. Certain people will thus switch to the new product from near substitutes to increase their total utility. Second, firms producing other products will suffer a decline in sales and higher production costs. Third, the consumers of these other products will, as a result, face higher prices and thus suffer a loss of utility. A similar situation exists if one variety of a product is replaced by another. Consumers of the old product will lose utility, those who switch to the new product will gain utility, and there will be further repercussions if the new product affects the sales of other existing products. The problem is that the market does not provide a way of measuring the utilities that are gained and lost.

In theory the solution to the problem is to maximise the aggregate net consumers' surplus, that is, maximise the difference between the total value of output to consumers and the total production costs. This task, if undertaken by an all-wise government, would involve calculating the total value to consumers and the total cost to producers of every conceivable combination of products. The information so obtained could then be used to impose the optimal production pattern. If there were an effective compensation mechanism whereby the gainers from any change would compensate the losers, the market would eventually bring about an optimum solution. But such a mechanism does not exist. The problem of standardisation versus variety can thus be seen to arise out of a combination of factors: the variety of tastes, economies of scale, and the absence of any mechanism whereby gainers can compensate losers.

However, failure of the market mechanism to achieve *the* optimum position need not concern us unduly. Far more important are the following questions: Are there reasons to suppose that certain market structures will result in far worse performance, in terms of the choice of goods available to customers, than others? And, is it possible for government intervention to improve performance, due allowance being made for the administrative costs of government involvement?

As far as market structure is concerned it has been claimed that, when it comes to combining scale and variety, monopolistically competitive markets represent 'a sort of ideal'. These are markets characterised by a large number of firms acting independently, a differentiated product with buyers' preferences fairly evenly spread among the different varieties available, and freedom of entry and exit. Under such conditions the existence of monopoly profits will attract new firms and new varieties of product. This will reduce the demand for the products of existing producers, and will continue to do so until all firms are earning no more than normal profits. In other words there will be a tendency for demand curves to be pushed to points of tangency with the unit cost curve. The final equilibrium under conditions of monopolistic competition is shown in Figure 6.1. As long as there are economies of scale, and since the individual demand curves are downward sloping, the 'tangency solution' must involve some degree of unexhausted economies of scale. Also the plant, depicted by the *SAC* curve in the figure, will be operated with some degree of excess capacity. However, it is clear that, if the demand curve is highly elastic, departures from minimum cost production will be small. The output of each individual firm will only depart substantially from least cost output if the *LAC* curve slopes very gently over a wide range of output. But if this were the case, cost conditions would favour large firms and the structural characteristics of the market would no longer be those of monopolistic competition.

Figure 6.1

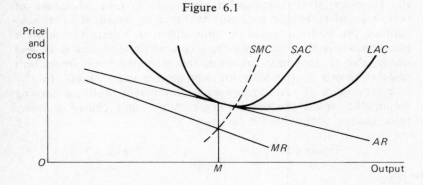

In theory Chamberlin's ideal of monopolistic competition cannot be accepted as a policy objective because it is not possible to demonstrate that the product mix associated with the final equilibrium position is an optimum in the sense defined earlier. However, it is also clear that the structure of the market is such that deviations from the optimum position are unlikely to be large. Consumers will have a wide choice of products at little cost in terms of technical inefficiency, and it is hardly likely that government interference will improve matters. If, however, market conditions favour oligopoly or monopoly rather than monopolistic competition, the outcome of the scale/variety dilemma is much less easily predicted and analysed.

6.33 *Monopoly and Oligopoly Pricing*
The rather reassuring picture presented by monopolistic competition is, indeed, of limited value, since markets of that kind are rarely found in manufacturing industry. The typical manufacturing industry is more likely to resemble an oligopolistic market structure, characterised either by the existence of one dominant firm and a

number of smaller competitors, or by a small number of producers accounting for a substantial share of total sales. In such circumstances the actions of at least some firms will affect the position of competitors, so that a general situation of interdependence between firms exists. If the firms find some way of pursuing a collective profit-maximising strategy, their market behaviour and performance will approximate to that found under pure monopoly.

The classical case against monopoly is that, as compared to competitive markets, the monopolist restricts output and raises price. In terms of Figure 6.2, the competitive industry would produce output ON at price P_c. A monopolist, however, assuming identical demand and cost conditions, would produce output OM at price P_m. However, if the monopolist were able to take advantage of economies of scale that were not available to several smaller competitors, the position would be quite different. Figure 6.3 shows a situation where the cost curve for a competitive industry is S_c, and where, due to economies of scale, the monopolist has lower unit costs as shown by the long-run average-cost curve, LAC. In this case economies of scale are so important that a profit-maximising monopolist would produce a larger output and charge a lower price than a competitive industry.

Figure 6.2   Figure 6.3

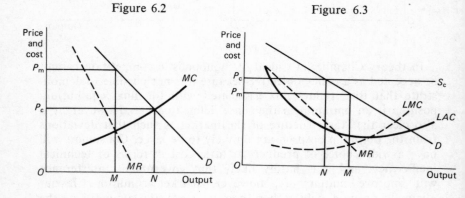

Which of the two outcomes is most likely is an empirical issue, depending in particular upon the extent of the economies available within different industries. Here we are concerned with the more general case; where economies of scale are sufficiently important to benefit consumers considerably and to lead to fewness of sellers, some degree of market power and interdependence between firms, but not sufficient to justify a monopoly situation.

Where oligopolistic market structures are the result of economies of scale there is an advantage in having such market structures, because the resource cost of producing a given level of output is minimised. There is, of course, a cost in terms of reduced variety, but there is also a further problem – which is that consumers may not benefit fully or even at all from economies of scale in the form of lower prices. If they don't benefit, they suffer reduced choice with little or no compensation in terms of lower prices. The extent to which consumers are likely to gain in terms of lower prices depends on the extent to which producers are successful in co-ordinating their price and output behaviour. The more competitive their behaviour the more will cost savings be passed on in lower prices. On the other hand, the more successful they are in co-ordinating their behaviour, the more the outcome will approximate to the monopoly one and the less benefit there will be for consumers.

What then are the factors that will facilitate or limit oligopolistic co-ordination? The answer to this question is a very complicated one, and a full treatment of it would require case study work on individual industries. However, the following factors are likely to have an important bearing on policy co-ordination.

The first point concerns the number of sellers. In general, the smaller the number of sellers, the easier it will be for firms to achieve agreement on prices, market shares, etc. and the more likely it is that such agreement can be achieved by tacit rather than overt means. As the number of firms increases it becomes more likely that one or more will be tempted to act independently, thus increasing competition.

Second, the possibility of co-ordination is affected by the size distribution of firms. For instance, where there is one dominant firm and the others are much smaller, price leadership may well be established with the dominant firm setting prices and the others following suit.

Third, the more homogeneous the product, especially in technical matters, the easier it will be to reach agreement on price. On the other hand, variations between products in terms of quality, technical specifications and so on will make for a complex price structure and render agreement difficult to achieve. Similarly, if the nature of the product changes substantially over time, either because of rapid technological change, as in electronics, or because of changes in fashion, as in clothing, price agreement will again be difficult to achieve.

Fourth, cost conditions are particularly important. The greater the similarity in the unit costs of competing firms the easier it will be to reach agreement on prices, either overtly or by the use of rules of thumb such as full-cost pricing. If unit costs are similar a co-ordinated price policy can be achieved merely through an understanding that firms should, in calculating price, adopt a common full-cost pricing formula, such as adding a given percentage mark-up to unit costs at normal capacity working. Should costs vary substantially between firms, however, it will be difficult to co-ordinate price policy on the basis of rules of thumb alone.

Fifth, success in co-ordinating policies will depend on the stability of demand. When demand fluctuates it will clearly be difficult for firms to adjust total production so as to maintain that rate of overall output which is necessary to maintain price stability. By allowing stocks to increase or run down, or by allowing order books to shorten or lengthen, firms can to some extent cushion the effects of demand fluctuations and thus stabilise price agreements. But the more violent the fluctuations the greater the stresses and strains that are imposed on co-ordinated behaviour, especially if firms are affected unequally.

Sixth, the variability of demand and the composition of costs may facilitate or hinder co-ordinated behaviour. Where demand comes regularly and in small lots, and where fixed costs form a small proportion of total costs, conditions facilitate agreement. But where demand comes infrequently and in orders that are large in relation to annual turnover, and when in addition fixed costs are high, agreement may be difficult to reach or, if reached, difficult to maintain for any length of time. G. B. Richardson has drawn attention to these problems in relation to the heavy electrical-engineering industry. In this industry, one order from the electricity-generating authority can be very large in relation to total annual output. Furthermore, with high fixed costs it is important for each individual firm to secure its share of demand. There is always a temptation, therefore, particularly when demand is low, to cut prices in order to secure an order. When fixed costs form a high proportion of total costs any tendency towards price-cutting behaviour can have serious consequences, since in the short run prices can be cut all the way to the level of average variable costs. Figure 6.4 contrasts a situation where fixed costs are important (*a*) with one where they are relatively unimportant (*b*). The greater scope for short-run price cutting in the high fixed-cost situation is obvious.

This very fact may of course produce a greater determination on the part of producers to avoid such competition. The dangers of price competition may result in more entrenched restrictive agreements. The history of at least some industries, such as heavy electrical engineering and cables, lends support to this view. And it brings us to the final factor bearing upon the likelihood of co-ordinated behaviour – to what Joan Robinson has called the 'animal spirits of businessmen'. If these are strong, competition will be strong also. But if they are weak, and there exists instead a strong determination to avoid competition, the latter may be extraordinarily difficult to enforce.

Figure 6.4

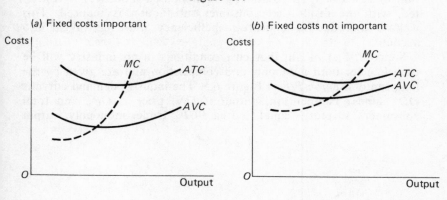

(a) Fixed costs important

(b) Fixed costs not important

Attempts have been made to establish whether firms have in practice been able to collude effectively so as to establish a monopoly position by estimating the effects of varying degrees of oligopoly upon prices. In the main these have consisted of statistical cross-section studies of the relationship between (a) concentration (which is a measure of the extent to which industry sales are concentrated in the top x firms) and other elements of market structure on the one hand, and (b) profitability or price–cost margins on the other. On the whole the evidence suggests that as far as concentration is concerned (concentration being used as a proxy measure for monopoly power), there is a tendency for profitability to increase and price–cost margins to widen as the level of concentration increases. The relationship need not be a continuous one, but may be rather a marked difference between, say, the average profit performance of industries with a high level of concentration and those with a low level. There is also evidence to suggest a positive association between changes in concentration and price–cost margins over time. It is not surprising, in view of all the various factors affecting the outcome, that the concentration variable alone provides only a part, sometimes only a small part, of the explanation of differences in, or changes in, profitability and price–cost margins. As should be clear from the factors listed above, all of which affect the likely success of firms in co-ordinating behaviour, the level of concentration is only one of several factors affecting the outcome. However, a general and positive relationship between profitability, or price–cost margins, and the level of concentration seems well established.

6.34   *The Welfare Loss of Resource Misallocation*

If, other things being equal, monopolised industries do have higher price–cost margins than competitive ones, this signifies a misallocation of resources. The output of monopolised industries is restricted, with the result that consumer satisfaction is reduced. This welfare loss due to allocative inefficiency must be taken into account.

Suppose, first of all, that cost conditions in an industry will be the same for both monopoly and competition and are given by the long-run cost curve P_cL in Figure 6.5. The industry demand curve is DD'. Under competition, output is ON, price is OP_c, and total consumers' surplus is equal to area DCP_c. Under monopoly, output

Figure 6.5

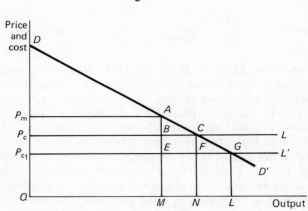

is restricted to OM and price raised to OP_m. An expenditure equal to area $BCNM$ is released for other purchases, and it is assumed that this is dissipated over a large number of competitive industries having only a marginal effect on each industry. For these diverted purchases, therefore, the price paid equals the marginal production cost, and there is no gain or loss of consumer surplus. In the monopolised industry there is, however, a loss of consumers' surplus equal to area P_mACP_c. Part of this loss, area P_mABP_c, is a transfer to producers' profits, so that there is a redistribution of income in favour of producers. The other part, area ABC, is what has become known as the 'dead-weight welfare' loss; that is, it is the net loss from monopolisation, which is not offset by any gain to another sector of the community.

The quantitative importance of this welfare loss clearly depends on the extent to which the monopoly price exceeds the competitive price and on the elasticity of the demand curve over the relevant range. One or two studies, such as Harberger's pioneering work on US manufacturing industry, have attempted to quantify the resource allocation loss from monopoly as a percentage of gross national product (GNP). These empirical studies invariably show the estimated loss to be very small – less than 0·1 per cent of GNP. Various criticisms can be made of this work, most of which suggest that the estimates are biased in a downward direction. First, the elasticities of demand assumed have been too low; second, monopolistic price distortions have been underestimated by relying on rather broad industry data, which conceals strong monopoly position in individual products; third, price distortions themselves do not fully reflect the degree of monopoly, and fourth, the neglect of price distortions in non-manufacturing activities introduces another serious downward bias into the estimates.

However, not all the errors operate in this direction. Some part of the price distortions attributed to monopoly may, for instance, be due to other factors, such as exceptional managerial ability or risk. Again, the assumption that the expenditure released by the output restrictions of monopolists is worth no more than marginal cost in alternative uses is questionable. Expenditure elsewhere may well yield consumers' surplus, which would have to be subtracted from the welfare loss in the monopolised sectors. Further doubts about the resource misallocation effects of monopoly stem from the new managerial theories of the firm. Large firms are in general management controlled, and it is often argued that these firms are motivated more by growth than by profit maximisation. Certainly a minimum profit has to be earned in order to satisfy shareholders and to reduce the likelihood of takeover, but once this is achieved the firm's goal, so it is argued, will be to extend output to maximise sales revenue. Firms that maximise sales revenue subject to a minimum profit constraint will produce a larger output than the profit-maximising firm, as long as the minimum profit level is itself lower than the maximum attainable. Thus in so far as, in general, the firms with monopoly power are also those which are motivated most strongly by the desire to grow, resource allocation will be nearer to the optimum. However, while this is possible it is by no means clear that it must be so. For instance, firms may expand by diversification while restricting output in each individual market.

Even if, on balance, the net outcome of all these factors is that the welfare loss has been underestimated, it can hardly be the case that it would amount to much more than about 1 per cent of GNP.

There are two major qualifications to this conclusion. First, a shift from monopoly to competition may lower costs as well as prices. When firms have monopoly power they may, for various reasons, fail to minimise costs. Internal inefficiency may occur, because management effectiveness is impaired by the extended hierarchical chain and communication systems, and by organisational problems. Or it may simply be the fact that, if competitive forces are seriously blunted, there is no incentive to strive continuously to minimise costs. Irrespective of the degree to which ownership and control are separated, the determination to minimise costs at the expense of other objectives declines as monopoly power, and the security it brings, increase. In terms of Figure 6.5, suppose that a shift from monopoly to competition lowers costs to $P_{c_1}L_1$. This means that the allocative benefits could be as high as area AEG. Furthermore, there are substantial benefits to be achieved in the form of an increase in internal efficiency. These benefits, equal to area $P_cBEP_{c_1}$, are related to the whole of the monopolist's output and not, as in the case of allocative improvements, merely to the difference between monopoly and competitive output. Since OM is likely to be very large relative to ML, and unless cost reductions are very small, the welfare gain due to improved internal efficiency will be large relative to the gain attributable to improved allocative efficiency. If, therefore, monopoly is associated with internal inefficiency, the potential welfare losses are substantially increased. It is this point that Leibenstein has emphasised so strongly in his analysis of 'X-inefficiency'.

The suggestion that the welfare losses due to a decline in internal efficiency are more important than those related to allocative inefficiency is likely to hold good at least in terms of the range of goods actually being produced. Our second qualification, however, suggests that the usual method of estimating the welfare losses of allocative inefficiency may seriously underestimate these losses for a reason not yet mentioned. As indicated earlier, the calculations are based upon data on profitability or price–cost margins. This data must of necessity refer to products that are currently being produced. But an important cost of monopolies to society may be that monopoly behaviour restricts the choice of goods and services available to consumers. This loss cannot of course be picked up by empirical work using cross-section analysis of data for the set of products that are actually produced. An assessment of the practical importance of this loss depends on case studies of individual industries. The welfare loss of restricted choice where it occurs is probably quite impossible to quantify, but it is none the less important for that.

6.4 THE POWER OF LARGE FIRMS

The last subsection was concerned with monopoly power as it arises from the exploitation of scale economies. However, if we are to explain the size of firms and the structure of industries at all adequately, we must recognise that firms grow with the deliberate intention of securing the financial benefits that market dominance and sheer size confers. We move on, therefore, to consider the nature and welfare implications of the benefits that large firms secure in the fields of marketing and finance, diversification and multinational operations.

6.41 *Marketing and Finance*

As far as marketing is concerned, advertising in particular raises a whole series of questions: What is the relationship between advertising and market structure? Does advertising result in increased concentration? Is there a relationship between advertising and profitability?

A considerable amount of effort has been expended by economists in attempting to identify the type of market structure that is associated with the most intensive advertising effort (defined as the ratio of advertising expenditure to total sales revenue). If a systematic relationship existed, it would clearly be of theoretical and practical importance, so it is worthwhile spending a little time on the matter.

First, however, it is important to emphasise that the nature of the product is an important factor, indeed the single most important factor determining the level of advertising expenditure. Advertising is a more effective technique in the sale of soap and cars than in the sale of paper clips and nuts and bolts. The important factor that distinguishes those products which lend themselves to advertising is the opportunity for differentiation. This may be based on the technical complexity of the product, which makes it difficult for the consumer to form a judgement on the relative merits of competing goods, or it may be created by advertising itself, with elaborate packaging, for instance, concealing the fundamental homogeneity of the product. In both cases consumer ignorance is important. Consumers may be unable to judge the relative technical merits of competing goods or may be unaware of the extravagant claims made by advertisers. This in turn reduces the effectiveness of price reductions and makes consumers more responsive to advertising messages.

There is little point, therefore, in comparing the advertising expenditures and market structures of products such as paper clips on the one hand and toiletries on the other. We must always be careful to compare products that differ in terms of the number and size distribution of firms, but that are similar in terms of the scope for advertising and of the other factors that influence the advertising decision. With this important point out of the way we can now turn to the question of the relationship between advertising intensity and market structure.

The hoped-for effect of advertising to the firm is that it shifts the position and/or slope of the demand curve, enabling the firm to sell more at the existing price, or to sell the existing output at a higher price, or indeed a larger output at a higher price. Concentrating on sales expansion, the relative attractiveness of advertising compared to a reduction in price as a means of increasing sales depends on the responsiveness of sales to advertising expenditure and on the price elasticity of demand.

Under conditions of perfect competition, where the firm's demand curve is infinitely elastic there is no incentive for the firm to advertise, because price elasticity is greater than advertising elasticity, although the industry as a whole may, of course, find it profitable to advertise. Under conditions of imperfect competition, where elasticity of demand is less than infinite firms may find it profitable to advertise, and an inverse relationship between advertising intensity and elasticity of demand may be expected – that is, the more inelastic is the demand curve facing the firm, the more likely it is, other things being equal, that the firm will resort to advertising. If such a relationship exists, however, it will be in the form of a general tendency rather than an iron law. Salt, for instance, has a low price elasticity of demand, but very little advertising expenditure is incurred in promoting sales.

Clearly, if we are comparing different products, the nature of the product and the scope that exists for increasing consumption are important factors in determining the level of advertising expenditure. Differences between products in these respects will weaken the relationship between advertising intensity and elasticity of demand.

Even if a strong negative relationship between these variables did exist, however, for it to be translated into a systematic association between advertising intensity and market structure there would have to be a strong association between structure and elasticity of demand, so that the more concentrated the market structure the lower the elasticity. In general, however, there is no reason to expect a systematic relationship of this kind. Therefore, if we were describing market structure in terms, say, of the number of firms making up 80 per cent of industry sales, we should not expect to find a simple relationship between this measure and advertising intensity such that the latter increased as the number of firms decreased. Further information is clearly needed before we can arrive at any hypotheses about the relationship between advertising and market structure. For instance, one factor that is important is the behaviour of oligopolists. If danger of retaliation is an important factor, this is likely to make the firm's demand curve highly inelastic and so to increase the importance of non-price competition, including advertising.

So far we have focused attention on price elasticity, but, as indicated above, we must also take into account the responsiveness of sales to advertising expenditure in explaining a firm's propensity to advertise. Attacking the problem from this side, it seems on *a priori* grounds that the incentive to advertise will be strongest in industries with relatively few sellers. The reasoning is as follows. Advertising expenditure may expand the demand for a firm's products in two ways. First, it may increase industry demand as a whole at the expense of the products of other industries – the market expansion effect of advertising. Second, it may change the pattern of demand within the industry, shifting demand in favour of the firm doing the advertising – the market redistribution effect of advertising. In industries with a large number of competitors of similar size, any individual firm will benefit from the market redistribution effect of its advertising, but since it is a small part of the market it will derive little benefit from the market expansion effect. A large part of any market expansion that is due to the advertising efforts of one firm will accrue as benefits to its competitors, so that on this score individual firms will be reluctant to engage in heavy expenditure. Conversely, for the monopolist the market expansion effect of advertising is important, while the market redistribution effect does not exist at all. In the cases of atomistic competition and monopoly, therefore, only one of the inducements to advertise will be important. In the oligopolistic market with few sellers, on the other hand, both types of stimulus are relevant. Since each firm is large in relation to the market each one will expect, or at least hope, that its advertising campaign will result in worthwhile gains, both by capturing a substantial part of any overall expansion of the market and by diverting sales away from its competitors.

The analysis so far cannot be said to have resulted in any startling conclusions. We have learnt that it will not pay a firm to advertise when the industry is perfectly competitive, since the demand curve is perfectly elastic and the firm can sell all that it is capable of producing at the going price. However, when the demand curve facing the firm is downward sloping it is difficult to arrive at any definite conclusions. As far as price elasticity is concerned there is no simple relationship with market structure that leads to a clear-cut hypothesis. As far as the effectiveness of advertising is concerned it seems plausible to argue that, because an oligopolist stands to gain both from market expansion and from an increased market share, advertising intensity is likely to be at its peak in oligopolistic markets. This conclusion, however, is of rather limited value, for two reasons. First, when comparing different products, the outcome depends on the quantitative importance of the inducements. A firm in industry x, which is oligopolistic, may well have the two-fold inducement to advertise, but the sum total of the two effects may be less than the market expansion inducement to advertise that governs the behaviour of the monopolist in industry y. As mentioned above, differences between products in the scope for increasing consumption will materially affect the results. Second, in terms of the number and size distribution of firms, oligopoly covers a very wide range of market structures.

What we seem to have, therefore, is a theory that says, all other things being equal, that advertising intensity will be low in industries where there are a large number of firms and no dominant positions – that is, industries with 'low concentration'; that it will be substantially higher over a wide band of industries with moderate-to-high levels of concentration; and that it will fall below this level in industries characterised by a single dominant firm.

To proceed any further we must clearly know a great deal more about conditions in the oligopolistic industries. The more successful oligopolists are in avoiding price competition, the more important perhaps will advertising become as the outlet for competitive spirits. But why, it may be asked, will oligopolistic competitors not collude in order to limit their advertising expenditures in the same way as they tend to collude to limit price competition, especially when it is manifestly the case that the advertising efforts of firms are simply offsetting each other? There are reasons to believe, however, that attempts at collusive behaviour to limit advertising are less likely to be successful than price collusion. For one thing, unlike a price cut, an advertising campaign cannot be matched immediately. For another, the outcome of an advertising campaign is more uncertain, depending as it does not only on the total expenditure involved but also on whether the firm has hit upon a successful gimmick. Because of this a successful advertising campaign may not be easily counteracted. If indeed there is no tendency towards collusion, then there is no reason on this score to expect advertising intensity to be lower in the more highly-concentrated oligopolistic industries than in the more moderately-concentrated ones. If, however, collusive tendencies did exist, then there might be good reason to distinguish between highly concentrated industries containing a small number of large firms of similar size, and looser oligopolistic structures having a greater dispersion of firm sizes and a larger number of firms in total. The expectation would be that the incentive to collude would be stronger in the former and the incentive to advertise stronger in the latter.

Another factor that will distinguish one group of oligopolistic industries from another is the importance of non-advertising barriers to new competition. Advertising intensity will often be greatest where these barriers to competition are low. The heavy advertising expenditures of firms in highly concentrated industries, which seem to a large extent to be mutually offsetting and to have no rational foundation, can often be explained by the advantage that they give to established firms in the form of high barriers to entry.

This last point illustrates that there is a two-way relationship between market structure and advertising expenditure. As well as being affected by market structure, advertising may also result in changes in structure. In industries where advertising is an important competitive weapon, firms will use it in an attempt to achieve greater market shares. Because of this, advertising intensity may be greater in a situation of disequilibrium, and perhaps of relatively low concentration, when firms are jostling for market position, than when the industry has reached greater maturity. For this reason the tendency for high advertising expenditures to be associated with *increasing* levels of concentration may be found to be stronger than the tendency for them to be associated with *high* levels of concentration.

There are in fact reasons to believe that size confers important advantages in advertising. As a result, when some firms have gained a size advantage, possibly as a result of pure chance, this will secure a number of other advantages over their smaller competitors, which will result in more concentrated market structures and the stabilisation of high market shares once they have been attained. First, the cost per unit of advertising may be lower for large firms because of discounts that are offered by the media to important customers. Second, advertising effectiveness is subject to thresholds. A small expenditure sufficient only to purchase one or two television messages is less likely to influence consumers than an expenditure large enough to finance a regular stream of messages. Third, the prime advertising times that correspond with peak-hour viewing are obviously limited in duration, and only large firms can afford the very expensive advertising time available. Fourth, there is an important time factor involved. Advertising may be cumulative in its effects, so that a given annual expenditure is likely to be more effective for a firm that has been advertising over a number of years than for a newly established firm. Finally, advertising and the associated product differentiation advantages can impose formidable entry barriers to new competition. Further barriers may result if large firms succeed in establishing dealer networks, as in the case of the UK brewing industry. In order to compete with established firms, newcomers either have to match their marketing expenditures or must offer substantial price discounts to customers in order to offset their marketing weakness. Clearly, there will be instances where small firms will be successful in competing with their much larger competitors, but in general this competition will be blunted by the sales promotion advantages of large firms. As a result the latter will be able to widen their price–cost margins.

The empirical evidence that bears upon these inter-relationships is still rather limited, and much of it is unsatisfactory. As can be imagined from the foregoing discussion, there are severe difficulties in obtaining satisfactory data to test the various hypotheses. There are, for instance, great difficulties in obtaining a satisfactory sample of industries – that is, a sample of industries that have different levels of concentration but that are otherwise similar in terms of the scope for advertising and of the various factors, such as the price elasticity of demand and non-advertising barriers to entry, that influence the advertising decision. Again, the use of concentration ratios as a measure of industrial structure is not sensitive enough to enable a satisfactory test to be carried out. For example, a five-firm sales-concentration ratio of 80 per cent may mean that five firms of more or less equal size control 80 per cent of sales, or it may mean that one firm controls 70 per cent and the other four the remaining 10 per cent. This sort of summary measure will inevitably conceal a range of different market structures and, more important, will overlap the ranges that are significant for the analysis.

In view of the data problems and of the absence of a solid theoretical base it is hardly surprising that opinion is divided in this field. On the relationship between market structure and advertising intensity the findings range from no significant associations to reasonably strong ones. The latter findings can be divided into two camps: linear relationships with advertising intensity increasing with concentration; and non-linear relationships with advertising intensity reaching a peak at medium-to-high levels of concentration. On balance it is probably safe to say that advertising intensity has more often than not been found to be substantially higher in medium and high concentration industries than in low concentration ones, but that the picture at the top end of the concentration scale is still in some doubt. Somewhat stronger evidence, however, exists to support the hypothesis that heavy advertising leads to the emergence of highly concentrated industries, and that it also allows firms to widen their price–cost margins.

In addition to marketing advantages large firms also have considerable financial advantages over their smaller competitors. For instance, their financial muscle enables them to buy up any small innovative firm that poses a competitive threat, and to buy up or to contest patents taken out by small competitors. During times of financial stringency the large firm can enforce the prompt payment of bills by small customers and delay its own payments to small suppliers. The importance of retentions in financing the investments of large firms means that they are not so exposed to market discipline as firms whose investments have to be financed to a large extent by external funds. Finally, the large diversified firm has the ability to switch funds from one part of the business to another – a strategy not available to the small, primarily specialist, producer.

6.42 *The Large Diversified Firm and Resource Allocation*

The emergence of the large diversified firm has created one of the most important problems for the analysis of resource allocation. The 100 largest companies in UK manufacturing industry now account for over 40 per cent of total output. A similar picture of the dominance of the largest companies is to be found in the United States and in most other Western economies. The significance of this for the theory of resource allocation can be seen most clearly by contrasting the present real world position with a theoretical world where there is no such dominance, where each firm's activities are restricted to one industry, and where each firm is small in relation to that industry. In such a world the economist could safely ignore the co-ordination of productive activities within the firm, since the market mechanism would be overwhelmingly more important. The growing dominance of large companies, however, means that the integration of economic activity is increasingly taking place by planning within the firm rather than by means of the market mechanism. Thus the process of managerial decision making and the manner in which resources are allocated within the firm have become much more important matters for investigation. What in general terms can be said about the consequences of the dominance of large diversified companies for the process of competition and for the performance of the competitive system?

Some economists as yet see little need to feel concerned about the emergence of the large diversified company and indeed point to some actual or potential advantages. Thus, for instance, it is argued that, if the aggregate level of concentration were even higher than it is today, this would still be quite compatible with each large firm lacking significant monopoly power in any one individual market. In other words, individual market shares could be relatively low yet competition between firms in each market very intensive.

Looking at the diversified firm in a dynamic context, it can also be argued that it improves the performance of the economic system in two important related respects. First, it enhances competition by facilitating entry into industries where the barriers to entry are too high for the smaller, more specialised, firm. Second, there is some tendency for diversification to be directed towards industries characterised by above average profitability and growth rates. Given the fact that large companies finance a high proportion of their capital expenditure from retained profits, the diversified company may therefore facilitate more rapid resource reallocation and thus contribute towards a more adaptable economic system.

This advantage of flexibility in the allocation of investment funds may also be promoted by the internal organisation of the large diversified firm, and especially by the division of function between different levels of management. Here the multidivisional form of organisation may be of importance. In such an organisation the formulation of investment plans will be made by branch or divisional managers who compete for the finance available to the firm. Top management, however, is responsible for allocating funds, and the fact that it has not been deeply involved in the formulation of plans means that it is not committed to them and is therefore free to accept, reject or modify them. An internal capital market of some sophistication may thus emerge. By contrast, in more specialised firms where the division of labour in management is less and where top management is more closely involved in the formulation of plans, the degree of commitment to investment projects may be such as to lead to inflexibility.

There are, of course, arguments that put the large diversified firm in a less favourable light.

First, there is the problem of co-ordination and internal efficiency may deteriorate within large firms. Problems of communication between different levels of management become more severe as the organisation gets larger; vested interests within the firm may be powerful enough to succeed in delaying needed changes; the capacity of the top executive to co-ordinate effectively is limited, especially for firms operating in constantly changing environments. The decentralisation of management, the development of more sophisticated accounting and budgetary techniques, and the use of computers may have helped to reduce these problems, but they have not eliminated them. Clearly it is dangerous to generalise. There are examples of large diversified firms that seem to be efficiently managed, but others could hardly be put forward as models of efficiency. Even in an age when it is fashionable to speak about management as a team effort, a great deal of the efficiency or inefficiency of very large companies probably depends on the presence or absence of the organising genius of one or two people.

Second, the existence of large diversified firms opens up the possibility of a number of monopoly practices that may further impede efficient resource allocation. The first, and most familiar, is the danger of cross-subsidisation. Price cutting in one market subsidised by profits from other markets where the firm has monopoly power may be used in an attempt to eliminate rivals or to forestall the entry of new firms. There are clearly limits to the profits that can be sacrificed in this way, and whether such a strategy is worthwhile will depend on whether entry barriers can be raised sufficiently to ensure higher long-term profits. However, it must not be forgotten that the mere existence of a large diversified firm in an industry previously consisting of specialist producers only, may be enough to dampen the competitive spirits of smaller specialist firms and to deter the entry of new competitors.

Just as important is the use of excess profits in one market to engage in heavy marketing activities in another, so as to extend a firm's sphere of monopoly influence. The danger is particularly great where marketing rather than production skill is the main basis for diversification. It is in the field of marketing that large firms have perhaps the greatest advantage over smaller ones – especially where such factors as brand names, national advertising and style changes are important. In this case a small number of diversified firms may well build up a position of dominance in several industries, using their monopoly position in one industry to finance heavy sales-promotion expenditures in another.

It has to be recognised that such developments, although leading to positions of greater dominance for large firms, could still be consistent with substantial competition between large firms themselves. Thus the exploitation of a monopoly situation by one large firm carries with it the danger of attracting competition from another. It is highly unlikely, however, that large firms will develop the same pattern of diversification. Rather, it is likely that in many cases the main activity of one firm will be a secondary activity of another and that, recognising the danger of spoiling one another's markets, firms will develop 'spheres of influence'. If mutual inter-penetration of markets does occur and profits are eroded, then this may be followed either by restrictive trading agreements or by mergers, or by other (perhaps government-sponsored) schemes designed to 'rationalise production'. There is certainly a danger that an increase in aggregate concentration resulting from the diversification of large firms will subsequently result in increased market dominance in the interests of a more rational structure or of more 'orderly marketing'.

Finally, as large firms increase their dominance their interdependence as buyers and sellers also increases. There will be a tendency, therefore, for an increasing proportion of interfirm transactions to be based, not on a comparison of prices and quality from alternative sources, but on bargaining power. That is, preference in purchasing of inputs will tend to be given to firms that are good customers. Such tendencies inevitably favour large firms and increase the barriers to new entry.

6.43 *Multinational Firms*
To round off this discussion of the large firm, something needs to be said about multinational companies. Everything that has so far been said about the power of large firms applies to the multinationals with even greater force. They have all the advantages that have been noted on the marketing side, and even greater financial power than firms whose operations are restricted to the domestic market. As an example of this power, a multinational with a subsidiary in a country with a relatively high level of profits tax may be able to reduce its tax liability by the manipulation of transfer prices – that is, the prices that the subsidiary 'pays' for materials imported from other parts of the company and that it charges for exports to other subsidiaries within the organisation. Thus by overpricing imports and underpricing exports the subsidiary can gain a financial advantage over domestic competitors.

It is argued that the multinationals have had a favourable effect on efficiency, for a number of reasons.

First, the entry into a market of a subsidiary of a multinational may have a shock effect on the management of local firms and thus boost efficiency. This is likely to be particularly important if the national producers have traditionally operated within the protective cocoon of restrictive agreements. However, this sort of effect could also be achieved by other means, for instance an aggressive restrictive practices policy, and so the benefits cannot be associated uniquely with multinational operations.

Second, the multinational is less likely to build plants of sub-optimal size than national firms. This is because it has the alternative of importing supplies of a product from another country. Take, for instance, an American multinational that is considering building new plants in Belgium and Denmark. If the size of each market is too small to justify an optimal-sized unit in each, the firm may decide to build one optimal unit in, say, Belgium and use this plant to supply both markets. Subsequently, as the size of the market expands, a separate optimal-sized unit may be justified for the Danish market. In this way multinationals may be able to benefit more fully from economies of scale and thus put competitive pressure on national firms.

Third, there may be gains in allocative efficiency. The products of a multinational subsidiary may, for instance, offer the consumer a genuine widening of choice. In other words, they may differ from domestic products in a non-trivial way in terms of price, style, quality, etc. Again, multinationals are not likely to be deterred by barriers to entry, especially when existing barriers favouring domestic firms derive from the advantages of product differentiation. Finally, price warfare in any one market has less effect on the overall profitability of a multinational subsidiary than on that of national firms. Consequently, in markets where multinational subsidiaries are present collusive price behaviour may be somewhat less well entrenched. These points suggest that deviations from the optimum are likely to be smaller when multinational companies are present than when they are not. But it is not clear that these advantages would not be realised just as fully by free international trade. Free trade would also widen consumer choice, and limit the market power of domestic producers possibly on a more permanent basis. There is always a danger that multinational subsidiaries will sooner or later enter into collusive agreements with their competitors – a tendency less likely to develop between firms operating in different countries.

Fourth, direct overseas investment by multinationals speeds up the transfer of technical knowledge. The host country gains by the more rapid introduction of both process innovations and new consumption goods. Again the force of this argument depends on how effective alternative channels of communication for the transfer of technical knowledge might be in the absence of multinational subsidiaries. The strong arguments in favour of multinational operations as a mechanism for transferring technical knowledge across national boundaries rest on two conditions. The first is that alternative methods of communication – the embodiment of knowledge in freely traded goods, licensing agreements, joint ventures between multinationals and domestic firms, the state purchase of knowledge, and so on – would be substantially less rapid or more costly. The second condition is that domestic firms are more responsive to competition from goods produced on their 'own ground' than to that from goods imported from foreign competitors.

It is not entirely clear, therefore, that there is much to be gained from direct overseas investment as compared to a regime where such investment is non-existent and where there is free international trade in goods. Given the existence of tariffs and other constraints on imports, the advantages that have stemmed from the operation of multinationals are more clearly seen, but that is another matter.

If the effect of multinationals on market structure were limited and the effect on business conduct and performance enduring, there might be little to add to the foregoing account. However, there may be longer term forces at work that make the beneficial effects on performance significant only in the short term. Take, for instance, the argument that the entry of a multinational subsidiary into a market widens the choice of goods to consumers because of the different national characteristics embodied in certain products (for example, the American taste for large engines and ample luggage space in their cars). This wider choice would disappear if over time the subsidiary products adopted the characteristics of the host country or if the subsidiary drove out several competitors and came to dominate the market.

Indeed there are dynamic forces at work that tend to promote high concentration and monopolistic behaviour.

First, if one multinational subsidiary enters a particular economy, it may well be followed by the subsidiaries of other competing oligopolists from the homeland. This entry in itself may do nothing to increase concentration, and indeed may initially reduce it if entry is secured by building new plant rather than acquiring an existing firm.

Second, however, competition between the multinational subsidiaries and large domestic firms may drive smaller firms from the market. This is particularly likely where strong product differentiation exists and where advertising and other sales promotion activities are the main form of competition. Multinationals are indeed most highly represented in industries characterised by strong product differentiation. We have noted earlier the advantages that large firms have in advertising and how this is likely to lead to increased concentration. By increasing the resources devoted to non-price competition, and by increasing, through increased monopoly power, the level of prices above what it would otherwise be, the operation of multinational subsidiaries may result in a social loss.

Third, the tendencies towards the emergence of more highly concentrated markets will be strongly reinforced if the entry of multinationals sparks off a wave of defensive mergers by domestic firms, as they attempt to hang on to their share of the market. Domestic firms are liable to regard mergers as necessary because, in part, they see the threat of the multinational as due to the latter's sheer size. Mergers also reduce the number of competing units and serve to offset the increased competition brought about by the multinational subsidiary.

Fourth, the setting up of overseas subsidiaries is not a one-way process. The large firms of one country whose domestic markets have been raided by subsidiaries from another will tend in turn to reciprocate and establish their own overseas subsidiaries. In this way an oligopoly situation may develop at a transnational level, with the main actors competing in several national markets. Competition is likely to be intense in the early stages of this development, but there is clearly a danger that, recognising their transnational inter-dependence, the firms will attempt to restrict competition by various forms of collusion.

6.5 BIG BUSINESS, COMPETITION AND THE STATE

We turn now to a brief consideration of the policy issues raised by the above analysis. Our starting point is the view that wherever possible it is desirable to maintain and strengthen effective competition.

Over the last twenty years economies in the Western world have in general experienced a substantial increase in the level of industrial concentration. At the same time, however, there has been a large increase in competition at the international level, with the market shares of domestic firms threatened by imports and multi-national subsidiaries. These developments have not been independent of one another. For instance, part of the increase in concentration within national markets has been a consequence of increased international competition. On balance, and for a large number of firms, there can be little doubt that the net outcome of the increase in national concentration and in international competition has been an intensification of competitive pressure. This, however, is not to say that nothing needs to be done. In part the increase in concentration has been the inevitable outcome of the competitive process, but part has also been due to institutional factors that may need modification or radical change. There is also the major problem of distinguishing between the process of change and the end result of that change. The process of change may bring advantages in terms of increased competition which disappear when market structure has stabilised.

What then can be done to counteract the strong trend towards size and increasing market power? Essentially there are two alternative approaches open to us. The first may be called the structural approach, the second the cost–benefit approach. The former would identify non-competitive situations purely on the basis of the structural characteristics of different industries – concentration levels, the extent of barriers to entry, etc. It would seek to reintroduce and confirm competitive forces by instituting changes in the structure of the industries selected for attention. The cost–benefit approach would seek to sort out non-competitive industries by an analysis of the conduct and performance of the firms involved, taking account of such factors as profit levels, costing and pricing behaviour, and collusive practices. It would seek to check monopolistic tendencies by constraining or modifying the conduct of these firms where necessary.

Given the fact that monopolistic situations may well generate significant benefits for consumers via economies of scale, research and innovation etc., a rigorous cost–benefit approach may well appear to be the first-best solution. However, the arguments in favour of the structural approach deserve careful attention. First, it is argued that the cost–benefit approach is expensive to operate. Second, that it cannot possibly handle the number of examples of non-competitive behaviour necessary to significantly affect the course of the economy. Too many instances will go by unchallenged. Third, conceptual problems surrounding the measurement of economies of scale, normal profits, X-inefficiency, and research and development effects, will make the process of assessing monopoly situations tortuous, possibly inconsistent and too often inconclusive. Fourth, the means for constraining firms' conduct are limited. As long as the industry's structure is conducive to non-competitive behaviour, firms are likely to find ways round the directives and constraints placed upon them. It will thus be impossible to establish competition where it has virtually disappeared, as opposed to simply preventing further erosion elsewhere. Fifth, though the structural approach is at first sight arbitrary and drastic, it may well be necessary and indeed the only effective policy left to us, given the extent to which monopoly trends have already progressed. Finally, those favouring the structural approach cite the evidence from past cost–benefit-type approaches to monopoly. The number of instances where, after extensive and costly study, important economies of scale and other benefits have been found is very small. Many of the claimed benefits have been limited and of questionable long-term significance as far as society as a whole is concerned. Against this the benefits of competition, which are so hard to regain once lost, seem very considerable.

Whatever the broad approach adopted, a long list of potential policy instruments exists for individual situations. What follows draws attention to six possibilities.

First, monopoly policy could be used to curb the power of established monopolies. Where the competitive forces facing the monopolist are too weak to act as an effective control mechanism the intervention could take the form of an efficiency audit, with a body such as a monopolies commission or prices commission empowered to investigate the firm's prices and profit. Such direct measures would also have to apply in controlling some of the activities of multinational companies. A more radical approach would be to break up large companies into a number of smaller units. This would obviously be most easily accomplished where the firm owned several plants that could be operated independently without loss of efficiency.

Second, a strong merger policy could do much to prevent the emergence of more market power. Merger activity, as will be shown in Chapter 7, has contributed substantially to the growth of leading firms and to the emergence of monopoly situations. Policy might be directed at allowing mergers only when there were strong reasons, in terms of the achievement of scale economies, for doing so. The onus here should be on the firm involved to substantiate the existence of the claimed benefits, and not upon the government's agency to prove that the merger would be detrimental to the public interest.

Third, policies aimed against restrictive trade practices might succeed in enforcing competition. Such policies have indeed been introduced, albeit with unequal firmness, in most Western economies. A major problem with this type of policy is its uneven impact. It succeeds in eliminating the more overt practices, but nothing like so well in ferreting out and eliminating many kinds of tacit collusion that are common in well-established oligopoly situations. In addition, a tough restrictive practices policy may itself generate forces leading to higher industrial concentration.

Fourth, a policy aimed at reducing heavy advertising expenditure in certain industries would seem to be amply justified. As we have seen, the marketing power of large firms gives them a considerable advantage over smaller competitors and also makes it difficult for new firms to enter the market. A curb on advertising could be effected by imposing direct controls upon those industries where advertising is most intense, or by introducing a progressive tax on advertising expenditure above a certain minimum level.

Fifth, competition from imports will often serve to constrain the market power of domestic producers who control a large proportion of national output. It is worth making the point that, on balance, we see competition from imports as preferable to competition from the subsidiaries of multinationals as a means of controlling the market power of domestic producers. Competition from imports is probably more effective in widening consumer choice, and also in constraining the monopoly tendencies of domestic producers. Indeed, as multinational subsidiaries get established they may develop their own monopoly power, which has to be controlled. Any edge that multinational enterprises may have in the more rapid transmission of technical knowledge has to be set against the problems that they raise for government policy, stemming in particular from their financial strength and ability to switch funds within the organisation.

Finally, there is a strong argument in favour of establishing special financial institutions whose job it would be to make finance more readily available to efficient small firms and also to assist in the formation of new firms. This would help to remove one of the main disadvantages of small firms and thus provide larger competitors with more effective competition. The state could also involve itself more directly in confronting large firms with more competition where necessary, either by starting and operating new ventures or by participating in joint ventures with small- and medium-sized firms in the private sector.

Chapter 7

Problems of Adjustment

7.1 INTRODUCTION

We turn now to a different set of problems – those associated with the process of market adjustment. In Chapter 2 it was shown that in a highly competitive system where there were no impediments to the free play of market forces there would be a tendency for resources to be allocated so as to exhaust all opportunities for making further profit. Consequently, in the long-run equilibrium position and for a given distribution of income, resource allocation would be optimal. However, in the course of our analysis of the competitive process a number of difficulties were glossed over, particularly those relating to the model's dynamic properties. For instance, just how efficient is a competitive system in adjusting supply to changes in demand in the short term and in adjusting capacity to changes in demand in the long term? Is the competitive system superior to all others with regard to the process of invention and innovation? Does a highly competitive system have a built-in mechanism to maintain competitive balance within industries, between regions and between countries, or does the competitive process itself contain forces leading to severe imbalances that only government intervention can check? It is to these questions that we now turn.

7.2 SHORT RUN ADJUSTMENT OF SUPPLY TO CHANGES IN DEMAND

According to the theory of perfect competition, the profit-maximising firm will produce the output where price equals short-run marginal cost and where the marginal cost curve is positively sloped. In Figure 7.1 the market demand curve is D. We assume that each firm in the industry has the same short-run marginal-cost curve, shown as SMC. This is also the firm's supply curve. The industry supply curve, SS', is the sum of the marginal cost curves over the various firms involved in the industry. In the short run no entry or exit takes place. If full equilibrium exists initially, this means that each firm produces OM units of output at price P. If market demand then falls to D_1, price will fall to P_1. The firm's demand curve therefore falls, and each firm reduces its output. A new short-run equilibrium is established when firm output is ON, selling at price P_1. If market demand increases to D_2, each firm will expand its output to OL, selling at price P_2, and so on. Price, therefore, is perfectly responsive to short run fluctuations in demand, and profits will vary accordingly. For the firm depicted in Figure 7.1 the price of the product can fall as low as P_0 before it stops production. At that point revenue is just sufficient to cover the firm's prime or variable costs.

Figure 7.1

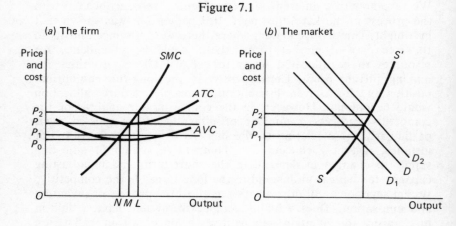

(a) The firm   (b) The market

It appears, therefore, that perfect competition has certain highly desirable dynamic-adjustment properties. Unfortunately, in practice, there will be considerable difficulties associated with market behaviour of the kind described above, especially when it comes to planning future production.

First, frequent price changes impose costs upon the firm and are a nuisance to customers. The theory of perfect competition gets around the problem by assuming a perfect knowledge of price offers. In fact, of course, customers have to be kept informed of all price changes. Manufacturers would therefore often have to issue new price lists to retailers. Customers for their part would have to engage in frequent search activity. Changing price lists and search activities are costly, a factor that must inevitably act as a constraint on the desirability of frequent short-term price changes.

Second, the problems of short-run price competition are particularly acute when fixed costs form a large proportion of total costs. In this case competition can drive price well below the level that is required to cover the total costs of production. This situation is depicted in Figure 7.2, where the lower limit to price, P_0, is considerably less than P, which is the price required for receipts to cover the total costs of production. In such circumstances firms will be particularly anxious to avoid price warfare, especially since there is no guarantee that they will even survive the competition,

Figure 7.2

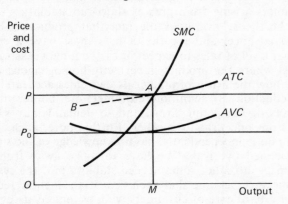

let alone earn compensating surpluses during the next upswing in demand. This point was fully recognised by Alfred Marshall:

'In a trade which uses very expensive plant, the prime cost of goods is but a small part of their total cost; and an order at much less than their normal price may leave a large surplus above their prime cost. But if producers accept such orders in their anxiety to prevent their plant being idle, they glut the market and tend to prevent prices from reviving. In fact, however, they seldom pursue this policy constantly and without moderation. If they did, they might ruin many of those in the trade, themselves perhaps among the number; and in that case a revival of demand would find little response in supply, and would raise violently the prices of the goods produced by the trade. Extreme variations of this kind are in the long-run beneficial neither to producers nor to consumers, and general opinion is not altogether hostile to that code of trade morality which condemns the action of anyone who 'spoils the market' by being too ready to accept a price that does little more than cover the prime cost of his goods, and allows but little on account of his general expenses.'

It follows that, if competition is threatening to push prices below P, firms are more likely to move along a path such as AB rather than along the short-run marginal-cost curve SMC. They thereby maintain prices near to the normal level. This means, of course, that prices will diverge from marginal costs, in this case being higher, and, therefore, that output will be below the optimum level. Thus there will be a misallocation of resources in the static sense. The extent to which output falls short of the ideal will be small, however, if the demand for the product is inelastic, which may well be so in the short run. Furthermore, against any resulting welfare loss must be set the very real long-term welfare gains to both producers and consumers arising from greater short-run stability.

Third, the theory overlooks the fact that production has to be planned in advance, and for this a firm must have a reasonable idea of what level of sales to expect in the coming weeks or months. In a model where the product is perfectly homogeneous it is difficult to see how the firm can predict its own sales accurately enough to plan production. By definition, customers are indifferent between the products of competing firms, and so demand may swing substantially from one firm to another. Furthermore, each individual firm, acting quite independently, has no knowledge of the supply that is being planned by rivals. We have to move away from perfect competition to introduce some needed stability into the system. We may, for instance, assume that each firm has somehow secured the goodwill of a hard core of customers who, as long as its price is not significantly higher than those elsewhere, will continue to buy its product. Apart from any natural imperfections of this kind, firms will usually endeavour to introduce greater stability into the short run situation by attempting to reduce the incidence and extent of price competition. They may do this by means of express or tacit price agreements. In oligopolistic markets where interdependence is recognised, price stability may be achieved simply through each firm acknowledging the possible damaging consequences of short-run price competition. Any one firm will expect a price cut to be matched by rivals, so that it can expect to gain little in terms of increased market share. Indeed if short run demand for the product is inelastic, all firms may lose revenue, the extra sales induced by the price cuts being insufficient to offset the lower margin on each unit sold.

We can, therefore, expect greater price rigidity in oligopolistic markets than in atomistic ones. Firms recognise that the actions of any one of them will affect others, and in consequence a measure of industry discipline is established. Prices will not respond as fully to short run changes in demand as would be the case under perfect competition. If prices were to increase so as to eliminate excess demand following an increase in demand, the high profits would tend to attract new entrants, which would endanger collusive behaviour, undermine industry discipline, and perhaps leave firms in a worse long-run situation than if they maintained stable prices.

If oligopoly prices do not adjust to clear markets in the short run, then there must be some other adjustment mechanism. This is found in changes in stocks and/or the length of order books. When demand increases, stocks will be reduced and order books lengthened, and conversely when demand falls. There are clearly limits to the extent to which these quantity adjustments alone can be sustained. As demand increases, stocks cannot be run down indefinitely, nor order books lengthened continuously, without loss of consumer goodwill. The latter may be of less consequence to any one individual firm if all producers of the product are finding it equally difficult to meet demand. But then there may be a danger of losing demand to substitute products and also to overseas suppliers. Similarly, with declining demand, stocks will not be allowed to increase beyond a certain point because of the costs involved, and prompt delivery of goods to customers will only offer a safety valve for a slump of limited duration. Nevertheless, subject to these qualifications, we should expect to find that, in general, oligopolistic prices will be less responsive to short run changes in demand than competitive ones.

The above arguments suggest that continuous rapid adjustments to short-run demand changes are not always desirable. Less competitive market structures may well bring a certain amount of necessary stability and thus, overall, represent more efficient means through which to allocate resources than highly competitive markets.

7.3 LONG RUN ADJUSTMENT OF CAPACITY TO DEMAND

In the case of short run adjustments we have seen that, although it is perfectly feasible for firms to adjust prices in response to changes in demand, it will often not pay them to do so, nor be consistent with dynamic efficiency. The case of long run adjustments involving capacity changes is rather different. Here the problem is basically one of insufficient information. Under highly competitive conditions each firm must obtain the market data necessary to guarantee that investment decisions lead, overall, to an equality of supply and demand at the equilibrium price level. To illustrate the problems involved in this, consider a simple perfectly competitive situation operating under the conditions described in Figure 7.3.

The initial equilibrium situation is given by the point of intersection of the demand curve D_1 and the long-run supply curve SS'. Price is equal to P_1, and output is OM. Assume that demand increases, due say to a change in tastes, so that the new demand curve is D_2. Using a comparative static approach we conclude that, in the new equilibrium situation, price will be P_2 and output ON. But what is the process by which this equilibrium position is attained? Is the adjustment process likely to function more efficiently under perfect competition than under alternative market structures?

Figure 7.3

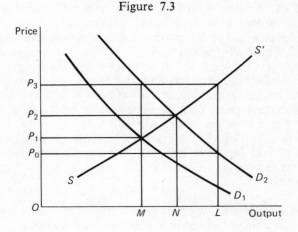

For an efficient overall adjustment to take place each individual firm must correctly foresee that the new equilibrium price will in fact be P_2. In other words, firms must base their investment plans on the product price that will prevail when their output comes to be sold. Similarly, to maximise profits their plans for purchasing factors of production must be based on factor prices when they are bought. Because the construction and implementation of investment plans takes time, most firms are forced to estimate prices a long time in advance of any buying and selling. Even the best guess about the future is therefore unlikely, except by chance, to be completely accurate. Having insufficient information is a problem that of course besets all firms, whatever market structure they happen to operate in, but the problem is likely to be particularly acute under perfect competition. This is because each firm acts independently, taking no account of the effects that its own plans will have on future prices, and basing its plans on the assumption that existing market prices will continue to prevail.

In the short run, before capacity can be extended to produce more output, and assuming for simplicity a perfectly inelastic short-run supply curve, the perfectly competitive response to the increase in demand will be an increase in price to P_3. It is this price that, together with prevailing factor prices, will influence the investment plans of each firm, including new entrants. If all firms respond at much the same time, output will be expanded to *OL*, too much capacity will be installed and price will fall. The assumption of unchanged product prices on which individual investment plans are based is bound to be falsified by events, for what is true for any individual firm is not true for all of them taken together. The same applies on the factor side. The technology used by firms in the industry may require a special type of labour that is in short supply, and any significant expansion of the industry will require an extensive training programme to increase the supply of the particular labour skill in question. While the expansion of any one firm will not have a significant effect on the wage and availability of the labour concerned, the expansion of the industry will cause wages to increase and produce a shortage of labour. However, if all firms are pushing ahead independently with their expansion plans, they will fail to anticipate these labour market changes, and the whole industry may be unable to find sufficient labour to operate the newly constructed plant.

The simple market situation that has been described so far is unlikely to persist indefinitely. Producers will no doubt learn from experience, and some at least will become more cautious when it comes to expanding capacity during the next upswing in demand. We have assumed that all firms are able to respond immediately to profitable opportunities for expansion, but this is unlikely to be the case. Existing firms are likely to have an advantage over outsiders. Among existing firms, differences in the quality and energy of management will mean that some firms will recognise the opportunities for profitable expansion sooner than others. Differences in the extent to which firms have access to finance will mean that some firms will be better placed than others to proceed with their investment plans. As a result of such differences, some firms will be quicker off the mark than others, so that the implementation of industry expansion plans will be staggered. The stability of the adjustment process will then depend on the length of time over which producers' expansion plans are spread and the gestation period of investment – that is, on the time it takes for the first batch of expansion plans to result in increased output. If output from the extra capacity of some firms comes on to the market before others have put their expansion plans into effect, then the laggards are likely to modify their plans in the light of price movements. This will increase the chances of a smooth movement to a new equilibrium. If, however, expansion plans are closely bunched and every firm has embarked on new investment on the basis of current levels of prices and output, then overexpansion is the likely outcome.

Subject to these qualifications, our analysis suggests that market structures characterised by large numbers of firms acting independently will have a certain tendency towards instability in the process whereby capacity is adjusted to demand. Industries that come nearest to this description, such as agriculture and construction, do indeed suffer from such instability. Market structure is not the whole explanation, of course, but it is undoubtedly an important contributory factor.

What, therefore, are the reasons for supposing that long run adjustments will be more efficiently carried out in oligopolistic industries? First, to the extent that prices, as argued earlier, are rigid under oligopoly, firms are less likely to mistake short term fluctuations in demand for permanent demand shifts. There should also be less of a tendency for capacity to be overextended as a result of high short-run profits. Second, each oligopolistic firm is aware that its own investment will have a considerable effect upon its competitors. Third, given the small number of firms involved, each one will have a greater awareness of the intentions of its competitors than is the case under atomistic competition.

However, the waters are considerably muddied when account is taken of non-price competition. It is possible that non-price competition, particularly the importance attached by firms to their ability to meet orders promptly as a means of maintaining consumer goodwill, may be a source of instability. There are two aspects to this thesis, both of which apply to conditions of increasing demand. First, when demand is increasing there is always a danger that new competitors will enter the market. If existing producers can keep capacity ahead of demand, this may clearly act as an important deterrent to new entry. On the other hand, the attempt to keep capacity somewhat ahead of demand during the upswing may lead to existing producers having more spare capacity than they have bargained for. This possibility is increased by the second point which is that each existing producer will be concerned that through lack of capacity it will be unable to meet orders from its customers and will, as a result, permanently lose their goodwill to rival producers. Competition in the creation of capacity may then develop, facilitated by the large cash flow of big firms and their easy access to outside finance. Competition between oligopolists may therefore result in capacity being pushed too far, and when it becomes clear to firms that capacity has outstripped demand a sharp cut-back in investment is inevitable.

Thus for different reasons both atomistic and oligopolistic markets may be inefficient in adjusting capacity to changes in demand. *A priori* it is not possible to say anything much, on the basis of a broad distinction between atomistic and oligopolistic markets, about the relative strength of the forces at work.

Whatever the market structure, however, persistent excess capacity is likely to provoke firms into seeking some sort of remedy. If the protection afforded to firms by market imperfections, such as product differentiation, is not sufficient, they may well resort to artificial imperfections, such as price agreements and market sharing. If these also prove ineffective, either because of the problem of maintaining discipline among a large number of firms or because they are declared illegal by government competition policy, an alternative remedy may be sought involving a reduction in the number of firms by means of merger and acquisition. This of course poses a real dilemma for the analyst. The attempts made by firms to increase the information that they have on market conditions will increase dynamic efficiency, but they will also strengthen their power to behave in a monopolistic manner. The number of firms is reduced, possibly even to the extent of creating a single dominant firm. Restrictive agreements can have the same effect less directly. Capacity may then be restricted well below the optimum level.

Another possible way in which firms may overcome the excess capacity problem is for them to exchange views on future demand conditions and their investment intentions. Thus without entering into any restrictive agreements they would each be able to form a better assessment of future market prospects, which would make adjustment a more efficient process. Although the exchange of information might improve matters there is no guarantee, of course, that it would do so. For instance, if a firm learns that its closest competitors are planning an extension of capacity, this may induce it to speed up its own investment. It is also difficult to see how the benefits of increased information can be achieved without some form of market-sharing agreement. Imagine, for instance, that firms in an industry have embarked upon some joint-planning process. After an exchange of views they agree on the most likely rate of expansion of demand, including exports, over the next five years. Allowing for the market share likely to be taken by imports, this will then enable them to see what new investment will be needed in total. To ensure that this total will be forthcoming, however, they will also have to reach agreement on how much is to be contributed by each firm. Furthermore, they will be particularly anxious to establish some form of market-sharing agreement if economies of scale are so important that investment must take place in large chunks. The problem then is to balance the advantages of competition as a way of controlling monopoly behaviour, against the advantages of restricting competition as a means of ensuring that each firm has sufficient information for dynamic efficiency to be achieved. In some markets natural imperfections may be sufficient to produce an acceptable performance in terms of dynamic efficiency; in others, further restraint on competition may be required, in the form of restrictive agreements, planning agreements or a reduction in the number of competitors. In the latter case, however, there is no guarantee that these restraints will be kept to the minimum necessary for efficient dynamic adjustment.

It is worth noting just one instance where, on balance, a joint-planning exercise by firms would probably be desirable. This is where technical economies of scale are important and where new plant of optimal size is large in relation to the annual increase in demand. In this case there is the danger not only that investment in total will exhibit an unstable pattern, but also that competitive investment plans would lead to suboptimal capacity increments. To build an optimal-sized plant under competitive conditions a firm would have to be prepared to wage all-out price warfare on its rivals in order to gain the larger market share necessary to achieve the full utilisation of the new plant. Since firms are usually reluctant to pursue such a policy, particularly where fixed costs are important, and since collusion is unlikely to operate successfully over non-price competition and capacity extensions, each firm might well expand by building plants of suboptimal size. To avoid a serious loss of efficiency, two alternative solutions are possible: first, mergers to reduce the number of competitors, and second, agreement between existing firms, for instance, to build optimal-sized plants as joint ventures.

Similar problems to the above arise when the government resorts to some form of national indicative planning. This is potentially an important vehicle for providing firms with the information necessary for investment planning. Introduced into a situation that is basically competitive, indicative planning theoretically offers genuine opportunities for improving dynamic efficiency. A dual policy of stimulating competition and formulating an indicative plan seems the optimum strategy. There are, however, many practical problems associated with the application of these ideas to the real world, of which possibly the most vital for the present analysis is whether indicative planning itself actually encourages non-competitive behaviour.

Consider an industry containing a number of competing oligopolists. The planning organisation cannot, as under perfect competition, simply aim at identifying a set of prices that will equate future demand and supply by means of some iterative process. The problem is made much more complicated by the various dimensions of non-price competition that have to be taken into account and also by the interdependence of company plans. Each firm's plans for the future will be based on some set of assumptions relating to the behaviour of its competitors. In answering questions about investment plans each firm is liable to say: 'On the basis of the information that we have about competitors, suppliers and customers, our plans are as follows . . .'. Even if the information supplied to the planning body is not deliberately misleading, the complicated set of interdependencies that exist between firms will make a consistent overall plan extremely difficult to achieve.

Assuming that the planning body does succeed in arriving at an internally consistent overall plan, information will then be given to firms, setting out their production targets over, say, a five-year period. However, another problem will now arise, for even if each firm has agreed to behave in a way that is consistent with the fulfilment of the plan if others do so, there is no reason why any one firm should believe that the others will keep their part of the bargain. For instance, firm X may be dependent on a 50 per cent expansion in the capacity of firm Y over the five-year period in order to ensure adequate supplies of a particular input. X may have cause to doubt the willingness or ability of Y to undertake such an expansion, and may decide to invest in its own capacity for the production of at least part of its requirements of this input. If such doubts are general, no firm will take much notice of the plan. The obvious way to avoid this is to bring the firms together in an attempt to convince each of them that the intentions of the others, as revealed in the plan, are genuine. But this is where problems would arise. Even if firms are entirely honest in their replies to the planning agency, we can hardly expect them to give accurate information when they know that it will be fed directly to their rivals. Indeed their strategy may be deliberately to mislead. Furthermore, in bringing firms together the government may well play host to collusive agreements, and may indeed actually encourage this in order to make the planning process easier to handle. In addition, the government will in practice only be able to negotiate with large firms, and by cutting out the smaller elements in any market it will encourage stable market-sharing agreements, which hitherto the firms may have found difficult to establish. To the extent that, in reality, all markets are to some degree oligopolistic, indicative planning will always, on the above arguments, tend to weaken competitive forces.

The problem of dynamic efficiency does not, it seems, lead to any clear-cut conclusions or any firm guidelines for policy makers. No specific type of market structure can be identified as being clearly superior to all others. This is not to say that because all markets are likely to be dynamically inefficient, to a greater or lesser extent, some form of central-government interventionist planning is superior. There is no escaping the fact, however, that the more it is found necessary to reduce competition in order to improve dynamic efficiency, the more will it be necessary to find some other control mechanism, and this will itself involve more government intervention – direct or indirect – in industry.

7.4   INVENTION AND INNOVATION

Another aspect of dynamic adjustment that needs to be considered is the allocation of resources to invention and innovation. It has long been argued that, whatever the merits of a highly competitive market structure in allocating a given collection of goods and services, it can hardly be presented as an efficient mechanism for creating and developing new knowledge, whether in the form of new processes of production or as new products. For this activity to be pursued on any significant scale, both large firms and monopoly power are required. Furthermore, so the argument goes on, the benefits to be gained from a highly advanced invention and innovation effort far exceed the benefits to be gained from static allocative efficiency.

The argument in favour of large firms has three strands. First, invention and innovation are very costly activities, requiring the commitment of resources on a scale that is only available to large firms. In fact, the research and development process consists of several stages that vary a great deal in costliness. The most expensive stages are the later ones, involving the development of the project to the point of commercial application and the commercial application itself. It is here that large firms have their major advantage. How large they have to be in order to command the resources necessary will vary considerably from one industry to another, but there seems little doubt that, as we have seen in Chapter 6, large firms do have an advantage over small ones.

Second, invention and innovation involve considerable risk, a factor that again favours the large firm. Small firms are vulnerable because they must concentrate their resources on a relatively small number of projects, which clearly poses a considerable risk to the commercial viability of the firm. Large firms, on the other hand, can afford to support several projects, the cost of each one being small in relation to total profit. The risks of research and development are thus spread, the failure of some projects being set against the success of others.

Third, there are economies of scale in the invention and innovation process itself, which give a further advantage to the large firm. There may, for example, be economies of scale associated with the scientific and technical part of research and development, especially in the employment of specialised equipment and specialist research workers. More important perhaps is the advantage that the large firm often has on the marketing side. To a very significant extent, the profitability of investing in the development of a new product depends upon the speed with which the newly developed product penetrates the market. With its superior marketing skills and considerable sales activities the large firm will achieve faster market penetration. Furthermore, the large firm has an obvious advantage in input and process innovation. Having a greater output it can spread the costs and reap the benefits of the new development over a wider area.

Where the size necessary to achieve the benefits of scale is large in relation to the size of the market, these arguments also represent a case in favour of firms with some degree of market power. Such firms have the *ability* to undertake research and development, because they have access to accumulated supernormal profits. They will not be preoccupied with continual short-run price competition, and the market discipline that exists among oligopolistic competitors with regard to this aspect of competition offers an important element of safety to each firm. However, for there to be an adequate *incentive* to undertake research and development work the firm must also be able to look forward to monopoly gains stemming from its successful innovations. Invention and innovation require a considerable investment commitment, and there must be some financial incentive to ensure that the investment takes place. Only with market power will the firm be able to secure a high enough proportion of the total benefits from an innovation to make the investment in research and development worthwhile. In the absence of any monopoly advantage it would normally be virtually impossible for the owner of a new product or new process to obtain an adequate return on his investment, because as soon as his innovation became known it could be copied by rivals. Firms in competitive, atomistically structured, markets therefore have neither the depth of resources nor sufficient financial incentive to be prominent in research and development work.

Competitive pressures do, however, play an important role in speeding up the introduction of new knowledge. The danger that competitors, old or new, will get in first with a new product or process acts as a spur to the firm's efforts. Remove competition altogether, and the incentive to produce results sooner rather than later is eliminated. Thus in industries where there is one dominant firm and a number of small rivals, the former has little inducement to show urgency in introducing new products. In terms of market share there is simply not much that the large firm can gain at the expense of its small rivals, and if any of the latter produce an important innovation the large firm always has the resources to react quickly to the threat.

The best balance between safety and competition is likely to be found in an intermediate situation, where there is effective competition among relatively few, evenly matched, sellers and where the recognition of interdependence imparts some discipline to price competition. Even then rapid imitation remains a threat to the innovating firm. The existence of certain market imperfections gives some protection without detracting from the effectiveness of the competitive threat in the long run. Thus, for instance, there are time lags involved in imitation, the length of the lag depending on such factors as the expected profitability of the innovation, the magnitude of the investment required and the complexity of the new technology. The greater the profitability the faster will imitation tend to occur, other things being equal. The larger the investment required and the more complex the technology, the slower the response of existing and potential competitors. The firm may also find sufficient protection from competition in the form of product differentiation advantages and other barriers to competition.

In free enterprise economies, however, these market imperfections have rarely been relied upon to ensure the existence of an adequate incentive to the innovator. Additional protection has been given by patent laws that give the owner of an invention a temporary monopoly in its use. Here, however, there is a fundamental dilemma. For the production of new knowledge, some monopoly power, based either on 'natural' market imperfections or patent legislation, is required to give an adequate inducement in the form of a financial reward. But once the knowledge has been created it would clearly. be most beneficial, from society's point of view, if it were freely available to all who wanted to use it. Knowledge, once created, has all the properties of a public good, in the sense that the use of the knowledge by one firm does not preclude its use by another. For the maximisation of welfare, therefore, it should be available to all users free of charge. Figure 7.4 gives a simple illustration of the problem. The demand curve for a new commodity is DD' and the cost of production SS'. The social optimum requires a production of ON at a price OS equal to the costs of production. Consumers' surplus will then be equal to area DSP. A monopolist, however, will produce output OM at price OP_m. The sum of consumers' and producers' surplus is area $DQRS$, which is area QRP less than the social gain when output is extended to the optimum position. The monopolistic exploitation of new knowledge will therefore result in its use being restricted below the optimum level. But it is at the heart of the public good's analysis that without such restrictions no single firm would have the incentive to innovate. Everyone would always want someone else to go first.

When it comes to assessing alternative market structures, perfectly competitive conditions would ensure the rapid diffusion of new knowledge, but there would then be little incentive to innovate. The incentive and the ability to innovate exist when firms have some degree of market power, but this power shields the firm from market pressures and thereby retards the diffusion of new knowledge, and if it is too great it may also weaken the incentive to innovate. Furthermore, in the conduct of research, and particularly in basic research, it seems important to have a number of competing centres of initiative. This may mean that some duplication

Figure 7.4

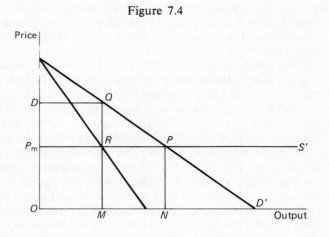

in research will occur, but such an apparent 'waste' of resources will be justified if it speeds up the process of research and prevents a much more serious misallocation of resources arising from a premature commitment to one set of ideas. At the same time, when major discoveries are made it is important that the new knowledge should be rapidly disseminated, so that resources are not wasted either by attempts to replicate the success or in research work that the new knowledge has shown to be fruitless. Such a free flow of information between research centres, however, is alien to the whole nature of the free enterprise system based on independent business units and the private profit motive.

Neither atomistic competition nor monopoly can therefore be expected to perform ideally in the field of research and development. Nor is it possible within any one market structure to achieve the best of both worlds – the optimum rate of production of new knowledge, and the immediate and free disposal of that knowledge to all who want to use it. However, a more relevant issue is not what could be achieved in an ideal world but whether anything can be done to improve matters as they stand. On the basis of the analysis above, it appears that there are at least two government measures that may be justified.

First, there is a very strong case for government-financed research institutions, particularly in the area of basic research, where the free enterprise system is most likely to result in an incorrect allocation of resources. Both the risks involved in basic research and the problems of appropriating the results of new discoveries tend to be greater than for other forms of research, and this will tend to result in an underallocation of resources. In basic research it is also particularly important, because of the risk and costs involved, to have a free flow of information between research centres – an arrangement that, as we have noted, does not fit comfortably into a free enterprise system.

Second, there is a strong case for specific government measures to assist smaller firms. As we have seen, the large firm has several advantages in the conduct of research and development, but there are also weaknesses associated with size that have not yet been noted. It has been argued that research in large firms may suffer from being overorganised, with insufficient freedom being given to the individual to pursue what may be regarded as unorthodox ideas. There may also be a tendency in management-controlled firms for the really revolutionary and high risk projects to be neglected in favour of more trivial and safer developments. On the other hand, it is in invention and the early stages of development, where ideas and a flexible approach are most important and where financial requirements are frequently modest, that the small firm has an important role to play. However, the overwhelming advantages that large firms have in finance and marketing ensure that at the stage of commercial application the small firm is a much smaller competitive threat. There is a good case, therefore, for government financial assistance to small firms, which would strengthen their position at the more expensive later stages of development and at the point of commercial application. The importance of measures designed to assist small firms will become even more apparent in the light of the analysis of the next section.

7.5   STRUCTURAL CHANGE WITHIN INDUSTRIES

One final problem that we must look at in relation to the process of adjustment is that of structural change. This is another large subject that we cannot hope to deal with at all fully, but failure to include anything on the subject would be a serious omission. This section will look at structural change within industries and at the question of whether competitive market structures are sustainable. The next section will examine the problems of adjustment to structural change within regions and countries.

7.51 *The Transfer and Innovation Mechanisms*

The specific question we are concerned with here is whether competitive market structures tend to sustain themselves over long periods of time or whether the competitive process is such as to lead inevitably to the emergence of highly concentrated industries. In a static context this question is generally looked at by examining the importance of economies of scale in relation to the size of the market. However, it is also instructive to look at the problem within a dynamic framework. Firms do not accept the pattern of demand and techniques of production as given. Indeed they often attempt to change them to their own advantage. The incentive and the ability to do so are related to the firm's short-run circumstances in terms of both efficiency and profitability.

A convenient starting point is the analysis of the competitive process developed by Downie. His theorising is constructed around two fundamental competitive mechanisms: the transfer mechanism and the innovation mechanism. The former is the process whereby efficient firms gain market share at the expense of the inefficient, and the latter summarises the forces that bear upon the incentive to innovate.

At any moment in time an industry will be composed of firms of varying degrees of efficiency. This follows because innovations come about as a result of the efforts of individual firms and because any new knowledge embodied in these innovations is diffused only slowly. Thus, currently, the most efficient firms are the ones that have been the most successful innovators in preceding periods. The inefficient firms are the ones that have consistently failed to undertake research or to seek access to improved technology. Given the pattern of relative efficiencies, the more efficient firms will steadily expand at the expense of the less efficient, so that output becomes concentrated in fewer hands. The transfer mechanism will be particularly powerful where there are many firms and where differences in efficiency are initially very large. As the most inefficient firms are successively eliminated from the market, however, efficiency differences will diminish, so that the transfer mechanism is weakened. This weakening will be reinforced if the move towards more concentrated oligopolistic structures accompanied by more entrenched collusive behaviour.

The transfer mechanism, it seems, will push an industry, at first quickly and then more slowly, towards higher levels of concentration. However, the very threat to the existence of the inefficient firm embodied in this mechanism is the stimulant to the innovation mechanism. The incentive to innovate is strongly related to external trading conditions, so the greater the competitive pressure upon firms the more they are forced to look to a technological breakthrough for economic salvation. At the same time the most efficient firms, whose current market leadership is based upon their past technological superiority, will feel little pressure to continue their search for new advances. If the innovation mechanism is governed mainly by these forces acting upon the incentive to innovate, it will tend to undo the work of the transfer mechanism and arrest the move towards higher concentration. Leadership in innovation will change hands, and this will mean continual changes in the efficiency ranking of firms.

However, the conditions necessary for the innovation mechanism to be powerful enough to offset the transfer mechanism are clearly very stringent indeed and are unlikely to be fully satisfied in practice. For instance, even if there is a strong tendency for innovative leadership to change hands, there is the question of the time lags involved, which may be very long given the intervals between innovations. If the time interval is a long one, the transfer mechanism may well result in the emergence of a small group of large firms with market power, which a much smaller innovative firm would find difficulty in dislodging. Furthermore, large firms may well adopt the strategy of acquiring any small competitor likely to pose a threat because of its technological expertise. Failing ·this, they may adopt predatory tactics to drive such firms into bankruptcy. Again, for the innovative mechanism to operate effectively it has to be responsive to competitive pressures and highly unresponsive to such factors as luck and the availability of finance.

Another important element in Downie's analysis is the role of new entry, which is seen to be dominated by the diversifying activities of large firms moving in the main from high concentration to low concentration industries. In highly concentrated industries the transfer mechanism will be weak, because only very small differences in efficiency between firms persist and because collusive behaviour is highly probable. The innovation mechanism will also be weak, since there will be little threat to the existence of individual firms. Consequently there will be a tendency for market shares to stabilise. The growth aspirations of firms will therefore have to be satisfied by diversification into industries with lower concentration and considerable dispersion of efficiency. It follows that there will be a certain irreversibility about the process of concentration. Industries that have become highly concentrated will tend to remain so, and the diversification of large firms from high concentration to low concentration industries will tend to push the latter in the same direction by speeding up the transfer mechanism.

Overall, therefore, Downie's analysis predicts that there will be a general tendency in a free enterprise economy for industries to become more highly concentrated, and, furthermore, that large firms will come to hold positions of market power in more than one industry. This is clearly an oversimplified account of the competitive process. There are several factors not mentioned that must be taken into consideration, some of which would tend to strengthen Downie's conclusions, others of which would tend to weaken them. Let us first consider some of the reinforcing factors.

First, there is the element of chance. Assume that each firm in an industry faces the same distribution of growth possibilities, regardless of initial size and past history. Actual growth rates will nevertheless differ over any particular period, simply because some firms will have more luck than others. Consequently, starting from a situation where there are many firms of equal size, at the end of, say, a five-year period some firms will have jumped ahead of the pack. In the next period each firm will still have the same chance of growing by a given proportion, and this will make it very difficult for the laggards to catch up. Applying this to investment in innovation, the more important that chance factors are in explaining success or failure, the less likely it is that success in innovation will change hands in a systematic fashion to allow the inefficient firms to catch up on the leaders. Where chance plays an important part, the firm that has forged ahead on the strength of past innovations may further strengthen its position with more successful innovations. There would be no expectation, therefore, that firms that had fallen behind would in general be able to close the gap; rather it would be expected that large differences in firm sizes could quickly appear and persist. Stochastic models of the growth of firms do indeed show that market structures characterised by a highly skewed distribution of firm sizes would quickly evolve.

Second, if the growth rates of firms from one year to the next are not independent of each other, the forces that favour some firms and penalise others may be even more powerful. Thus, for instance, if a firm is fortunate in the appointment of a chief executive, it will reap the benefit over a run of years, while other firms may suffer over several years the misfortune of incompetent management. Where such periods of good or bad management occur, cumulative forces may come into play, with success breeding success in one group of firms and failure breeding failure in another.

Third, the initial boost to a firm's fortunes as a consequence of pure luck may be reinforced if over a range of output there are scale advantages to be reaped. The firms that are first to span this range of output will gain a competitive advantage over their rivals, and this will accelerate the trend towards high concentration.

These factors tending towards high concentration will not of course operate with equal force across all sectors of the economy. They will not, for instance, apply as powerfully in the service industries, where location is an important factor, as in the manufacturing industries. Within manufacturing the strength of the tendency towards higher concentration will vary substantially because of differences in the nature of the product, in technology, in the importance of economies of scale and in demand conditions.

We should mention one other factor that, at least in part, works against those forces making for greater monopoly. This is the introduction of new products. In a world in which products, processes and inputs remained basically unchanged and fixed in number, concentration in individual industries would undoubtedly increase at a much faster rate than it has actually done. Product innovation in particular has created entirely new industries. This has opened up completely new opportunities for all firms, and thus it represents an important offsetting factor to the forces tending towards more monopolistic market structures.

7.52   The Role of Mergers

So far we have said nothing about the role of mergers in facilitating the growth of firms and in changing industrial structure. Mergers have in fact played a very important part both in the emergence of large firms and in the increase in industrial concentration. To what extent can this be viewed simply as part of the process whereby industry becomes more efficient? The answer to this question depends largely upon our answere to three other questions. Is there a strong tendency for the inefficient firms to be acquired by the efficient ones? Do mergers typically lead to cost savings? If they do, do they also lead to price increases, and how are we to trade off the gains against the losses? We shall deal with these questions in reverse order.

Mergers are frequently defended on the grounds that they give rise to economies of scale. The argument has been most rigorously developed in the literature on welfare economics by Williamson. His analysis can be explained with the aid of Figure 7.5.

Consider the case of a merger that changes a competitive industry into a monopoly. The industry demand curve both before and after the merger is D. The unit cost curve before the merger is C_1C_1', constant cost conditions are assumed for simplicity of exposition, and price is equal to unit cost C_1. As a result of the merger it is assumed that costs are reduced to C_2C_2'. If the profit-maximising price after the merger is lower than C_1, then, ignoring second-best considerations, both price and cost movements have been beneficial. However, if, as shown in Figure 7.5, price increases to P_m, then to establish the net effect on welfare we have to balance the gain from the cost reduction, c, against the allocative loss brought about by the increase in price, which is equal to a. (The total loss of consumers' surplus is of course equal to $a + b$, but b is matched by an equivalent increase in producers' surplus.) If $c > a$, then, ignoring income distribution and other complicating factors, in this simple model the merger should be allowed. It is clear from Figure 7.5 that the greater is the price-raising effect of the merger and the higher is the elasticity of demand, the larger must the cost saving be to offset the fall in consumers' surplus a. In addition, if there is premerger market power that maintains price above unit cost, the cost saving must be even greater if the merger is to result in a net increase in economic welfare.

Figure 7.5

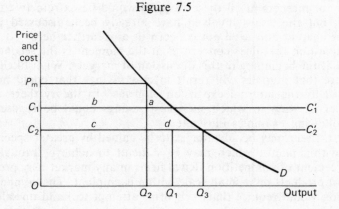

To make this analysis operational, a number of factors that we have so far ignored have to be taken into account. The analysis is of course a partial equilibrium one and abstracts from all inter-actions between the various sectors of the economy. If these inter-actions were introduced, it might be that the postmerger price rise had a beneficial allocative effect. This is only one possibility, of course, and whenever the opposite is true a trade-off approach must be adopted, as indicated in the above analysis.

The distributive effects of the merger are to redistribute income from consumers to producers, and this will normally mean a redistribution in favour of the better-off. If such a change were regarded as undesirable, it would count against the merger, and allowance would have to be made for this.

It is also clear that, if the merger leads to cost savings as suggested by the new cost curve C_2C_2', the *potential* welfare gain is not restricted to $c - a$. If output could be expanded to OQ_3 and price kept at the competitive level C_2, then a further gain equal to d could be achieved. In this case a comparison of the pre- and post-merger situations shows an increase of consumers' surplus of $c + d$. The second-best problem remains, and it is possible that allocative efficiency would be worsened by a fall in price, but where this is not the case the total gain is clearly larger when cost savings are achieved. To achieve such a gain, however, public regulation of the monopolist would be needed, to keep price near the competitive level.

There are many other additions and qualifications to be made to the analysis, such as the effect of the merger on technical progressiveness and on internal efficiency. If a merger produces a market structure that affects technical progress adversely, this will tell against it, and vice versa. Needless to say, an assessment of the effects of mergers in all these respects would be extremely complicated, but the issues involved have already been discussed in an earlier chapter and need not concern us any further here.

A question that does concern us at the moment is the second one posed at the beginning of this discussion of mergers: What likelihood is there that mergers will result in cost savings that could not be realised by the internal expansion of firms? In theory there are a number of ways in which such cost savings could be realised, as the following examples illustrate.

First, there may be advantages to be gained by greater specialisation within plants, which may be difficult to achieve through the enforcement of competition. Rival firms in any market may produce several products on a small scale within each plant. The competitive solution would require that such firms attempt to build up sales on a smaller range of products through the offer of lower prices on selected products. However, if there is a great deal of overlap in the products that rivals produce, this attempt may lead to competitive price cuts across the board, with the end result that prices are lower but nothing much has been achieved in terms of longer production runs. By combining plants into a smaller number of firms, mergers may lead to economies of rationalisation, which could not be achieved, or at least could take much longer to achieve, through internal expansion.

Second, mergers may lead to plant scale economies. For instance, existing industry capacity in aggregate may be sufficient to meet demand, but many individual plants may be of suboptimal size. A firm may not be prepared to build an optimal-sized plant for fear that severe price competition would follow. A merger, however, would allow the firm to close down suboptimal units when new plant came into production. Similarly, if economies of scale are large in relation to the annual rate of increase in demand, firms may invest in suboptimal units in order to reduce the danger of the emergence of excess capacity and price warfare. This tends to occur in oligopolistic markets, where competitors exercise price discipline but still compete vigorously in non-price ways, including the provision of sufficient capacity to maintain customer goodwill. Here again, mergers resulting in a reduction in the number of competitors may be necessary if scale economies are to be fully realised. The same result may be impossible to achieve through internal expansion because of market imperfections, such as control over distributive outlets, product differentiation advantages, or simply an unwillingness on the part of businessmen to take the risks of competitive expansion.

Third, a merger may be beneficial because it makes it possible for firms to time their capacity extensions more efficiently. When the time-phasing factor is taken into account, and if economies of scale are important, firms will typically have to find the most profitable compromise between building large plants infrequently, and extending capacity more frequently by building smaller units. If a large plant is built, there are advantages to be derived from economies of scale. If a number of smaller plants are built at more frequent intervals, there is the advantage of postponing part of the total investment and so reducing the incidence of excess capacity. Given knowledge of the rate of increase in demand and of cost functions, it is possible to calculate the optimal policy with respect to the size of plant built and the time interval between capacity extensions. Assuming a constant arithmetic growth of demand for the product; zero excess demand at all times, with no imports; constant costs; a constant discount rate; infinite plant life; and an infinite planning horizon – it can be shown that the optimal policy is to construct a given plant size at constant intervals, as shown in Figure 7.6.

DD' shows the constant annual increase in demand. At time t capacity K is just sufficient to meet demand, when a new plant of size x comes into production. Immediately excess capacity of x is created, but this diminishes until at time $2t$ capacity again is fully used, when another plant of size x is brought into commission. The correct timing and scale of capacity extensions ensures the minimisation of the discounted total costs of meeting demand.

The potential savings from the optimal time phasing of capacity extensions are most likely to be realised where there is only one seller. A merger that creates a dominant firm could, in theory, therefore have important benefits in this area. However, if mergers change an atomistic industry into an oligopolistic one, then, as the analysis in section 7.2 showed, the result in terms of the incidence of excess capacity could go either way: towards an improvement or a worsening of performance.

Whether or not the potential benefits of a merger outlined above are actually realised is another matter. It is only in theory that a monopolist may be able to achieve a better timing of capacity extensions and exploit scale economies more fully than is possible where several competing firms exist. The benefits may not be realised at all if the monopolist uses his power to restrict capacity.

Figure 7.6

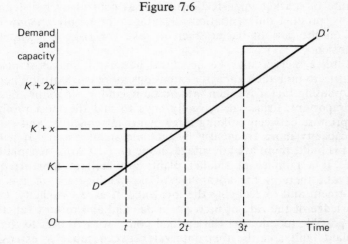

Furthermore, even if the benefits are realised they may be outweighed by a loss of internal efficiency. To forestall such possibilities would again require public regulation. Similarly, the potential advantages from greater specialisation within plants may not be seized, especially if the merger results in a sharp reduction in competitive pressure. It follows that a market structure best suited to encourage one type of economy may not be optimal from the point of view of another. Thus monopoly may be best for the timing of investment, but at least some competitive pressure may be required to achieve the benefits of greater specialisation within plants.

Attempts to assess the effects of mergers have generally concluded that, more often than not, most of the potential benefits have not been realised or have been offset by the costs. Even when management is keen to exploit the advantages of a merger it may take several years for the fruits of their labours to be realised. It is therefore worth noting that, if industry demand is expanding rapidly, many of the benefits that have been discussed will be achieved by the internal expansion of firms.

The third question posed earlier was whether there is a strong tendency for merger activity to eliminate the most inefficient firms.

The research carried out in this field suggests that although such a tendency exists it is in fact a very weak one, and that a high proportion of mergers in practice have involved the acquisition of the efficient by the inefficient.

It seems, therefore, that structural change brought about by merger activity cannot be viewed simply as part of the process whereby industrial efficiency is increased. In large part, mergers must be viewed as attempts by the firms involved to increase or maintain their market power. Consider, for instance, the economic conditions of the 1950s and 1960s. In the United Kingdom this period was marked by a substantial increase in the competitive pressures facing domestic firms. The Restrictive Trade Practices Act 1956 heralded a determined attack on restrictive business behaviour. British firms were facing increased competition at home from the subsidiaries of American companies, and also from imports. There was a fundamental change, therefore, in the competitive environment within which British firms operated. An important part of the merger wave of the late 1950s and 1960s in the United Kingdom was probably an attempt on the part of British firms to protect themselves from these new competitive conditions by creating more concentrated market structures. Once the merger movement had started, a cumulative process began, with an acquisition made by one firm triggering off defensive acquisitions by competitors. Since these interactions often involve competitors in different countries, it is difficult to formulate an effective national merger policy to restrain merger activity.

In conclusion, therefore, we suggest that there are indeed strong forces at work in the competitive process that continually push markets towards higher levels of concentration. In part this is the outcome of the forces of efficiency and progressiveness outlined at the beginning of this section, but it is also in part due to the pursuit of market power and merger activity unrelated to efficiency considerations.

7.6 STRUCTURAL CHANGE WITHIN REGIONS AND COUNTRIES

In our analysis of structural change within industries we mentioned the part played by cumulative causation in increasing the concentration of individual industries. That is, circumstances may well be such that success breeds success and failure breeds failure. Such a process need not operate continuously to lead to the concentration of economic activity. If it applies for only a limited period of time in a firm's history, it can help the firm achieve a position of market dominance from which it is unlikely to be dislodged. We also noted how market imperfections and government policy, particularly the permissive policy towards mergers, can serve to strengthen this mechanism. Similar cumulative forces are at work on a much wider scale, influencing the pattern of industrial development within a country and also between countries. We conclude this chapter by considering some of the facets of structural change at this higher level of aggregation, starting with a look at the development of regions within a country and then extending the analysis to cover some aspects of the growth of economies as a whole.

7.61   *The Growth of Regional Disparities*
At the heart of the regional adjustment problem are the problems of dynamic efficiency, examined earlier in this chapter, and of externalities. If the regional allocation of resources took place quickly and smoothly, and on the basis of market forces that reflected all social costs and benefits, there would be no economic basis for any regional policy other than one that deliberately left things to the market. Government intervention becomes justified, however, if the market adjustment process, although ultimately leading to an efficient allocation of resources, works very slowly. The case for intervention is strengthened if the market does not lead towards an efficient allocation of resources because private costs and benefits alone are taken into account and because divergences between private and social costs and benefits are significant.

In a dynamic economy, changes in the pattern of demand will continually cause some industries to expand while others contract. If the two groups of industries are geographically concentrated, regional disparities in the level of economic activity will begin to emerge. This would not necessarily be cause for concern if the market mechanism functioned effectively. Ignoring externalities for the moment, if all the factors of production are highly mobile and at the same time responsive to price signals, forces will be set in motion to check regional disparities. Wages in the depressed region will fall, thus inducing labour to move to the prosperous areas where wages are higher and job opportunities more plentiful. As wages and other factor prices fall, the marginal product of capital in depressed regions will rise, increasing the rate of return on investment. If capital is mobile, the lower wages and more plentiful supply of labour in the depressed areas will encourage firms to locate there. The falling prices of products produced in less prosperous regions will increase their competitiveness and therefore increase the level of exports to other regions. The movement of factors will continue until regional disparities are removed.

However, in practice the adjustment process does not work as smoothly as this, for a number of reasons.

First, the movement of labour both occupationally and geographically may, for various reasons, be very difficult. Workers may possess hard-earned skills that are specific to the declining industries. Housing shortages, inadequate information and transfer costs may obstruct movement from one locality to another. Social and cultural factors may also tie households to particular locations.

Second, wages will be less than fully responsive to changes in supply and demand conditions. Pay differentials between workers in different regions will not reflect relative labour market conditions, partly because of trade union pressure to maintain traditional comparabilities. As a result, money wages in different regions will tend to show the same rate of growth. This being so, the decline and expansion of regions may then not only continue but also take on a cumulative aspect. While money wages are increasing at much the same rate, productivity growth will be faster in the more rapidly expanding and newer industries in the prosperous areas, and so the latter will acquire a cumulative competitive advantage. The high income levels of prosperous areas will attract firms even though they can expect only a small share of the market – a small share of an expanding market being more attractive than a large share of a declining one. Similar considerations apply on the labour side. Although, in the aggregate, the labour market in prosperous areas will be tight, it will also be large in terms of the range of skills. A firm may prefer to locate in these areas, even with the knowledge that labour is scarce, in the expectation that it will obtain its fair share of the labour available, rather than locate in a less prosperous area with an abundant labour supply of the wrong kind. The availability of skilled labour, ancillary services and other advantages will have a powerful effect in maintaining the forward momentum of the more prosperous areas. The declining regions, however, will suffer from forces operating in the opposite direction. The loss of a disproportionate number of the younger and the more skilled members of the working population, declining income, decaying social capital and the scars of earlier industrialisation will combine to make the regions unattractive to new firms. This will lead to further contractions in activity.

Regional disparities arise under competitive conditions not simply because of adjustment problems, but also because of externalities. Even if all the factors of production are mobile, market forces will eventually result in diseconomies of overexpansion in the prosperous areas, especially in the form of congestion costs and environmental pollution. In a market economy these costs are not fully reflected in the costs borne by individuals and firms, so that the optimal location pattern cannot be achieved. The fact that all location decisions are based on charges that fall short of marginal social costs means that expansion in the prosperous areas and contraction in the less prosperous regions will go beyond the socially optimal point.

To offset these tendencies government policies are needed to compensate for the imperfections of the market mechanism. The failure of wage differentials to respond to labour market changes could be compensated for by measures to subsidise employment in depressed areas and to tax employment in prosperous areas. This would give an incentive to employers to locate in depressed areas and at the same time contribute to solving the problem of externalities. Investment in the less prosperous areas could also be made more attractive by generous investment grants and tax allowances. Of particular importance is the need for retraining facilities and removal grants, which increase the occupational and geographical mobility of labour. It is also important to improve the infrastructure of depressed regions, including transport facilities within the region as well as between the region and other areas.

These and other policies for dealing with regional problems are of course well known and have been used in many countries. The problem is that in the past the measures taken have often been too weak and too long delayed, with the result that large structural imbalances have been allowed to develop. Policies that operate via the market mechanism are most effective when the adjustments required are small ones. The problem of adjustment becomes more and more intractable as the structural imbalances are allowed to grow.

7.62   *Disparities between Countries*
The same forces that fashion economic development in the different regions within a country also contribute to the explanation of the varying fortunes of different countries. However, whereas with regions the adjustment problem has been aggravated by government failure to compensate for market imperfections in time, in the case of countries the problem has been aggravated by the unwillingness of governments to allow the market mechanism to work.

Consider, starting from a position of equilibrium, the effect of an increase in the demand for the exports of country A and a decrease in the demand for the exports of country B. The increase in A's exports will cause an increase in income in A, and the fall in B's exports will bring about a fall in income in B. These income effects will tend to correct the balance-of-payments disequilibrium in the two countries, the increase in income in A resulting in an increase in the demand for imports, and the fall in income in B causing a decline in the demand for imports. This mechanism will be weakened if, for instance, the public sector deficit in B increases as the government, despite falling receipts from taxation, increases its expenditure to compensate for the fall in exports. But there is another adjustment mechanism – a change in the exchange rate. The increase in the demand for *A*'s currency to pay for the increased exports from *A* will cause *A*'s currency to appreciate, while the fall in the demand for *B*'s currency will cause its currency to depreciate. This will make *A*'s goods less competitive and *B*'s goods more competitive in world markets. Forces are thus set in motion that generate structural changes in *A*'s industries. Import substitution is fostered, and new export opportunities are opened up. The currency changes will continue until a new equilibrium is reached. They are not panaceas in themselves, but they provide a breathing space, and an incentive for the more fundamental structural changes that are necessary if income levels are to be maintained.

However, these exchange rate adjustments have not always been allowed to occur. Over the greater part of the 1950s and 1960s a regime of fixed exchange rates existed, and the important role that exchange rate adjustments play in rectifying imbalances was ignored. Because of this, very powerful cumulative factors were allowed to develop, which benefited some economies and harmed others. Thus, for instance, the success of German exports resulted in a fast growth of manufacturing outputs, which induced a high level of investment, which in turn resulted in a high rate of increase in productivity, and this further strengthened Germany's position in world markets. In a free market the deutschmark would have appreciated, thus increasing the price and/or reducing the profitability of German goods in export markets. The maintenance of a fixed exchange rate, however, prevented this adjustment and allowed the cumulative forces to work unchecked. In the United Kingdom, in contrast, a weakening of competitiveness in export markets had adverse effects on the growth of output, which in turn weakened the incentive to invest. The result was a low rate of growth of productivity and a further deterioration in the competitiveness of UK products, but the required depreciation of the pound was not allowed to occur. In addition, whereas in Germany the undervalued currency and the fast rate of domestic growth encouraged businessmen to invest at home, in the United Kingdom the overvalued currency and the slow growth rate encouraged overseas investment.

In a free market these cumulative movements would not be allowed to develop to any marked extent but would be nipped in the bud. Of course, because of lags in the adjustment mechanism imbalances would appear, but these would tend to be short-lived. The maintenance of fixed exchange rates, however, resulted in the build-up of extremely large imbalances, with the British economy suffering a long-run competitive decline with ever increasing structural weakness. By the second half of the 1960s, therefore, the British economy had suffered from a long period of slow output growth and low investment, and thus slow technical advance compared to many other countries.

We noted earlier that the market mechanism works most efficiently when the required adjustments are small. When very large structural changes are required, as was the case with the United Kingdom by 1967, the efficiency of the market mechanism is considerably weakened.

For instance, in the case under consideration, the longer a structural imbalance is allowed to develop, the greater the devaluation that will eventually be required, the greater the adverse effect of the devaluation on inflation and real wages, and the longer the period over which real wages must be depressed below what they would otherwise be, before any headway begins to be made in dealing with the underlying competitive weakness. The strain that this imposes on labour may well wreck the whole policy, whereas action taken earlier might have been successful because it would have necessitated much smaller sacrifices. It is not altogether surprising, therefore, in view of the fact that it has had to correct an imbalance accumulated over a long period of time, that the market system has not appeared to be an impressive mechanism for dealing with the problem of dynamic adjustment.

Chapter 8

Externalities and Public Goods

8.1 INTRODUCTION

So far we have been primarily concerned with the allocation of goods and services where all costs and benefits in production and consumption are taken into account by the normal workings of the market. Prices, costs, factor rewards and profits are then all complete signals of the utilities and opportunity costs involved in economic activity. In this chapter we turn to consider the problems of resource allocation in those situations where market forces and signals do not reflect the full range of benefits and costs associated with production and consumption. Where market signals are inadequate in this sense, the goods and services involved are said to generate externalities (alternatively referred to as external economies and diseconomies, spillovers, or neighbourhood effects) – that is, direct effects upon another's profit or welfare position arising as an incidental byproduct of some person's or firm's activities.

The extent to which the market does encompass all benefits and costs is a matter of degree, varying from one activity to another. There are instances where virtually no effective market exists, as with the case of noise, so that the externality is very large. There are other instances, as with the case of the extraction of minerals, where a market exists but works imperfectly, so that benefits and costs are not accurately reflected. There is, then, no rigid dividing line between activities that involve externalities and those which do not. Indeed, it is possible to cast the net very widely and define externalities in such a way that very little of what goes on in the world is excluded. For instance, Meade defines an external economy (diseconomy) as 'an event which confers an appreciable benefit (inflicts an appreciable damage) on some person or persons who were not fully consenting parties in reaching the decision or decisions which led directly or indirectly to the event in question'. On the basis of this definition we have in fact already touched upon several externalities in earlier chapters of this book. Consider the case of price discrimination in postal charges. If the authorities decide that it should cost the same to post a letter irrespective of the distance it travels, people who send letters over long distances will not pay the marginal cost of that service. A decision in which they are not involved thus confers on them a benefit for which they will not pay. Similarly with advertising. Firms make decisions relating to advertising campaigns without consulting the consumer. The consumer's utility function may, however, be affected – adversely or beneficially – so that an externality exists. If working conditions in a factory are substantially improved or worsened as a result of a decision made by an employer without consultation with his employees, again an externality is involved. And virtually every act of government is likely to involve an external effect, since any government policy is almost bound to have an appreciable effect on someone who has not been fully consulted. Meade's definition of externalities is so wide that very little of what goes on in the world fails to fall within its scope.

A narrower definition identifies an externality as simply any change in the value of a firm's production function or a consumer's utility function arising from the activity of other decision-making units. In the competitive model of Chapter 2 it was assumed that each consumer's utility depended only upon the goods purchased by the consumer, and that each firm's production function depended only upon the inputs used by that firm. But if in the process of consumption or production certain costs are imposed on others and no compensation is paid, or benefits are conferred but no payment is received, the utility and production functions of individual consumers and firms cannot be separated in this way. Private costs will not accurately measure the costs to society of producing goods, and market prices will not accurately measure the value of goods.

Four different types of non-market interrelationship between consumption and production can be identified. First, there are consumption-to-consumption externalities. In this case a particular variable enters into the utility functions of two or more people. Thus A may purchase high fidelity equipment that excites B's envy and reduces the enjoyment that he obtains from his old-fashioned record player. The hi-fi equipment is thus a variable in B's utility function as well as A's. This interdependence between utility functions is no doubt played upon and strengthened by the heavy advertising of consumer goods. Second, there are production-to-production externalities. The emission of chemicals into a river by firm A may increase the costs of production of firm B located downstream, because B's production process requires clean water, which it can obtain only by installing water-purifying equipment. A classic example of a beneficial effect is the beekeeper's bees, which pollinate the fruit grower's trees, and the reciprocal benefit that the blossom on the trees confers on the beekeeper. Third, there are production-to-consumption externalities. This category includes the adverse effects on people's utility functions of the smoke, noise, smell and unsightliness of many productive activities. Finally, there are consumption-to-production externalities. A recent example of a diseconomy of this type is the claim that the increased use of low-foam detergents in the home has reduced the efficiency of power stations. If the high potash content of these detergents enters the water used by power stations, it causes scaling on the inside of the condenser tubes that cool the steam from the turbines, thus reducing the efficiency of the plant and increasing the amount of coal needed to generate a given power output. An example of a consumption-to-production external economy is the long run benefit of education on economic efficiency.

Although, as just indicated, there are external economies as well as diseconomies, the latter pose by far the most widespread problems for a modern society. Our attention will thus be focused largely upon the diseconomies, and in particular upon production-to-consumption and production-to-production diseconomies, which in practice are some of the most serious impediments to efficiency. They include the well-known problems of noise, congestion, smoke and the discharge of poisonous chemicals into air and water, referred to above. In addition to the pollution of the environment, however, our analysis is also relevant to the problem of the too rapid exploitation of both replaceable and irreplaceable resources. External diseconomies of this kind have recently become much more widespread as a result of the growth of population and increased industrialisation.

It would be a mistake to think of externality problems as a peculiarly twentieth-century phenomenon. Mining communities, and industrial cities, suffered acutely from external diseconomies in the eighteenth and nineteenth centuries, and in many respects the position then was far worse than it is today. However, this is not to deny that there is a major problem to be dealt with.

8.2 A SIMPLE ECONOMIC MODEL OF EXTERNAL DISECONOMIES

Consider the case of a production-to-consumption externality where the problem is, say, the emission of smoke by a factory, which imposes uncompensated costs on nearby households. Assume initially that there is only one method of production and that the emission of smoke and the level of activity are directly related. In Figure 8.1 the gains and losses are measured in money terms on the vertical axis and the scale of activity is measured on the horizontal. The area $a + b$ under the marginal private-gain curve measures the total profit to the producer at each level of activity. The area $b + c$ under the marginal social-cost curve measures the losses incurred from the externality by those who are not party to the activity. If the producer's freedom is in no way constrained and his aim is to maximise profits, then he will operate at a scale of activity equal to Q_4, where the area under the marginal private-gain curve is maximised. This is clearly not an optimum position from the point of view of society as a whole, for at this scale the marginal loss, of those who suffer from the externality is very much greater than the marginal gain of the producer. The socially optimal scale of activity is Q_1, where the marginal private gain equals the marginal social cost. At any larger scale of production, marginal loss exceeds marginal gain, and so net benefit can be increased by a reduction of output. The converse is true for a scale of production below Q_1.

Figure 8.1

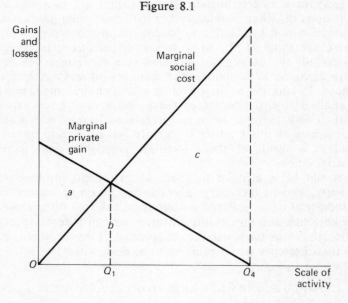

Assume now that there is not one but two possible technologies. Figure 8.2(*a*) reproduces Figure 8.1 and is associated with the use of production process *A*. The marginal social-cost curve in diagram (*b*) shows the losses associated with production process *B*, which for each scale of activity involves a lower level of pollution than process *A*. The use of this alternative technology means higher costs for the firm, and thus lower net gains, because it has to substitute other inputs for pollution in order to maintain a given level of output.

As drawn, the optimal position is now one in which production process B is used, at a scale of activity equal to Q_2. At this point marginal private gain is once more equal to marginal social cost, but the amount left over for the producer, or his net benefit, is greater than at Q_1 using process A; that is, $d > a$. However, it should be noted that with complete freedom of action the producer, in order to maximise his private gain, would choose process A and operate at a scale of Q_4, because $a + b > d + e$.

Figure 8.2

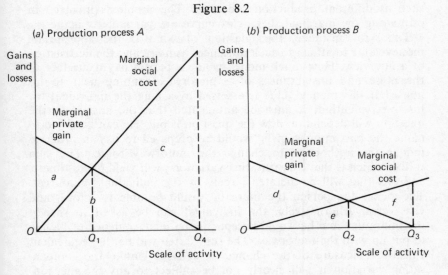

(*a*) Production process *A*

(*b*) Production process *B*

This analysis points to a number of important conclusions.

First, only externalities that occur at the margin are relevant from the point of view of resource allocation.

Second, because the solution to the resource allocation problem involves the balancing of gains against losses, in general this will mean that some level of external diseconomies will still remain when an optimum position has been attained. In other words, the cost of the complete abatement of an externality may be so high as to outweigh the benefits achieved. The prohibition of an activity that gives rise to external diseconomies will therefore rarely be in the social interest.

Third, the solution to the external diseconomy problem may involve changing the type, or nature, of an activity as well as its scale. This is a particularly important point to bear in mind when it comes to policy, because some policies are likely to be more effective than others in encouraging producers to search for, and to introduce, new methods of production that will reduce pollution.

Fourth, there is the important problem of identifying the optimum position. Since adjustment to the optimum does not usually mean the complete elimination of the activity, but rather the balancing of costs and benefits, there is a major problem involved in measuring those costs and benefits. In terms of Figure 8.2, information has to be obtained that allows the policy maker to plot the two pairs of marginal gain and loss curves. In other words, estimates have to be obtained of the gains and losses associated not only with different scales of activity, but also with different types of activity as well, such as different production processes. The problems involved in estimating the marginal social-cost curve are particularly acute.

Take, for instance, the question of what is the appropriate money value to attach to such nuisances as noise and the destruction of a fine view. How much money would a person pay to be free of the noise and unsightliness of a motorway running near to his house? If this money value is assessed by asking the individual for his own valuation, it must be anticipated that the answer to the question will depend on how the question is put. He can be asked to name the maximum sum he would be prepared to pay in order to induce the authorities to change the motorway route. The sum stated, which is the 'compensating variation', will yield one estimate, and one that will be dictated largely by the individual's resources. The richer the person the more he would be able to afford, and vice versa. Alternatively, the individual can be asked to specify the minimum sum he would accept for the inconvenience of having to put up with the motorway. The sum stated will be the 'equivalent variation' measure of the change in welfare. Unlike the compensating variation it will clearly not be subject to any income constraint, and as a result it will typically be much larger. If a person is poor, the maximum sum that he would be prepared to pay to get rid of or avoid a nuisance will inevitably be small, but the minimum sum that he would be prepared to accept to put up with it may be high. Neither of these two measures is likely to give an accurate measure of the value of a pleasant environment. The first is likely to be too low, especially where the people involved are in the lower income brackets, and the second may be too high, since people may deliberately overstate their demands when it is a matter of receiving compensation.

The difficulties of measurement are compounded if a particular situation is regarded as desirable by some but undesirable by others, for then there is the problem of deciding what weights to attach to these different preferences. In many cases the conflict may be between the rich and the poor, with the former putting great emphasis on conservation of the environment, and the latter favouring the devoting of more resources to industrial expansion in order to increase job opportunities and to augment the total supply of goods and services.

A further complication worth mentioning is that in estimating the social costs of pollution future generations as well as the present one may be involved. This is obviously the case with the exploitation of irreplaceable resources. It may also, on occasion, be an important factor when considering the side effects of new products, especially in the pharmaceutical and chemical industries.

Needless to say there is a cost involved in collecting information on the benefits and costs of pollution abatement, and this cost has to be taken into account both when deciding whether certain policies are likely to lead to an improvement and when selecting which particular policy to introduce. However, one should not fall into the trap of using the difficulties associated with data collection as an excuse for doing nothing. While it is important, wherever possible, to quantify costs and benefits, it is even more important to recognise that it will seldom, if ever, be possible to obtain a complete quantification of all the relevant variables, and that this should not be allowed to delay the introduction of measures for dealing with an important problem.

8.3 POLICY APPROACHES TO CONTROLLING EXTERNAL DISECONOMIES

Various solutions to the problem of externalities exist.

8.31 *Internalising the Externality*
The problem could be solved by internalising the externality, that is, by changing the institutional structure so that the people affected by the externality become part of the decision-making process associated with it. This is likely to be most effective when the numbers involved are small. Thus, for instance, in the case of production-to-production diseconomies involving a small number of firms, the diseconomies could be internalised by means of a merger.

8.32 *Bargaining*
A solution could be achieved by means of bargaining. Consider Figure 8.3, which shows the gains and losses associated with some polluting activity of a firm. Assume that only one type of activity is possible, so that there is only one pair of marginal gain and loss curves. The social optimum position is therefore at scale of activity A. However, if the law imposes no constraints upon the firm, it will choose to operate at Q. To get to the optimum position the people suffering the diseconomy would be prepared to pay a sum up to a maximum of $c + d$, that is, a sum equal to the total losses incurred

at Q minus the losses incurred at A. Of course, if they could bribe the producer to reduce his scale of activity by paying a smaller sum, so much the better, and any sum less than $c + d$ would leave them that much better off than before the change. The producer, on the other hand, would be prepared to shift from Q to A in return for a payment of not less than c, which is the extent to which his total private gains are greater at the initial as compared to the optimum point. If he could get more than this, so much the better as far as he is concerned. The difference between the maximum sum that the sufferers are prepared to pay and the minimum that the producer is willing to accept equals d, which represents the over-all gain to the economy if the adjustment is made, and is available for sharing between the two parties.

Figure 8.3

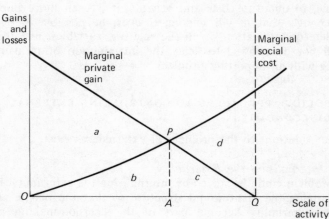

If there are no legal sanctions and it is left to the aggrieved people to bribe the producer to move from Q to A, they will pay a sum somewhere between c and $c + d$. Suppose, however, that by law the producer is compelled to compensate those who suffer from his polluting activity to the full extent of the costs he imposes upon them. Then the best adjustment he can make is to move from Q to A, pay b to the victims of his pollution and retain a sum equal to a. As far as efficiency is concerned, the outcome is the same as when no legal sanctions apply. The optimum position is reached whether it is the producer who has to compensate the sufferers or whether it is the latter who have to pay the producer. As far as equity is concerned, however, the two outcomes are very different – the alternative ways of reaching the optimum have markedly different effects on the distribution of income.

The feasibility of arranging bargaining solutions is crucially dependent on the numbers involved. Unless numbers are small the transactions costs of organising the two sides are likely to be prohibitive. For both parties to the agreement these transactions costs include the costs of identifying and getting together the members of the group; agreeing on the joint offer to be made or on what offer would be acceptable; agreeing on individual contributions; negotiating with the other side; and implementing and policing the agreement. If numbers are small on both sides, involving say a handful of firms, then no doubt it will be perfectly possible to negotiate a joint agreement. But many of the most important externalities, especially of the production-to-consumption kind, involve very large numbers. For instance, thousands of households may suffer from the emission of smoke from factory chimneys, and in such cases a privately negotiated settlement will be impractical.

An important issue raised by the bargaining model is the state of the law relating to externalities. In the case of air and water pollution, for instance, should the law give industries the right to pollute, or should it give individuals the right to clean air and water? There are strong arguments for favouring the latter state of affairs.

First, if the law gives industry the right to pollute, it will often be difficult for the injured parties to take effective steps to reduce the pollution, because it is the sufferers who are usually large in number and badly organised. A law that gave the rights of clean air to the individual would, on the other hand, place the responsibility for bargaining and compensation on industry, and one can presume that the smaller number and greater organisational efficiency of firms would mean that more effective action would be taken.

Second, if industry knows that it will have to pay full compensation to the victims of pollution, this will act as a powerful spur to research and development in the field of pollution-reducing technology.

Third, the people who are worst affected by pollution are often poor as well as badly organised. If the law gave industry the right to pollute, the money that the sufferers could afford to pay in order to compensate firms for the costs of reducing pollution might be well below the true social damage caused by pollution. If this were the case, then, even if negotiation between the two sides did take place, there would still be a general tendency for the level of pollution to remain above the optimum level.

Of course, a bargaining solution need not involve money payments. Many externalities between neighbours, for instance, are settled amicably without money payment. Furthermore, the whole problem of externalities may be lessened by the fact that very often people do not behave in an entirely selfish way and do take account of externalities. A less charitable view is that people may be induced to behave in such a way only because of the reciprocal nature of the situation. Neighbour *A* refrains from throwing rubbish into *B*'s garden, not because he likes *B* but because he does not want *B* to use his garden as a garbage can. In other words, it is not so much altruism that lessens the magnitude of the problem but the fact that neighbours recognise their interdependence, and that it will be to the benefit of all if certain standards of behaviour are maintained. Even so, neighbours do not always live in harmony, and sometimes the conflict is sufficiently serious for the law to be called in to settle matters. This brings us to the third possible solution of the problem of externalities: litigation.

8.33 *Litigation*
One problem with this course of action is that it is expensive, so that even with the levels of legal aid currently available it is beyond the reach of a large proportion of the population. Apart from the expense, legal processes are not well understood, and this again tends to put litigation out of the reach of ordinary people. Furthermore, for the purposes of law it is essential to be able to identify the precise extent and cause of the suffering or of the deterioration in the environment, and this task is again by no means an easy one. For example, certain illnesses associated with industrial occupations have not always been easily attributable to the working conditions involved, and as a result many people continue to suffer without compensation. Finally, litigation can be extremely prolonged, and this is a further important deterrent. Large companies may use the complicated processes of law to delay settlement, especially when the sufferers are large in number and not well organised. It would be a great advantage if the law could be simplified and speeded up, so that it could be effective in safeguarding the interests of more people.

8.34 *Quantitative Regulations and Charges*
The two remaining solutions to external diseconomies that we shall discuss here involve the imposition of charges on polluters, and the introduction of some form of quantitative regulation. The latter solution involves the government in introducing legislative and administrative pressures to bring polluters into line with some predetermined standard. The standard set might be a zero level of pollution activity, and the sanctions would involve fines and even prison sentences. Such a solution has been used in the past, the Clean Air Act and the Rivers (Prevention of Pollution) Act being just two examples in the United Kingdom. The particular problems of this

solution are fairly obvious: the arbitrariness of the standards set (especially a zero level); the costs of policing a system based upon such high standards; and the legal prohibition of any choice.

Alternatively, a system of charges might be built around a tax per unit of pollution. In Figure 8.4, DQ is the curve showing the marginal cost of pollution abatement (which is just another way of looking at the marginal gain curve in our earlier analysis), with firms using the cheapest means available to them of reducing pollution by a given amount. OC is the marginal social cost of pollution. If the authorities imposed a tax of OP per unit of pollution, they would succeed in attaining the optimum amount of pollution OA, where the marginal cost of pollution abatement equals the marginal social cost of pollution.

Figure 8.4

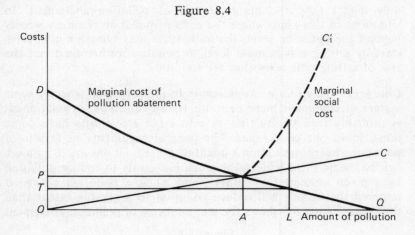

An alternative to a tax per unit of pollution is for the authorities first of all to decide upon the level of pollution that they wish to establish and then to issue licences, or rights to pollute, up to this fixed amount, the licences being sold to the highest bidder. A less demanding variant of this would involve the government in setting standards for individual production units and imposing high and strongly progressive taxes on firms going above the limit. Both variants of the acceptability standards solution enable the government to adjust its strategy through time. For example, if the government finds that the standards it sets are achieved very easily and at little cost (that is, if the tax revenue is low), it can raise the standards. On the other hand, if the government observes that certain pollution activities and certain production units provide very high revenue, it can adjust the standards so as to permit the firms concerned to operate at pollution levels that are higher than those generally prevailing.

The choice between using the tax per unit and the acceptable standards method of charging depends in part on the shape of the curves shown in Figure 8.4. Suppose, as is very likely, that the authorities have not hit upon the optimal tax per unit of pollution and have in fact set it too low at OT. Given the marginal cost of pollution abatement, the consequences of setting this suboptimal tax depend on the shape of the marginal social-cost curve. If it is OC, then the effect is not particularly serious. The level of pollution OL will certainly be higher than the optimum, but the marginal social costs of pollution at this level are not very much higher than the marginal costs of pollution abatement. If, however, the relevant curve is OC'_1, the marginal social cost of pollution at OL is considerably higher than the marginal cost of pollution abatement. In situations of this kind, where the costs of pollution rise very steeply beyond the optimum level, the authorities may consider it safer to start by setting a maximum level to pollution rather than run the risk of setting unit taxes that are too low.

Charges or Quantitative Regulation? In the debate on whether some system of charges is more desirable than quantitative regulations it is probably true to say that by and large economists have come down in favour of charges. The general arguments in favour of pollution charges and against quantitative regulations are as follows.

First, some firms will find it much less costly to reduce pollution by a given amount than others, and when a pollution charge is imposed the former will reduce pollution to a greater extent than the latter. Figure 8.5 shows the marginal cost of pollution abatement

Figure 8.5

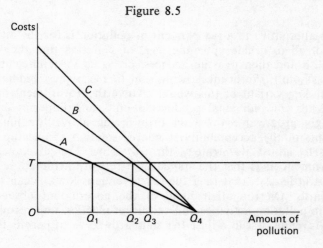

for three firms, A, B and C, on the assumption that they all initially emit the same amount of pollution OQ_4. The cost of pollution abatement is lowest in firm A, highest in firm C. The introduction of a pollution tax of OT will result in A reducing the amount of its pollution to Q_1, B to Q_2 and C to Q_3. When all three firms have fully adjusted to the charge the marginal cost of pollution abatement will be the same. Quantitative controls, however, will by comparison be a much cruder method of control, since without becoming too cumbersome they cannot distinguish between the different circumstances, and possibilities for adjustment, of different units. Regulations will tend to impose the same requirement of pollution abatement on all firms. A given reduction in pollution will therefore be achieved at less cost by pollution charges than by regulation.

The same arguments apply to the case of the overexploitation of resources due to ill-defined ownership. Take, for instance, the case of deep sea fishing. There the social costs are greater than private costs because the sea is treated as a free factor. As the number of fishing boats and the rate of fishing increase, the real resource costs of a unit of output will eventually increase. There is no incentive for any individual firm to restrict its catch because this will only make life easier for others. If the sea were privately owned a rent would be charged for fishing rights, which would bring private and social costs into line, but the absence of property rights to the sea prohibits such a solution. It is possible to restrict fishing by regulation, but this has the disadvantage of imposing a uniform restriction on all firms – efficient and inefficient alike. A tax, however, would restrict output but would do so in a way that would discriminate in favour of the more efficient firms.

A second advantage of pollution charges is that they allow each firm to adopt the cheapest method available to it of reducing pollution. Because of the different circumstances of different firms they will tend to respond differently in their efforts to reduce pollution. For some the best response may be to invest in new plant; for others it may be to relocate a plant in a less densely populated area, and so on. Controls, however, might specify the methods to be used by firms to reduce pollution and would again, therefore, lack flexibility.

Third, charges give an incentive to firms to seek, through research and development, new methods of production, for the more successful firms are in reducing pollution the less tax they pay. With controls, however, since firms are simply instructed to reduce pollution by a given amount there is no incentive to go further.

Fourth, to be effective any system of quantitative regulation requires a force of inspectors to see that the standards are being observed and also to enforce fines. The latter must be heavy enough to act as a real deterrent to the law breaker. Those found guilty of not complying with the regulations would have to be prosecuted, and this adds further to the administrative costs of the system. In practice we generally find that where controls are used the fines are far too low and the inspectorate is grossly undermanned, so that the enforcement of the regulations is at best uneven, and at worst grossly inadequate to achieve the standards set.

Notwithstanding the general argument in favour of pollution charges, there will always be instances where quantitative regulation is the most appropriate policy measure. An attempt to levy charges might involve the installation of a highly sophisticated metering system, the cost of which might be so large that a charging system would become less attractive than some form of regulation. There will also be instances where regulation seems to be the most appropriate policy on grounds of general principles. There would be little sense in allowing some people to drive on the right hand side of the road when everyone else drove on the left, even if those individuals were willing to pay a price equal to the social costs of their actions. There is also a fundamental case for using regulations to prevent the emergence of pollution problems rather than waiting for them to appear. For instance, sensible land-use planning which separates residential and industrial areas could prevent the emergence of many problems. Integrated planning at the local level which takes an overall view of the residential, recreational and work needs of the population, together with what these imply for transport policy, is one of the most important and difficult tasks which policy makers must tackle.

Another instance where regulation is appropriate is where the costs of finding the social optimum are very large but where the gains are expected to be large and widespread. The creation of smokeless zones, speed limits, and restrictions on aircraft flights are examples. Or the problem may be the uncertainty surrounding social costs. In the use of chemicals and pharmaceutical products, for example, where the long-term effects on health or the environment are very uncertain there is a great deal to be said in favour of a play-safe policy to restrict or indeed, in some cases, to prohibit the use of certain products.

A final example of the usefulness of regulation occurs where, because of varying tastes, it is desirable to maintain choice. For instance, some people might enjoy popular beaches. Others might place a much higher value on finding a quiet retreat. One possible solution is a system of private and public beaches where the private beaches would discriminate in favour of those who place a high value on peace and quiet. However, this system would also discriminate against those with low incomes, many of whom also enjoy quiet beaches. An alternative solution would be to ensure that some beaches are not accessible by motor vehicle so that access to open spaces is dependent on the willingness to walk rather than on the ability to pay.

Before leaving this analysis of the relative merits of charges and quantitative controls, two further points need to be considered. First, in some cases it is not possible to measure the pollutant itself. In such cases both charges and controls would have to be imposed on some related activity, such as the input of a raw material into the productive process. The relative merits of charges and controls could then be assessed as in cases where the pollutant is directly measurable. Second, it may be thought that an alternative to a tax per unit of pollutant would be a subsidy per unit of pollutant of equal amount. In either case an existing firm starting with a given level of pollution would have the same incentive to reduce pollution. The equivalence of taxes and subsidies, however, only applies if we are considering the reduction in pollution below an initial level by a given number of firms. Looked at from a wider perspective, subsidies have certain major disadvantages when compared with taxes. If the subsidies apply to all firms, they may in the long run have the perverse effect of increasing pollution by encouraging the entry of more producers. Furthermore, subsidies have to be financed by increased taxation elsewhere in the economy, which may further distort the allocation of resources. On the other hand, the taxation of external diseconomies improves resource allocation directly by compensating for market failure in the polluting industries. The revenue that is raised also enables the government to reduce other taxes, with further indirect benefits for economic efficiency. Alternatively the extra revenue could be devoted to increasing welfare payments to the poor, thus improving the distribution of income.

8.35 *Policy Conflicts*

Finally, it should be noted that policies for dealing with externalities may well produce results that conflict with other policy goals. For instance, an external diseconomy may occur in an industry that is monopolised. In this case it is not clear whether the scale of activity is above or below the optimum level. The externality is a factor that tends to make the industry too large from the social point of view, but the monopoly element works in the other direction. It is not clear, therefore, in which direction the level of activity in the industry should be changed in order to move to a more optimal allocation of resources. The best approach to this problem is to use two policy weapons: one for dealing with the monopoly aspect and another for dealing with the diseconomy. Thus the authorities might attempt to use antitrust legislation to increase the competitiveness of the industry, and at the same time adopt fiscal measures to deal with the externalities.

Another example of the conflict that can arise between policy objectives occurs where policies for dealing with externalities lead to unemployment in a particular region because of the concentration there of pollution-intensive industries. If the unemployment produced is other than very short-lived, it clearly will have to be taken into account in deciding upon the most appropriate policy package. Again it seems that the most appropriate course of action will be to press ahead with the most effective method of dealing with the externalities and to introduce other policies for dealing with unemployment. Thus, for instance, pollution charges might be imposed on the industries and the proceeds, supplemented if necessary from other sources of revenue, used to finance retraining schemes and to attract new industry into the region. However, careful consideration would have to be given to the time factor. The full introduction of pollution charges in one step might lead to substantial unemployment almost immediately, whereas the measures introduced for tackling the unemployment problem might take a very long time to have any effect. Where this was the case it would be desirable to modify the policy by introducing the pollution charges over a number of years, starting well below, and gradually building up to, the optimum level. In fact a phased introduction of charges would probably be desirable in any case. An alternative but possibly less attractive step would be to change the pollution policy itself, from one of pollution charges to the payment of subsidies to local industry for installing less pollution-producing technology.

As a third example of policy conflict, measures for dealing with external diseconomies may lead to an undesirable redistribution of income. In particular a move towards a more optimal allocation of resources may lead to the poor becoming worse off. As in the previous example, it seems that the best solution will be to adopt the most effective method of dealing with externalities, and to use other policy weapons – particularly fiscal policy – to achieve the most desired distribution of income. However, so long as fiscal policy has not or cannot be used to obtain the best distribution of income, the equity effects of policies for dealing with pollution must be considered. And there may be strong arguments for compensating some of the people who suffer a decline in real income as a result of the adoption of policies to deal with externality problems.

It should be clear from the above analysis that there is no one solution to the externality problem that is best in all instances, and that whenever government intervention is considered several factors have to be taken into account in the choice of policy instruments. It is necessary first of all to determine whether or not any form of intervention is likely to improve matters. If the answer to this question is yes, the most efficient policy must be sought. In considering each policy the authorities have to decide whether the benefits are likely to exceed the costs of implementation. They must also consider whether the adoption of each policy is likely to frustrate the attainment of other policy goals and, if so, what modifications are required. Finally, the effects of a given policy on equity have to be considered. If they are adverse, the policy may again have to be modified and possibly dropped altogether. Alternatively the policy can be implemented and consideration given to some device for compensating the losers.

8.4 URBAN ROAD CONGESTION

We turn now to consider in some detail a specific example of an external diseconomy that is particularly important in modern society – the road congestion in towns and cities.

The costs of transport may be divided into three categories: costs such as oil, petrol (excluding tax) and wear and tear, which are costs both to the individual and to society: costs such as fuel tax and the vehicle licence, which are costs to the individual but not to society; and costs associated with congestion, accidents and air pollution, which are borne by society but not, or at least not fully, by the individual. The private motorist, of course, complains that he already pays a great deal to the government in the form of fuel tax and the vehicle licence. But these payments do not relate at all closely to the costs of using the roads, partly because they are not assessed according to the amount of road use and partly because the owners of vehicles do not take into account the costs that their road use imposes upon others.

As a starting point to our analysis, consider the highly simplified situation shown in Figure 8.6. The demand curve DD' relates to the demand for the use of an urban motorway. The marginal social-cost curve shows the costs of congestion only, that is, the time delays that an additional user imposes upon other motorists. The horizontal axis measures the volume of cars per unit of time. Below a volume of OM there is no congestion and the marginal social cost is zero. Up to this volume of traffic no charge is required from the point of view of efficiency, since an additional person's use of the motorway in no way hinders existing users. If a charge were imposed, this would restrict the number of users and thus the total net benefit derived.

As the volume of traffic increases beyond OM each additional vehicle causes some measure of congestion in that it increases journey times for existing users. Marginal social cost becomes positive, and as the volume of traffic increases the costs of congestion increase at an increasing rate. Given the demand and cost conditions shown in Figure 8.6, if no attempt were made to restrict demand, the volume of traffic would increase to OQ and congestion would be considerable. The optimal position is a traffic volume equal to ON, where the benefit to the marginal user of the motorway is equal to the marginal social cost. There are a number of ways of restricting the volume of traffic to this level.

Figure 8.6

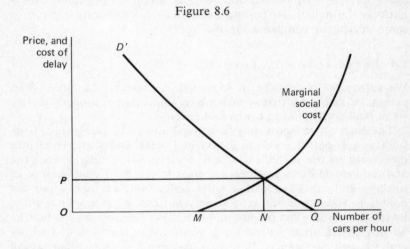

8.41 *Policies to Control Congestion*

From the analysis of the last section we know that one way of achieving the optimal position is to impose a congestion tax on the motorist equal to OP. If the policy maker is to calculate the correct level of tax to impose, he must clearly have some knowledge of the demand and cost conditions. The following simple example gives an idea of how estimates of congestion costs have been made. Suppose that the volume of traffic is 3 000 vehicles per hour and that average speed is 10 miles per hour. Then if we know the extent to which an additional vehicle will reduce the average speed, we can arrive at a figure for time lost per mile. For each existing vehicle the time lost due to an additional vehicle using the road will be small – let us assume it to be 0.01 minute per mile per vehicle. But the sum total of time lost is 3 000 times this figure, that is, 30 minutes' delay per mile. To convert this to a money figure we need an estimate of the value of time to those using the motorway. Taking a figure of £1 per hour, a delay of 30 minutes per mile means a cost on others of 50p per mile. The same calculation can be made for different volumes of traffic, so that it is possible to trace out a curve for the marginal cost of congestion. Given this information, and also the appropriate information on the demand side, a congestion charge approximating *OP* could in principle be calculated.

The above analysis, of course, grossly oversimplifies the estimation exercise. Several complicating factors have to be taken into account. First, an optimal charging system should take account of the fact that congestion varies according to the time of day, and this should be reflected in multiple charges. Second, congestion costs are also related to the type of vehicle, so that in principle there should be different charges for different types of vehicle – higher for private motor cars than buses, and higher still for heavy commercial vehicles. Third, the optimal tax must take into account not only mutual congestion costs but also the whole range of other social costs, such as noise, smell, damage to buildings, danger to life and limb, and so on. Fourth, there are problems of measurement. In the simple example used above the most difficult problem is that of valuing time. This particular measurement problem, and others, is discussed in detail in Chapter 9. Anticipating the outcome of that discussion, however, it is clear that, whatever figures are finally used, some rather arbitrary assumptions are likely to have been made in the process of arriving at them.

Nevertheless, as we have already pointed out, the difficulties in arriving at reasonably accurate measurements, in this case of the social costs of traffic congestion, should not be used as an excuse for failing to introduce appropriate policies. Failure to take all the social costs into account, for instance, simply means that the calculated marginal social costs will be an underestimate of the true costs and that a tax based on the calculations will be too low. Inaccuracies of this kind are not a justifiable reason for failing to tackle the problem. A problem clearly exists, and as long as a policy approach exists that can improve matters that policy should be introduced.

So far we have analysed the problem and its solution solely in terms of a tax on vehicle users. What is required, however, is to restrict the volume of traffic to *ON*, and a tax is only one of the possible ways of achieving this. Other possibilities are some form of administrative regulation, and subsidies for public transport.

The quantitative regulation of traffic includes not only parking restrictions but also such schemes as one-way systems, bus-only lanes, traffic lights and pedestrianised areas. Such measures clearly have an important part to play in smoothing the flow of traffic, but in general they may do little to deter the vehicle user in urban areas. Parking restrictions as such may even make matters worse, if they simply force people to drive around for longer periods looking for a space. Increased parking charges would certainly have some deterrent effect, but they would not affect through traffic and other vehicles that go into town centres without actually parking. Pedestrianised shopping areas, which are out of bounds to private vehicles and which are accessible to delivery vehicles at restricted times, also have an important part to play in improving the urban environment. But car-free zones are practical only for relatively small areas within any city. Introduced on a large scale such schemes would lead to a far greater reduction in the use of cars than was required, and would be grossly unfair to those living within the designated zones.

An alternative, or additional, policy approach is to subsidise public transport. A major part of the urban transport problem is the fact that relative prices are out of line with relative costs – specifically, that, in relation to costs, the price of private transport is too low relative to the price of public transport. If it is not practicable, possibly for political reasons, to impose substantial extra charges upon private transport so as to bring relative prices into line with relative costs, the alternative is to lower the price of public transport by means of subsidies. Here after all is a case of two services – private and public transport – that are close substitutes, one of which generates important external diseconomies. If for any reason the charges for the latter cannot be brought into line with marginal social costs, the alternative way of adjusting relative prices is to subsidise the competing service.

There are, however, a number of problems associated with such a policy. First, it is possible that the two services are not such close substitutes as is often supposed. If this were true, public transport charges would have to be lowered very substantially to have a worthwhile impact, and subsidies would have to be correspondingly large. Second, there is the usual problem with subsidies of ensuring the internal efficiency of the organisation that receives them. Third, subsidies will tend to encourage commuting over longer distances. This will increase the number of people working in town centres, and in the long run it may even lead to increased traffic congestion if, as real incomes increase, people switch back to private transport.

The logical solution then is to impose taxes on those causing the external diseconomy. A congestion tax has the merit of tackling the problem directly. Furthermore, an optimal tax has the advantage that it not only limits social costs in the short run within reasonable bounds, but also provides accurate information for investment appraisal. Without a tax the demand for road space might on the surface be so great as to indicate the need for a large extension of road capacity. However, a tax that equated what motorists pay to short-run marginal social cost would probably mean a substantial reduction in the use of private vehicles, which in turn would indicate a substantially lower level of investment in extra road capacity. Indeed it is conceivable that the volume of traffic would be so much reduced that no additional capacity at all would be required. An optimal pricing policy for the use of roads is therefore essential for making efficient investment decisions.

8.42   *The Problems of Implementing a Congestion Tax*

As noted earlier, in order to keep the flow of traffic continuously at the optimum level, a number of different charges would be required for different types of vehicle, at different times of the day and week, and in different parts of the city. However, it is necessary to distinguish between what is required for an ideal theoretical solution and what is practical, and considerations of practicality will dictate the selection of a highly simplified version of any theoretical solution. Even then, a simple tax scheme would not be without its problems.

First, care would have to be taken to make such that the charges were known well in advance, so that people could plan their adjustments to them. It would also be wise to introduce the estimated optimal tax over a period of time rather than in one fell swoop. In some cases the level of congestion might be so great that the implementation of a charging system based on short-run marginal cost would involve exceptionally high charges and a great deal of hardship to some people. A phased introduction of charges, announced in advance, would ease the situation and make for more efficient adjustment.

Second, there are considerations that suggest that a congestion tax would be best introduced at the local rather than the national level. This would have the benefit of enabling one area to benefit from the experience of another. Furthermore, both the severity of the congestion problem and the likely effects of introducing a tax vary from one area to another, and it is desirable that special local conditions be taken into account when formulating policy. As far as the magnitude of the problem is concerned, it is likely that congestion levels vary fairly systematically with the size of town, and that the case for introducing a tax is greater in large urban areas than in small ones.

As to the likely effects of a tax, this again will depend on circumstances. Any tax will have a number of effects, such as persuading people to change their route, to alter the time of their journey, to reduce the number of journeys, to make more use of public transport, to make greater use of pooling arrangements, and so on. The quantitative importance of these factors will vary from place to place, and special local conditions should be taken into account.

In some areas it may well be that the opportunities for adjusting to a tax are very limited, so that over a wide range congestion charges would have little effect. However, in general, and in view of the several different responses that can occur, it may well be that a modest tax would have a substantial effect on the pattern and volume of traffic. In this context it is also worth noting that the required reduction in peak period traffic is probably small, say of the order of 10 per cent. Furthermore, a tax would induce certain changes in institutional arrangements – such as more flexible office hours – which would increase the possibilities of adjustment. A reduction in the level of congestion would make bus services more attractive by increasing the reliability and frequency of service, and this would offer a further stimulus to people to change from private to public transport and thus reduce congestion.

It is worth emphasising here the important problem of the availability of public transport. The rapid growth in the use of the motor car and the decline of public transport mean that a sudden change of policy that induced a move towards the latter might well be frustrated by insufficient capacity. Certainly the frequency and reliability of public transport services in many areas would have to be improved and an adequate service be made available when a tax was introduced. This serves again to emphasise the importance of forward planning, and also of the need to base such planning at the local level, because here again the quality of public transport varies from place to place. The provision of public services and the introduction of a congestion tax on motorists would therefore have to be looked at as a whole. There are difficulties involved, of course, such as anticipating beforehand the likely need for extra public-transport capacity. The more responsive the motorist to a congestion tax the greater the increase in public-transport capacity that will be required. But an attempt must be made to foresee the likely consequences of a tax, and this will be facilitated by the recommendation made earlier of introducing the tax in stages over a period of time. And on the question of planning, the important interrelationship between housing and transport policy cannot be overemphasised. In many cities the problem of transport has been exacerbated by the large scale demolition of inner city housing, with the people herded out to large housing estates on the outskirts of the city, that are very often badly supplied with public transport facilities. An integrated urban development that took full account of the transportation consequences of housing decisions might well have put rather less emphasis on rehousing and more on the renovation and rebuilding of houses in the inner city.

The third problem likely to arise even from the most simple tax system concerns the income distribution consequences of the policy.

A congestion tax discriminates in favour of those who place a high value on speed or time saving. It also favours those who can afford to pay. In fact, the value that people attach to time is related to income, so the two are interrelated. But even if this were not the case, there would, as in all markets, clearly be discrimination in favour of those with higher incomes who could best afford to pay. This would not constitute much of a problem if the distribution of income was generally accepted to be fair, but where this is not the case, equity considerations assume importance. As pointed out earlier, the best way of tackling the problem of equity is directly, by the use of fiscal measures. There are cases, such as in the provision of health services, where there are also strong arguments in favour of the manipulation of price on grounds of equity, but it is not clear that the price of road space is a good candidate for such treatment. In so far as a satisfactory fiscal corrective to the problem of income distribution is some way off, however, this aspect of the problem cannot be ignored.

To what extent, then, is it likely that equity considerations will be a powerful argument against the introduction of a congestion tax? There may be cases where people on relatively low incomes have to pay the tax because of the absence of public transport, or because even though public transport is available it means substantially longer travelling time in getting to work. The importance of this factor depends on circumstances – for instance, the extent to which car sharing is possible, the quality of public transport and the elasticity of demand for road space. If the latter is high, and if many people in residential areas near to the city centre do make adjustments, then the charge required will be modest. On the other hand, if the elasticity of demand is low, the congestion charge will have to be high, and so considerable hardship will be imposed upon certain sections of the travelling public. There may be a case, therefore, for compensation, possibly in the form of a reduction in the car licence fee or the tax on cars. This would, of course, encourage car ownership, and it would mean that the congestion tax would have to be higher in order to achieve a given reduction in the volume of traffic. There is something to be said, however, in favour of a system that increased the spread of car ownership but discouraged the use of cars in urban areas at peak periods. It would bring the advantage of mobility, which the car offers, within the reach ·of more families without, hopefully, the disadvantages of congestion.

There are other considerations to be taken into account on equity matters. First, we should not forget the benefits of improved public transport to the very poor, who do not own cars. Second, a tax, as well as relieving congestion, will raise revenue that can be put to good use. It might, as mentioned earlier, be used in part to compensate the motorist, but there is no compelling reason why it should be. Alternatively, the revenue raised might be used to finance improvements in social services or a higher level of welfare payments, which would benefit all low income families. The amount of revenue raised will, of course, be related to the elasticity of demand for road space. The more elastic the demand, the lower the tax required to achieve a given objective and the smaller the revenue raised. The more inelastic the demand, the higher the tax required to achieve a target reduction in congestion and the more revenue raised. Third, the heavily used urban roads tend to be concentrated in the poorer areas. Any policy measure that limits congestion and improves the possibilities for urban planning will benefit low income groups disproportionately. Fourth, it is worth remembering that 'the motorist' also breathes and is capable of appreciating cleanliness. The person who drives his car into town will appreciate the advantages of less congestion, both as a member of the travelling public and also as a pedestrian and shopper. In addition to the benefits of a smoother journey, there will then be wider benefits to be appreciated as well. Indeed there is no reason why those who pay the tax should inevitably be, or even feel, worse off.

On balance it seems that, taking a broad view of the effects of a congestion tax, considerations of equity do not add up to a powerful argument against its introduction. The more important obstacles in the way of introducing a congestion tax are the technical and administrative costs involved in setting up a system that would enable the authorities to tax motorists in relation to their use of cars in urban areas.

8.5   PUBLIC GOODS

The essential characteristic of a public good is that its consumption by one person does not detract from its availability to others. In other words there is non-rivalry, or a zero opportunity cost, in consumption. National defence, police protection, radio broadcasting and uncongested roads and parks and theatres are typically quoted as examples. Thus the fact that one person feels more secure as a result of expenditure on national defence does not prevent other people from also feeling more secure. The fact that one person tunes in to a radio broadcast does not prevent other people from doing so too. If a theatre is not full the presence of one extra person does not stop others from enjoying the performance, so long, that is, that the relevant variable is the ability to see and hear the performance rather than to see and hear it from a particular position. And if there are a number of people who smoke during the performance, and the smoke fills the theatre, one person's 'consumption' of the smoke does not limit that of another – an example of a public 'bad'. In contrast, private goods, such as bread and butter, feature rivalry in consumption, because the consumption of a unit of the good by one person precludes consumption of the same unit by others.

It should be clear from this that public goods and externalities are very closely related – the difference being one of degree rather than kind. Indeed we can think of public goods as extreme examples of externalities, or of externalities as activities with a public good content. Take the case of a well-kept garden. The fact that a passer-by benefits from being able to admire the garden does not detract from the satisfaction enjoyed by the owner or by other passers-by. This is an example of an external economy. A similar situation, however, arises in the case of a lighthouse, which is often quoted as an example of a public good. The benefit that the lighthouse gives to one ship does not prevent other passing ships from benefiting as well. There is, however, a difference between the two cases in terms of motivation. The benefit that the garden gives to passers-by may be quite unintentional, whereas the lighthouse is there for the express purpose of steering all ships clear of the rocks.

It should also be noted that the classification of goods may change with circumstances. Take, for instance, the case of a swimming pool. When there are only a few people in the pool it has the characteristics of a public good. The swimmers do not inconvenience one another, and an additional swimmer can be added without inconveniencing those already in the pool. As more and more people are added a point comes when they start competing for space. At this stage, additional swimmers cause congestion and all those in the pool will suffer – we have an externality. Alternatively one could think of the congestion itself as a public good (or bad) that all the users have to suffer. At the extreme we can imagine a situation where congestion is so great that the attendant will only admit another customer as someone leaves the pool. At this point swimming space has become a private good.

This example draws attention to the fact that public goods are produced under conditions of joint supply, and the question of whether or not it is possible to supply a public good by private enterprise depends on the excludability characteristics of the good. Exclusion by the producer means that he is able to prevent a consumer from using the good. Where this is the case, the producer can charge a price for the use of the good and it is possible for the market system to work. Where exclusion is impossible, a price cannot be charged and the market will not work. Excludability always exists for private goods but may or may not exist in the case of public goods. For instance, exclusion is possible in the case of an uncongested road bridge, but not in the case of national defence.

Exclusion is also a relevant concept for the consumer. It exists where the consumer can choose whether or not to consume the good. This is normally the case for private goods but not always the case for public goods. For instance, the consumer can choose whether or not to listen to a radio broadcast by switching the radio on or off, but the consumer is compelled to consume national defence whether he likes it or not.

Excludability is clearly a matter of degree, and it is possible to exclude in most cases – at a cost. In some cases, however, although it may be possible for the producer to exclude people from consumption and thus to introduce a charge for the use of the good, the costs involved in doing so may be so high that it will not be profitable to supply the good. Even where exclusion and a system of charges are feasible, it may not be socially optimal to supply the good on a market basis – for, if the marginal social cost of supplying an extra customer is zero, then, for allocative efficiency, price should also be zero. An important example of this problem, examined in the previous chapter, is that of the payment for new knowledge – for new knowledge, once discovered, is a public good. Its use by one person does not prevent its use by another. And yet by means of the patent system access to new knowledge is in practice often restricted, and when it is made available it is only at a price.

Having identified the nature of the public good case, let us now turn briefly to a simple analysis of some of the problems to which public goods give rise. Figure 8.7 shows the demand and cost con-

Figure 8.7

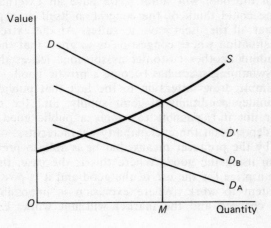

ditions for a public good, assuming for simplicity that there are only two consumers. D_A shows consumer A's marginal valuation of different quantities of the good, and D_B shows consumer B's marginal valuations. The sum of these curves gives the aggregate demand schedule, DD'. It should be noted that, whereas individual demand curves for private goods are summed horizontally, in the case of a public good they are summed vertically, so that at output OM the sum of the marginal valuation is equal to marginal cost. This is because individual consumers are faced with a given quantity of the good and are unable, as in the case of private products, to consume different quantities at a given price.

At output OM it is clear that the total benefit derived by the two consumers is greater than the cost of supplying that quantity. It is also clear, however, that each consumer's marginal valuation of quantity OM is less than the marginal cost of supplying that quantity. For the good to be supplied privately, consumers must be prepared to make contributions, and if the latter are to be related to benefits received, each individual must be prepared to reveal his true benefit from having the good. As we have seen, however, once a given quantity of a public good is made available to some it will, where exclusion is impossible or unprofitable, be available to other consumers at zero marginal cost. If individuals are motivated by selfishness, each one, hoping to get something for nothing, will attempt to conceal his own true benefits from having the good and hope that the financial burden will be shouldered by others. However, since everyone behaves in this way the amount of finance forthcoming from voluntary contributions may not be sufficient for the good to be supplied privately.

The magnitude of the problem depends upon circumstances. The more altruistic people are, for instance, the more likely they are to reveal their true preferences rather than selfishly to conceal them in order to get a 'free ride'. Again, individuals may behave selfishly because they suspect that others will do so, but if they can be assured that 'fair' contributions will be made by others, they may well be prepared to contribute their own fair share. Most important of all, however, in determining the feasibility of private provision, is the minimum scale at which the good can be supplied and the number of people involved. The smaller that the minimum feasible quantity of the good that can be supplied is in relation to an individual's resources, the more likely it is, other things being equal, that the good can be supplied by private enterprise. The more costly the good, however, and the greater the financial risks that individuals must take, the less likely it is that they will be prepared to reveal their true preferences in the contributions that they are prepared to make. As far as numbers are concerned, the smaller they are the more likely it is that an acceptable pattern of contributions can be established. With small numbers it is easier to reach an agreement of the 'if you contribute this much I will contribute that much' type. This is due both to the ease of communication and to the difficulty of evasion. As the number of individuals increases, however, so do the costs of communication, and the easier it becomes for some people to get lost in the crowd.

Where the private provision of a public good is not feasible, one alternative is for it to be supplied by charity. Otherwise it will have to be supplied by the state and financed by taxation. Public provision, however, ensures only that the good is supplied. It does not solve the problem of how much of it to supply. This has to be tackled with the aid of cost–benefit analysis, a subject that will be examined in the next chapter.

Chapter 9

Cost–Benefit Analysis

9.1 INTRODUCTION

We now turn to an examination of investment appraisal in the public sector, and in particular to the technique of cost–benefit analysis. At the outset we need to consider two questions. First, what are the theoretical foundations of cost–benefit analysis? Second, how and why is it different from investment appraisal in the private sector?

The theoretical foundations of cost–benefit analysis are found in the theory of welfare changes, which was examined in Chapter 3. It may be advisable to recap on some of the salient points of that analysis before proceeding to more practical matters. First, the theory is based on the value judgement that welfare is increased if one person is made better off and no one worse off. Optimality therefore requires that there is no way of increasing one person's surplus without reducing that of others. Second, the theory is concerned with the assessment of the benefits and costs that would result from a policy change and as far as possible attempts to bring these benefits and costs within the scope of the measuring rod of money. Third, the compensation principle states that, if benefits exceed costs, then it is *possible* for everyone to be made better off following a policy change. The implication is that the policy should be implemented so long as benefits exceed costs even if compensation is not paid. As was emphasised in Chapter 3, the theory of welfare changes has severe limitations. In particular the distributional effects of any policy measure must be taken into account. The fact that an investment appraisal reveals that benefits are greater than costs means only that everyone *can* be made better off and not that they *will* be better off. The implementation of the investment decision may in fact lead to adverse distributional effects. The recommendation of a policy therefore depends both on benefits exceeding costs and on the distributional consequences being acceptable.

Let us now turn to the question of what distinguishes cost–benefit analysis from investment appraisal in the private sector based on profit-maximising considerations. After all, private firms do take account of benefits and costs in arriving at investment decisions.

The answer is that private firms are concerned only with private costs and benefits whereas cost–benefit analysis is concerned with social costs and benefits. Thus, for instance, a private firm does not have to take into account any external costs that its investment may inflict upon others. These costs will, however, be included in a cost–benefit study. As another example, a firm's investment may result in the employment of hitherto unemployed workers who would otherwise have remained unemployed for the duration of the life of the project. The firm, in its profit and loss calculations, will include the cost of labour valued at the wage that is paid. In a cost–benefit study, however, the relevant cost is the opportunity cost of the labour employed, which in this case will be well below the wage paid and may indeed even be negative.

Under rather special circumstances, profit-maximising behaviour will result in the maximisation of economic welfare for society as a whole. Such circumstances, which were assumed throughout the analysis of Chapters 1 and 2, include the existence of universal perfect competition and the absence of externalities. All social costs and benefits would then be accurately reflected in market prices. In such a world, profit-maximising behaviour would, assuming an acceptable distribution of income, result in the maximisation of welfare. With indivisibilities absent and with prices everywhere equal to marginal cost, not only would the correct levels of output be produced in the short run, but also the profits and losses made by firms would provide accurate signals for the adjustment of capacity. This simple solution, however, does not apply when we move into a world characterised by imperfect competition and externalities. We have noted in earlier chapters many of the complications that arise. For instance, under conditions of decreasing cost, marginal cost pricing results in losses, so that unless price discrimination or multipart tariffs can be introduced a separate test is required for investment appraisal. In the case of public goods, provision is frequently made free of charge, so that again a separate test for investment is required. Another example is in cases where the supply of a good has important external effects, so that costs and benefits will not be accurately reflected in market prices. It is therefore in cases such as these, where prices are not charged or are below full unit cost, and where important externalities exist, that cost–benefit analysis is appropriate.

One further point needs to be made before turning to the details of cost–benefit analysis. In practice there are two types of investment decision that have to be made in the public sector. First, there is the decision on *how much* money should be allocated over a given number of years to the health service, or education, or coal mining, and so on. Second, there is the decision on *how* the given sum of money that has been allocated to a particular sector can best be allocated among the various investment opportunities within that sector. For example, should the £x made available to the health service be spent on building a new hospital or on opening a number of health clinics? And should the £y allocated to education be spent on equipment for universities or on building new primary schools in inner city areas? In principle the distinction between these two levels of decision making should be unnecessary, since investment funds should be allocated to any project, in whatever sector, that succeeds in passing some test, say a minimum rate of return. However, there are two major obstacles to planning investment in this grand centralised manner. First, the returns on all investments – whether in building hospitals, schools, roads, power stations, city halls or law courts – would have to be expressed in one common unit of measurement – a degree of standardisation that is most unlikely ever to be achieved given the diversity of goods and services produced in the public sector. Second, there would be considerable administrative problems. In practice, to make things manageable, top level decisions are made that determine the total budgets of individual government departments and corporations, and lower level decisions are then made on how to allocate the budget between investment projects. It is with these lower level decisions that we shall be concerned.

9.2 INVESTMENT CRITERIA

The returns to any investment project arise over a number of future time periods, and, as will be shown later, the time pattern of costs and benefits is crucially important in determining the outcome of project appraisal. Let us suppose for a moment that all the relevant costs and benefits associated with a number of investment projects are known with certainty and are quantifiable, that there is no problem in valuing future costs and benefits, and that there is no problem of income distribution. We are then left with the question of what criterion to use in order to choose between the investment projects. The two criteria most commonly used by economists are the net discounted present value (NPV) and the internal rate of return (IRR).

9.21 *Net Discounted Present Value*
In the case of (NPV) the benefits and costs of an investment project are estimated for each year of the project's life. Costs are subtracted from benefits, and the net benefits are expressed in terms of their present value. In order to perform this exercise we need a rate of discount that expresses our relative valuation of present and future sums of money, that is, a rate of time preference.

So that we understand the relationship between present and future values, let us start with the question of what is the future value of a given sum. Suppose that £100 is invested at 10 per cent per annum. In one year's time it will be worth $100(1 \cdot 10)$ or 110. Assuming the rate of interest to be the same for the second year, if the 110 is reinvested, it will at the end of the year be worth $110(1 \cdot 10)$ or $100(1 \cdot 10)^2 = 121$. And so on for subsequent years. Thus the future value F of an initial sum P is given by the expression

$$F = P(1 + i)^n$$

where i is the rate of interest and n the number of years. Let us now turn the question around and ask what is the present value of £110 due in one year's time, if the rate at which future values are discounted (that is, our rate of time preference) is 10 per cent. The answer is clearly 100. Similarly, if the rate of discount is the same for the second year as for the first, the present value of £121 due in two years' time is 100. In other words, the present value, V, of a given sum, B, available in the future is given by the expression

$$V = \frac{B}{(1 + r)^n}$$

where r is the rate of discount and n the number of years.

We can now proceed directly to the formula for the NPV investment criterion. Take the simple case of a project with a capital outlay of K in year 0 and a life of 3 years with net benefits of B_1, B_2 and B_3, all costs and benefits being in real terms. The stream of net benefits can be written as

$$\text{NPV} = -K_0 + \frac{B_1}{(1 + r)} + \frac{B_2}{(1 + r)^2} + \frac{B_3}{(1 + r)^3}$$

According to this criterion the investment should be undertaken if the discounted present value of the stream of net benefits is positive. Suppose, for instance, that a project with a life of 3 years involves an initial outlay of 100, and that the stream of net benefits in years 1, 2 and 3 is 40, 50 and 42 respectively. Let the rate of discount be 5 per cent. We then have

$$\text{NPV} = -100 + \frac{40}{(1 \cdot 05)} + \frac{50}{(1 \cdot 05)^2} + \frac{42}{(1 \cdot 05)^3}$$

The discounted present value of net benefits is equal to 120, and subtracting from this the initial capital outlay of 100 gives a net discounted present value of 20. Accordingly the project passes the investment test.

It is clear that a change in the discount rate will change the present value of net benefits, and that the higher the discount rate is the lower the present value will be. In the numerical example given above the present values of the net benefits, assuming discount rates of 10, 15 and 20 per cent, are 109, 100 and 92 respectively, and the net discounted present values are 9, 0 and −8. Thus if the appropriate discount rate were 20 per cent, this particular project would not be recommended. The relationship between the discount rate and the net present value is shown in Figure 9.1.

Figure 9.1

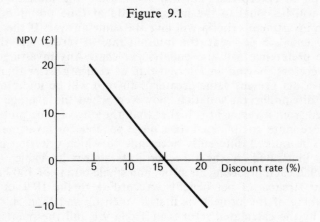

It will be noticed that there is a rate of discount, 15 per cent in the above example, that makes the present value of net benefits equal to the initial outlay. This is the internal rate of return (IRR) of the investment project.

According to the IRR criterion, an investment is recommended if the internal rate of return is greater than the predetermined rate of time preference. In this case, therefore, we have

$$K_0 = \frac{B_1}{(1 + i)} + \frac{B_2}{(1 + i)^2} + \frac{B_3}{(1 + i)^3}$$

where, as previously, the Bs represent the stream of net benefits and i is the rate of discount that makes the present value of this stream equal to the initial outlay K_0, that is, the internal rate of return. In the example given earlier we saw that the value of i was

15 per cent, so if the rate of time preference were 10 per cent, the project would be recommended.

The question now arises as to which investment criterion should be used. It should be noted first of all that in a general equilibrium situation they come to the same thing. With the NPV criterion we saw that future values are discounted at a rate that reflects our relative valuation of present and future sums of money. With a perfect capital market each individual will be confronted by the same market rate of interest, and each will adjust his borrowing and lending so that in equilibrium the marginal rate of time preference of all individuals will be the same and equal to the market rate of interest. On the firm side each enterprise will invest until the rate of return is equal to the interest rate, which again is the same for all enterprises. Thus in equilibrium the internal rate of return will be equal to the marginal rate of time preference, and the two investment criteria will give the same answer. If the rate of interest equals 5 per cent, the internal rate of return and the rate of time preference will also equal 5 per cent. Any investment project, therefore, having an internal rate of return greater than 5 per cent or a net present value greater than zero will be undertaken.

In a disequilibrium situation, however, when the average return expected from investment is higher than the rate of time preference, things are more complicated. It is quite possible for investment projects to be ranked differently according to which criterion is used. This is illustrated by the three projects shown in Table 9.1 and Figure 9.2, each involving an initial and single outlay of 100 but with different streams of net benefits. According to the IRR criterion, the ranking of the projects is first *B*, then *C*, and then *A*. This is shown by the calculated returns in Table 9.1 and the points where the discounted benefits curves cross the horizontal axis in Figure 9.2. Notice that the IRR ranking is not affected by the rate of discount.

Table 9.1

Project	Initial Outlay Year 0	Net Benefits Year 1	Year 2	Year 3	IRR (%)	NPV of Project at Rate of Discount of 5%	10%	15%	20%
A	100	40	50	42	15	20	9	0	−8
B	100	55	50	45	24	37	25	15	7
C	100	0	45	120	20	44	27	13	0

If the NPV criterion is used to rank the investment projects and the rate of discount used is 15 or 20 per cent, the same answer is obtained as for the IRR criterion. However, if the rate of discount used is 5 or 10 per cent, the NPV ranking is different, with *C* ranked higher than *B*. In Figure 9.2 the problem reveals itself in the intersection of the two curves *B* and *C*. At discount rates up to 12 per cent *C* is ranked higher than *B*, but at rates above 12 per cent the ranking is reversed. Thus the reason why a conflict may occur in the ranking of projects is that, as shown earlier, the IRR ranking is not affected by the rate of discount, while the NPV ranking may change as a result of using a different discount rate. A conflict in the ranking of investment projects, therefore, may or may not occur, depending on the discount rate used in the NPV criterion. These considerations will be important in practice because, with capital rationing, decisions will frequently have to be made on which of two worthwhile projects to undertake.

Figure 9.2

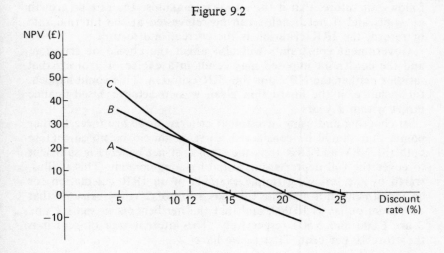

In the above numerical example, if the appropriate discount rate is 5 per cent, the NPV ranking differs from that given by the IRR criterion. Which criterion should be used? The answer depends on what is to be maximised, and on what constraints are imposed by government on the decision makers.

Throughout this book we have assumed that the objective of the government is to maximise consumers' welfare. Since the NPV criterion ranks projects according to the present value of net benefits, using the consumers' rate of time preference as the rate of discount, the choice of projects that results will be consistent with that objective. The IRR criterion, on the other hand, does not take account of consumers' time preference and is therefore inappropriate.

However, we should recognise that the government may have a different objective. Suppose, for instance, that the aim is to maximise the rate of growth of the capital stock. The government will then wish to plough back as much of the net benefits as possible into reinvestment. The IRR criterion does in fact assume that all net benefits can be and are reinvested as they accrue at the internal rate of return. Take, for instance, the example given earlier of an outlay of 100 and a stream of net benefits of 40, 50 and 42. The internal rate of return is 15 per cent. This implies that the 40 in year 1 are reinvested at 15 per cent so as to become 53 in year 3, and that the 50 in year 2 are similarly reinvested so as to become 57 in year 3. The net benefits accumulated by the end of the third year therefore equal $42 + 53 + 57 = 152$, which is what the initial outlay of 100 would amount to if invested at 15 per cent. It follows, therefore, that if the aim is to maximise the rate of growth of assets and if net benefits can be reinvested at the internal rate of return, the IRR criterion is the correct one to use.

Government constraints will also affect the choice of criterion, and the constraint imposed may result in a choice of projects that satisfies neither the NPV nor the IRR criterion. This could happen, for instance, if the instruction given was to achieve a self-finance target within 2 years.

In choosing and using investment criteria, there are three further points that should be considered. First, it should be noted that in both the NPV and IRR tests the stream of net benefits is sufficient to cover the full depreciation costs of the equipment. This is illustrated by the following simple example of an IRR calculation for an investment in a machine that has a life of 2 years. Assume that the initial outlay is 10 000, and that the net benefits in years 1 and 2 are 6 000 and 5 500 respectively. The internal rate of return is therefore 10 per cent. That is, we have

$$10\,000 = \frac{6\,000}{(1 \cdot 10)} + \frac{5\,500}{(1 \cdot 10)^2}$$

From this information we can derive the following table:

	Capital employed	Expected return	Capital Employed $\times$ 10%	Depreciation
Year 1	10 000	6 000	1 000	5 000
Year 2	5 000	5 500	500	5 000
				10 000

In year 1 the 10 per cent return on the capital employed leaves 5 000 available for depreciation. In year 2 the amount of undepreciated capital is 5 000, and a 10 per cent return on this leaves another 6 000 for depreciation in the second year. In each year, therefore, a return of 10 per cent is received, and at the end of the period the capital has been fully amortised.

Second, there is the importance of comparability. In comparing the returns from, say, investment in road and rail transport it is important to use the same criterion. In the case of past investment appraisal in the transport sector this has not always been so. There have been occasions, for instance, when investment in the railways has been based on a commercial-rate-of-return criterion while that in roads has been based on consumers' surplus analysis. Needless to say, such a procedure is bound to lead to an inefficient allocation of resources.

Third, if the NPV criterion is used, how should we rank alternative projects? There are three different ways of expressing the results of an NPV calculation: first by the excess of benefits over costs, $B - K$; second by the ratio of benefits to cost, B/K; and third by the ratio of net benefits to costs, $(B - K)/K$. Since the second and third methods give the same ranking we shall compare methods one and two.

Consider the following simple example, with the present values of outlays and benefits as shown in the K and B columns respectively

	K	B	$B - K$	B/K
A	200	250	50	1·25
Z	100	140	40	1·40

Assume that the government agency has a budget of 200. Should it choose project A or Z? According to the $B - K$ method project A is ranked first, but according to the B/K method it is ranked second. If there are no other opportunities open to the agency except to spend the 200 on A, or 100 on Z and return the other 100 to the government, then the correct method to use is $B - K$, which would select project A. However, suppose that other possibilities do exist. For instance, it may be possible to spend the 200 on two Z projects. In this case the Z project should be selected, because two of them give benefits of 280 and a $B - K$ of 80, which is higher than that obtained by spending the same sum of money on A. The B/K method of ranking is therefore correct. Or suppose that the Z project cannot be duplicated or expanded in size in any way, but that A is divisible into two equal parts. The best use of funds is to invest 100 in Z and 100 in A. The total benefits will be 265, and $B - K$ will equal 65. Once again the correct method of ranking the projects is seen to be B/K. The correct method of ranking the project thus depends on circumstances. If the only possibilities open to the agency are the two projects shown in the numerical example, the $B - K$ method is correct. However, if the size of either the A or Z project can be changed in any proportion, the B/K method is the one to adopt.

This discussion draws our attention to an important point, which is that in investment appraisal all feasible alternative projects must be compared. Let us illustrate this further by considering the choice between two other projects A and Z, using the NPV criterion. The initial outlays and net benefits over a number of years are given by K_0 and B respectively:

	K_0	B_1	B_2	B_3	B_4
A	200	80	80	40	40
Z	100	60	60	—	—

Project A involves an initial capital of 200 and a stream of net benefits over 4 years. Project Z, on the other hand, has a 2-year life and an initial outlay of 100. Assume that these are the only alternatives available, that the public agency has a capital budget of 200, and that the discount rate is 5 per cent. A will then be chosen, since it has the highest value of discounted net benefits minus initial outlay – that is, a net discounted present value of 16·20 as compared to 11·70 for Z. Suppose, however, that it is possible to repeat the Z project, the second 100 of capital outlay being expended in year 2 with net benefits of 60 in each of the subsequent 2 years. If this option exists, it is clearly possible for the agency to select it, because the total capital outlay involved does not exceed the budget. And indeed this will be the optimum choice, discounted net benefits minus capital outlay being equal to 21·70 for Z as compared to 16·20 for A. A correct selection of investment projects within the given political and financial constraints must therefore consider all feasible alternatives.

9.3   PROBLEMS IN INVESTMENT APPRAISAL

Now that we have considered the question of the choice of the investment criterion to be used, we turn to the practical problems involved in the evaluation of investment projects: what costs and benefits to include; how to value them and in particular how to value untraded goods; how to allow for uncertainty; and the choice of discount rate to discount future costs and benefits.

9.31   *The Costs and Benefits to be Included*
The simple answer to what should be included in the appraisal of an investment project is, of course, all relevant costs and benefits.

In so doing the analysis overcomes one of the deficiencies of the market, which is a failure to take account of externalities. However, in practice it is clearly impossible to take *all* the relevant cost and benefits, however distant, into account. This problem should not worry us unduly. The more distant effects of an investment will in general be small and can be safely ignored. Indeed it would be foolish to expend an enormous amount of effort in attempting to identify all repercussions, because the conduct of such investigations does itself impose a cost that has to be taken into account.

There are two particular pitfalls, however, which have to be avoided. The first is the handling of transfer payments and the second the danger of double counting. Briefly, transfer payments are not to be counted as costs or benefits, and real costs and benefits must be counted only once.

A transfer payment is a voluntary or compulsory passing of purchasing power from one individual to another that is not a payment for goods or services received. An obvious example is taxation. To the private firm that is considering an investment project the taxation that it will expect to pay out of the revenue from the project will be treated as a cost and deducted so as to arrive at a net profits figure. For society as a whole, however, it is clear that all that taxation does is to transfer part of the benefit of the investment project from the owners of the firm to other members of society. In cost–benefit studies, therefore, it is gross and not net profit that is relevant. At least, this is the case for investments made by a country's residents within the national economy. For investment overseas and for investment at home undertaken by foreign-based firms the position is a bit more complicated. In the case of overseas investment, taxation clearly has to be counted as a cost and deducted, for this part of the benefit goes to foreigners. On the other hand, in the case of inward investment the taxation of profits is part of the benefit, and the part of profit that is remitted overseas to the parent company should not be included as part of the benefit.

Another example of a transfer payment is the case of office dispersal. In recent years the UK government has adopted the policy of dispersing certain offices out of central London to other cities, such as Cardiff and Newcastle. As a result retail sales and profits are higher in Cardiff and Newcastle than they otherwise would have been. Not all of the increase in profits should be included as a benefit, however, because part of it will be due to a transfer of purchasing power and will be offset by lower sales and profits in London.

The second pitfall in identifying the costs and benefits of a project is the danger of double counting. Particular care must be taken not to include items in the list more than once. Consider an irrigation scheme that provides both a reservoir for fishing and sailing, and a controlled water supply that reduces the cost of producing the various crops cultivated in the area, say from C_2 to C_1 in Figure 9.3. Assuming competitive conditions, the effect is to increase consumers' surplus by an amount equal to area $C_2C_1P_1P_2$. This is a benefit and has to be added to the benefits of fishing and of sailing to set against the costs of the project. However, should the increased profits of farmers, wholesalers and so on be added to the benefits side? Clearly not, since this would involve double counting. The benefits arising from the cost-saving effects of the project have already been fully taken into account by measuring the gain in consumers' surplus that will occur if the cost saving is fully passed on to consumers in lower prices.

Figure 9.3

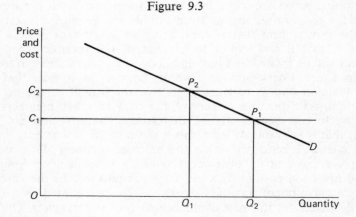

As another example take a project such as the extension of the M4 motorway in South Wales. One of the effects of this extension is to increase the price of houses located nearby. House prices rise because of the additional benefits that people gain in terms of quicker and cheaper access to jobs and shopping. Estimates of these benefits should be taken into account on an annual basis in the cost–benefit study. The increase in house prices should not be included as well, because this represents no more than the capitalised value of the stream of future benefits that residents receive from the building of the motorway.

9.32   *The Valuation of Costs and Benefits*
Having identified the costs and benefits to be included in the appraisal of a project, the next problem is how to value them.

Where a market price exists it often does not accurately measure the costs or benefits to society. In addition there are untraded goods that do not have a market price but that nevertheless have to be taken into account. This subsection considers the first of these problems, and the next subsection will consider the case of untraded goods.

On the costs side, what we are interested in is the opportunity cost of using a resource in one activity as compared to its value in alternative uses. If market prices always reflected opportunity costs, there would of course be no problem, but this is frequently not the case. 'Shadow prices', which reflect the full opportunity cost of resources used, must then be calculated and substituted for market prices.

This is best explained by taking the simple example of a project that employs hitherto unemployed workers. We shall assume, to simplify matters, that the workers would otherwise have remained involuntarily unemployed for the whole life of the project. Each worker, we shall assume, is drawing unemployment benefit of £20 per week. This is clearly not the opportunity cost of employing a worker, since unemployment benefits are transfer payments, which, as we saw earlier, must be excluded from costs and benefits. In terms of the output that is foregone by employing a worker the opportunity cost is zero, since no loss of output is incurred through diminishing the ranks of the unemployed. Matters are made slightly more complicated, however, by virtue of the fact that the unemployed worker may incur travelling costs in accepting a job and may also derive some pleasure from being unemployed, in the form, for instance, of having ample time to pursue his favourite hobbies. In this case the worker will have to be compensated in order to be induced to accept a job. Thus with unemployment benefit at £20 a week he may require, say, £24 to compensate him for the costs of travel to and from the place of work and the loss of leisure time. In this case the opportunity cost of employing the worker is equal to £4 per week. And if his marginal product in the project under appraisal is expected to be over £4, it will pay society to employ him. It may also be the case, of course, that the worker suffers such disutility in being out of work that he would be prepared to accept a job even if it offered only £18 a week. In this case the opportunity cost of employing him is −£2, and his employment would be a worthwhile proposition in any activity that promised a positive marginal product.

Similar considerations apply to the case of disguised unemployment. Assume that such a situation exists in the civil service. The wage paid to surplus labour will of course be positive, but it will in fact be a transfer from the productive sectors of the economy. In other words the loss of employment in the civil service would, up to a point, result in no loss of output. In terms of lost output, therefore, opportunity cost is zero. Displaced civil servants may, however, suffer costs in moving to another occupation – both costs of movement and perhaps the psychic costs of having to move to a less enjoyable job. The opportunity cost of placing the civil servants in productive employment would therefore equal the sum necessary to compensate them for these costs, and this is the sum that should enter the cost–benefit calculation – not their present wage.

9.33   *The Valuation of Untraded Goods*

Not only may market prices provide a misleading guide to social opportunity costs, but also in some cases they may not exist at all. For instance, in many investment projects time saving forms a substantial proportion of expected benefits. Correct investment appraisal thus depends crucially on being able to arrive at a reasonable measure of the value of time. Again, for many projects – and sometimes they are the same ones that give rise to time-saving benefits – the noise generated by the new activity is an important factor on the cost side. It is important to have some idea of the cost of this noise to those who suffer from it.

The Valuation of Time. Let us first take the problem of valuing time. It is customary to distinguish between time saved in working hours and leisure time. As far as work time is concerned it seems reasonable to value it at the going hourly wage rate, the argument being that this measures the marginal value of time to the worker and, also, the social value of an hour's labour. This will only be true, however, if the worker is free to choose the length of his working week and also, of course, in the absence of monopoly and external effects. In fact the length of the working week is determined by employers, government and unions. In some cases, university teachers for instance, there is considerable flexibility in deciding on the actual number of hours of work, and in other occupations absenteeism may give workers some degree of choice. In general, however, the number of hours to be worked is not something that workers are free to choose, and so there is no reason except chance why the wage rate should equal an individual worker's own valuation of time. As far as monopoly is concerned, if the workers are employed in a firm with monopoly power, then the marginal social product of an hour's work is higher than the wage. And if the worker is employed in an industry that generates an above-optimal amount of external diseconomies, the marginal product has to be adjusted downwards so as to make allowance for these external effects. The use of wage rates as a measure of the value of time savings is therefore only a very approximate measure.

The valuation of leisure time is even more problematic. The most common approach relies upon being able to infer a value of time from observing how individuals behave when faced with direct choices between travelling modes. Suppose that we observe in detail the travelling habits of a group of workers commuting from their homes to their places of work. Each worker will be faced with a choice between different travel modes – walking, cycling, car, bus, train, etc. Each of these modes will entail not only a different journey time but also a different money outlay. Observing each person's choice of travel mode will provide us with an indication of his time/money trade-off at the margin, that is, a measure of how much he values his time. For example, we might observe that an individual chooses mode A, involving 2 hours' travelling at a total cost of £1, in preference to mode B ($2\frac{1}{2}$ hours' travelling at 50p) and mode C ($1\frac{1}{2}$ hours' travelling at £1.70). This individual then appears willing to spend an extra 50p to save half an hour, but not an extra £1.20 to save an hour. We might conclude, therefore, that he values a 1-hour time saving at between £1 and £1.20. Over a large sample of individuals and many modal choices we should thus derive an average time value for each income group of individuals. Studies of this kind in Britain have arrived at a value for leisure time equal to about 25 per cent of the gross wage rate.

Of course, it is not only the time element that is important in decisions concerning the choice of transport. Other factors such as convenience, reliability, comfort, the ability to snatch forty winks, and safety also enter into the reckoning. Such factors have to be taken into account before an accurate measure of the value of time can be derived.

Another important problem associated with the valuation of time, whether in the form of work or leisure time, is the amount of time saved. It is common in cost–benefit studies in the transport sector to find that a particular road improvement is expected to make only a very small difference, a matter of seconds even rather than minutes, to each individual journey. However, if a large number of travellers are involved, the total benefit will look very substantial. It is doubtful, however, whether projects that rely on such calculations can be justified. If an investment results in only a tiny reduction in a person's travelling time, can it be said to have resulted in a significant increase in his welfare? No doubt there are cases where a minute one way or the other makes the difference between catching or losing a train or flight, and that minute can be quite valuable. However, this will only apply to a very small minority of cases. In the majority of cases one suspects that saving a minute or two on journey time is neither here nor there. The practice of multiplying these small time savings by the number of travellers in order to arrive at a figure of total benefit must therefore be regarded with suspicion.

The Valuation of Noise. Let us now turn to the cost side, and to an example of another item that figures prominently in the appraisal of many investment projects and is not properly valued by the market – the noise associated with such projects as investment in roads and airports. How are we to set about measuring the cost of noise, so that it may be entered into a cost–benefit analysis of, say, a proposal to turn a relatively little used regional airport into a major one? Increased noise levels resulting from such a change will affect many people. What is needed is a monetary measure of this inconvenience.

One possible line of attack is to observe what effect noise pollution has had on property values in an area that suffers from the inconvenience. Let us imagine two residential areas located near an airport, where the houses in both areas are identical except for the fact that in one case they are located directly under the flight path of incoming aircraft, whereas in the other case peace and quiet prevail. Assume also that the householders in the two areas have the same incomes but different tastes; that is, they have a different valuation of the noise inconvenience. We also assume for the moment that the costs of moving house are zero. When noise becomes a problem a general reshuffle in the pattern of house ownership will occur. Householders who live under the flight path and who have a low tolerance level for noise will take the first opportunity to move into the quiet area and will be prepared to pay a premium to get a house there. When equilibrium is established a differential will exist in house prices between the two areas, and the size of this differential will reflect the noise/income trade-off of the marginal householder, that is, the householder who finds that the existing price differential just offsets the noise differential and is therefore indifferent to where he lives. It may appear that the price differential times the number of houses in the noisy area can then be used as a monetary measure of the cost of noise.

We do in fact observe price differentials between identical houses in areas where polluting activities are undertaken. Will the above method, however, provide a reasonably accurate measure of pollution costs? The answer is almost certainly no.

The pollution changes likely to arise from public investment projects will be of the non-marginal kind. House price differentials, however, indicate only valuations at the margin. In this particular case they will in fact reflect the sensitivity to noise of the last householder to move to the quiet area or the householder in the noisy area who is on the verge of moving. The sensitivity to noise of these marginal householders, however, will be lower than that of other householders in the noisy area. In other words, the former are willing to pay a higher premium for a house in the quiet area than the latter. Consequently, to multiply the house price differential by the number of houses in the noisy area will overstate the true social cost of noise.

There are other factors, however, that indicate that this method of estimating social cost results in the undervaluation of the noise costs involved. First, there is the cost of movement. Such costs include not only the money cost of moving house but also non-monetary costs such as leaving old friends and a familiar environment and settling into a new neighbourhood. Second, many people have to live in areas of heavy pollution because those areas provide employment and because the costs of travel from outside the area would be prohibitive. Third, there will typically be very many people who would dearly like quieter surroundings but who live in noisy areas because they cannot afford to buy houses elsewhere. This point is most clearly seen if we assume that the householders within each area have the same sensitivity to noise but different incomes. The equilibrium price differential between houses in the two areas, after the adjustment to noise had taken place, would then be determined by the income of the marginal householder. The families left in the noisy area are there not because of a lower sensitivity to noise but because they are too poor to move out.

Thus even if differences in house prices were due only to differences in noise pollution levels, there is no reason to suppose that they would provide an accurate indicator of the social costs involved. In practice, it would of course be very difficult to carry out a study of house prices that fulfilled the conditions necessary for the above theorising to be applicable. Different areas vary considerably in the quality of housing, environmental facilities, population structure and so on, and it would be extremely difficult to standardise sufficiently to disentangle just the noise effect on the structure of house prices.

An alternative approach to the use of indirect market signals is to ask people to place a value on the inconvenience. There would clearly be a problem in asking people to put a value on a noise that they had not yet experienced. For some the actual noise level would turn out to be not as bad as they had anticipated, while for others it might be much worse. However, we could overcome this by conducting a survey of a similar sample of people who already suffer noise pollution in the vicinity of an existing airport similar in size to that of the proposed new one. More serious is the fact that the answers obtained from a questionnaire depend on the way in which the questions are put. As we saw in Chapter 3, a person can be asked to state the maximum sum that he is willing to pay in order to avoid noise, or he can be asked for the minimum sum that he will accept to put up with it. It is the latter sum, the compensating variation, that is relevant, assuming people are honest, since the first sum will be subject to an income constraint. A large number of people, for instance, will not be able to afford to do much about a noise nuisance and yet may suffer greatly from it. A measurement based on the maximum sum that they are able to pay will therefore greatly underestimate the social costs involved. On the other hand, a problem with the compensating variation is that people may exaggerate and claim sums well above the minimum that they would really be prepared to accept. As everyone who has conducted an interview will testify, the accuracy of the results obtained depends a great deal on the skills of the interviewer, and given interviewers who are good at their job there is no reason to believe that any alternative method of valuing noise is likely to get nearer the truth.

Finally on the problem of untraded items, it should be emphasised that in many cases it will be impossible to arrive at any money measure of the cost or benefit involved. What value do we attach, for instance, to the preservation of a beautiful landscape, and what is the cost of its destruction? Such items must not be omitted from a cost–benefit analysis simply because they cannot be brought within the scope of the measuring rod of money. The fact that certain costs and benefits arising from an investment project cannot be given precise monetary values is clearly a limitation of cost–benefit analysis, but this does not undermine its usefulness. Cost–benefit analysis is valuable first and foremost as a basis for well-informed decision making. Its function therefore is to present the various costs and benefits of a project in as complete and understandable a way as possible. Where it is not possible to calculate monetary values the investment analyst must present a full qualitative description of the costs and benefits involved. The significance of the non-quantifiable items has to be discerned by measuring the strength of feeling of the people involved. As was mentioned at the end of Chapter 3, pressure groups have an important function to play in resource allocation decisions.

9.34   *Optimal Prices and Investment*
The importance of having as accurate an assessment as possible of costs and benefits in project appraisal is so obvious that it may seem unnecessary to labour the point. Unfortunately one has only to listen to some of the pronouncements of people in authority to

realise that this simple point is still not fully appreciated. The suggestion, for instance, that because of a drought in some parts of the country work should proceed on developing a national water grid 'regardless of cost', or statements to the effect that traffic congestion always justifies more investment in road improvements and new road building, are examples of such pronouncements.

The basic problem is that, where market prices do not accurately reflect costs and benefits, the use of consumers' surplus analysis in the evaluation of investment projects may give very misleading results. Take, for instance, the case of investment in urban roads. The consumers' surplus derived from using a car in urban areas depends upon the price and availability of close substitutes. The more effective public transport is as a substitute for private transport the smaller the consumers' surplus will be, and vice versa. Actual traffic flows are of course a reflection of the existing pattern of charges, and, as we saw in Chapter 8, these charges fall below the marginal social cost of traffic in towns. And as well as being too low in general the price of private transport is too low compared to that of public transport. As a result the volume of traffic, especially private traffic, is pushed above the optimum level. This causes an increase in congestion. The higher the level of congestion, however, the greater will be the apparent benefits from road improvement schemes. This is because the higher the initial level of congestion the greater will be the time-saving benefits of the investment, and time saving forms a major part of the measurable benefits of road investment. Suppose, however, that an optimal system of charges were introduced and that the corresponding optimal traffic flows were established. The result might well be a substantially smaller traffic flow in urban areas, indicating the need for a lower level of investment. A correct system of charges is therefore vital to the proper appraisal of investment projects.

As another example of the relationship between price and investment policies, consider the case of the supply of water. The present position in Britain is that large industrial users are metered and pay a fixed charge plus a charge per unit consumed. The majority of consumers, however, simply pay a fixed charge per annum, so that there is no incentive at all to economise in the use of water. This means that, in terms of Figure 9.4, the consumption of water will be carried right up to point Q where the marginal utility is zero. If, as is very likely, the marginal utility curve for water consumption has a very shallow gradient over the higher levels of consumption, the quantity consumed, OQ, will be far in excess of the quantity, OM, where benefits and costs are equalised. By the same token a modest charge per unit of water consumed would result in a marked fall in consumption. The implications for investment appraisal are clear. The consumption of water will be very much higher than it would be if the supply of water were metered, and so storage capacity will also have to be much greater if water rationing is to be avoided. Costs, particularly the capital costs of installing meters, would be involved in changing over to a new pricing system. At the very least, however, investment appraisal in this sector should compare the benefits and costs of expanding storage capacity with the benefits and costs of changing to a system whereby the payment for water was related to the amount consumed.

Figure 9.4

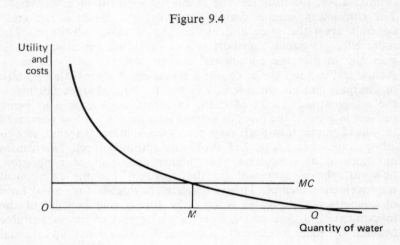

Quantity of water

9.35 *Uncertainty*

So far we have assumed that, in so far as they can be measured, the costs and benefits of an investment project are known with certainty. This assumes, however, that we have perfect knowledge of the future, of new discoveries of materials, of the development of new technologies, of changes in tastes and incomes, and so on. Clearly, we do not have such information, and some method of allowing for uncertainty about future costs and benefits has to be built in to investment appraisal.

A crude method of allowing for uncertainty – and one that might seem appropriate where the major element of uncertainty surrounded the life of a piece of equipment, because, say, of the embodiment of new technology – is to shorten the assumed length of life of the project. Thus a shorter life might be assumed for a nuclear as compared to a conventional power station, because of uncertainty surrounding the life of the nuclear reactor.

Another crude method is to increase the rate used for discounting future net benefits. This has a similar effect to the previous method since the higher discount rate will have the effect of reducing most heavily the present value of those projects where substantial benefits occur in the more remote future.

A more sophisticated approach, and one that goes to the heart of the matter, is to take each uncertain price and quantity and assess the probability of a number of values occurring. For instance, each uncertain item might be given three values: a low, medium and high value. Each value would then be given a probability weighting to reflect the likelihood that it will actually occur. Calculations of the net discounted present value would then be carried out for every combination of stated values. Each NPV result could be ascribed a probability measure equal to the product of the probabilities attached to each of its constituent items. In this way a probability distribution of net present values could be arrived at for each project. Thus for a particular project there might be a 75 per cent chance of the net present value lying in the range of £1 million to £1·5 million, a 10 per cent chance of its being over £2 million, and a 1 per cent chance of its being zero, and so on. The greater the number of uncertain items and the larger the number of probable values for each item, the more complicated the exercise. Even with only 6 items of cost and benefit and 3 alternative estimates of each, the number of possible NPV outcomes would be 729. Where the number of items to be handled is large the task could be made manageable by the use of computers. However, there is always a danger that impressive-looking computer print-outs will assume an authority that they do not possess. The value of this method of allowing for uncertainty depends upon our ability to attach sensible probabilities to the different possible outcomes for each uncertain item. The probabilities chosen will be subjective for they will be based upon the considered opinions of those who are consulted.

One specific problem with this approach is that of comparing overlapping probability distributions. Suppose that the distribution referred to above is to be compared with that of another project where the same capital outlay is involved, but where there is a 60 per cent chance of discounted net benefits less initial outlay lying in the range of £1 million to £1·5 million, a 20 per cent chance of its being over £2 million, and a 5 per cent chance of its being zero. If only one of the projects can be selected, which one should it be?

The problem of uncertainty is another problem to which there is no tidy solution. A great deal will inevitably depend upon the judgement of those making the decision, and no amount of clever statistical manipulation should conceal this fact.

9.36 *The Choice of Discount Rate*

So far we have assumed that the rate of discount to be used in discounting future benefits is one that reflects the rate of time preference of consumers. The correctness of this procedure is based on the assumption that the alternative to investment in the public sector is foregone private consumption. This, however, will not always be the case. Another possibility is that the opportunity cost of the capital is foregone private investment. If this is the case, the use of the rate of time preference for discounting benefits and costs in the public sector may lead to a misallocation of resources. For example, suppose that the ratio of net benefits to the capital cost of an investment project in the public sector is 0·1, using a rate of time preference of 5 per cent as the rate of discount. Suppose also that the ratio of net benefits to the capital cost of marginal projects in the private sector, using the same discount rate of 5 per cent, is 0·2. In this case, use of the NPV criterion in the public sector will allow the public investment project to pass the test, but it will yield a lower return than that available in the private sector.

The correct discount rate to use is the opportunity cost of the capital. This will depend on any constraints that the government may impose upon the public agency and on whether the funds raised for investment in the public sector are at the expense of private consumption, private investment or some combination of both.

Suppose first of all that a public agency such as British Rail has been allocated a given capital budget, and that the funds must be used for investment in rail projects or returned to the private sector. The correct discount rate to use depends on how the funds would have been used had they remained in the private sector. There are three possibilities. First, the funds may have been raised at the expense of private consumption only. The discount rate to use in this case is the rate of time preference. As long as net present value using this rate of discount is positive, the benefits produced by the investment will be greater than the benefits that would have been enjoyed if the same resources had been used instead for consumption. Second, the funds may have been raised at the expense of private investment only. If, further, the returns on investment in the private sector would have been wholly reinvested, the discount rate to use is the internal rate of return expected on private investment. The more likely case is of course one where the returns on investment in the private sector are partly consumed. The appropriate discount rate will then be somewhat lower than the private internal rate of return, and how much lower will depend on the marginal propensity to consume out of investment income, the discount rate being lower the higher the propensity to consume. It will always be higher than the rate of time preference, however, as long as the latter is below the internal rate of return. Third, the funds may have been raised at the expense of both private consumption and private investment. In this case the appropriate rate of discount will again lie somewhere between the rate of time preference and the internal rate of return expected on private investment. The actual discount rate will be determined by the apportionment of the funds raised between foregone consumption and investment in the private sector, and by the proportion of the private investment income foregone that would have been reinvested. The greater the proportion of the funds raised by reducing private consumption, and the lower the proportion of private investment income that is reinvested, the nearer will the discount rate be to the rate of time preference.

Suppose now that the government does not constrain the public agency to invest in its own projects in the public sector or not at all, but allows it to invest the funds where it can get the best return. Such an agency might be the National Enterprise Board, which was set up by the British government in 1975 in order to regenerate British industry. Since the aim of this agency is to strengthen the capital structure of the industrial sector, we can further assume that all investment returns will be reinvested. In this case the appropriate rate of discount to be used is equal to the rate of return expected on investment in the private sector – for in a disequilibrium position, when private investment is below the optimal level, the rate of return in private investment will be higher than the rate of time preference. The opportunity cost of investing in the public sector is thus the benefit foregone by not investing in private companies. Only if the net present value of public investment projects is positive, when using a discount rate equal to the internal rate of return expected in the private sector, should the projects be undertaken.

Although we may be able to decide in principle which rate of discount should be used in evaluating a particular public-investment project, there are still some rather hefty problems to be faced in evaluating the numerical value of that discount rate. These problems are important, because, as we saw earlier, the actual discount rate used will have important practical implications for the choice of projects. This is because the time pattern of costs and benefits may vary considerably from one project to another. The higher the discount rate, the less favourable will projects whose principal net benefits are further away in the future appear relative to projects whose principal net benefits come soon after the project has been undertaken.

The reasons why the calculation of the discount rate will pose difficulties should be clear from the preceding discussion. We need to know: what the rate of time preference is; what proportion of the funds that have been raised for public investment have been at the expense of private consumption; which investment projects in the private sector are to be taken for comparison; the expected rate of return on these investments; and the proportion of the annual returns that will be reinvested.

The most difficult problem of all is estimating the rate of time preference. What is required is an estimate of the rate of time preference for society as a whole, that is, the social rate of time preference. The first question to which we must address ourselves is whether market interest rates are likely to reflect at all accurately the social rate of time preference. To start with it should be pointed out that in equilibrium in a perfectly competitive economy there would be no problem. Any individual would be able to borrow and lend on the same terms as any other individual, so that everyone's marginal rate of time preference would be equal to the rate of interest. This interest rate would then be used to discount the stream of net benefits in the present value assessment of a project.

In practice, of course, there are several complications that have to be taken into account. First, there are differences in the terms at which people can borrow. These differences will reflect differences in such factors as the security provided, the duration of the transaction, and the nature of the activity for which the loan is required. As a result there are several market interest rates, each reflecting a different degree of risk. Differences in the terms of borrowing will mean that individuals will have different rates of time preference. Ideally, what is needed in the appraisal of any investment project is the rate of time preference of each individual who will contribute towards its financing. These rates would then be weighted according to the proportion of finance provided by each person, in order to arrive at a weighted average social rate of time preference. Needless to say, such information is hardly likely to be available to the policy maker. Second, market interest rates will be an accurate reflection of consumers' time preferences only if the information available to consumers is perfect. In reality, of course, information, especially about the future, is incomplete. Third, market rates are influenced by the government's macroeconomic policies, so that again factors other than time preference are being reflected.

In the face of such formidable difficulties the 'solution' that economists have often adopted is to take the yield on long-term government bonds as a reasonable approximation to the risk-free rate of interest – risk free, that is, in respect of default.

Even if this were generally accepted as being a satisfactory solution, however, or indeed if there were in fact only one interest rate in the market with none of the difficulties so far mentioned, there would still be other problems to face.

First, as a result of taxes on income or on capital the rate of return to the saver will be below the social rate of return on investment. Thus if the market rate of interest is 10 per cent, there will be an incentive to save and to lend money for investment if the yield on the investment is expected to be at least 10 per cent. However, if the return on the investment turns out to be 10 per cent before tax, this will of course mean a lower post-tax return, and the latter will clearly be below the real return to society. To allow for taxes, an individual who places the same value on £110 in one year's time as £100 now (that is, who has a rate of time preference of 10 per cent) will, if his marginal tax rate is 50 per cent, be prepared to lend only if the gross return on his investment is 20 per cent. The effect of income taxes and capital taxes is therefore to reduce the incentive to save and to invest.

Second, even in the absence of taxation, savings may be below the optimum level because when it comes to evaluating present and future consumption people are not good judges of their own well-being. As Pigou put it, they may have faulty 'telescopic faculties', which result in too much weight being put on present consumption and not enough on the future. In other words, future benefits are discounted too heavily, with the result that consumption is higher and investment lower than it should be in the interests even of members of the present generation. This is one reason why the market rate of interest may be above the social rate of time preference.

Third, and reinforcing the previous point, market interest rates reflect private, not social, rates of time preference. In particular, the market does not adequately take account of the interests of future generations. Now it may be that people are concerned about the welfare of future generations and derive satisfaction from the thought that by abstaining from consumption now they will increase the living standards of people as yet unborn, but this is not reflected in the level of interest rates. Certainly there are people who are concerned that continuing economic growth will result in a marked decline in the environment and the extinction of certain species, so that future generations' consumption of natural beauty will be at a lower level than their own is today. Similar concern exists over the rate of depletion of other exhaustible resources, such as oil and minerals. However, even if members of the present generation were not concerned about future generations, it could still be argued that the government should be. In either case, if the argument is valid, the implication is that the market rate is above the social rate of time preference, and thus discounting at the market rate would attach a lower value to future benefits than would be appropriate. It should be pointed out that the strength of this argument varies according to the type of investment being considered. It is stronger for the case of investments that lead to a depletion of exhaustible resources than for investments in man-made capital goods, which can be replenished, and where technical progress will in any case work to the advantage of future generations. As far as investment in capital goods is concerned, the argument that the market neglects the interests of future generations is stronger for projects with a short life span than for those with a long life.

What does all this amount to? We can be fairly certain that the social rate of time preference is below the average social yield of investment, partly because of the existence of taxation, and also because we are always in practice in a short-run disequilibrium position where investment has not reached the level that reduces the average yield to the rate of time preference. We do not have, and are most unlikely ever to have, the information that would allow us to calculate the social rate of time preference. The best that we can do is to use what seems to be a reasonable proxy – the rate of interest on long-term government bonds. It is possible, though on this point there is even less certainty, that such a rate would still be above the social rate of time preference, because of a failure of the market to have full regard for the welfare of future generations.

9.4   CASE STUDIES

We now turn to examine two cost–benefit studies that have actually been undertaken in the United Kingdom. The first study is an investigation of the social benefits of constructing an extension to the underground network in London. The second is an inquiry into the optimal siting of a third London airport. These studies illustrate very clearly a number of the difficult theoretical and practical issues in cost–benefit analysis that have been identified in earlier sections of this chapter.

9.41   *The Victoria Line Study*

The Victoria Line (VL) extends the London underground system by providing a north–south connection between Walthamstow and Victoria stations. At the date of commencement, total construction costs were estimated to be £48·1 million at 1962 prices. A cost–benefit investment appraisal was deemed appropriate for three reasons. First, the prices charged by London Transport on the underground system do not take externalities into account. The benefits to other users and to the suppliers of interrelated transport facilities would not therefore be adequately integrated into a purely private financial calculation. Second, underground prices are administered, not market, prices and thus may not accurately reflect either marginal costs or marginal benefits. Third, a complete new underground line represents a non-marginal output change. To measure the benefits to users adequately, therefore, requires an analysis of consumer surplus changes.

An outline of the results of the VL cost–benefit study is shown in Table 9.2. The methodology employed to obtain these figures is best understood from a brief examination of some of the items in the table.

The 11·3 per cent present-value rate of return shown in the table is an average rate-of-return figure. It is derived by estimating the net present values of all benefits minus operating costs using a discount rate of 6 per cent, then calculating the rate of return as the yearly sum of money (expressed as an interest rate) that over the life of the capital would increase the present value of the capital costs to equal the present value of the net benefits. Alternative discount rates were used, but neither a 4 per cent rate nor an 8 per cent rate produced significantly different present values. The calculations contain no explicit analysis of uncertainty in the estimation of individual costs and benefits, the figures shown being the authors' estimates of the most probable outcomes.

Table 9.2 *The Costs and Benefits of the Proposed Victoria Line*

	Amount (£m)		Net present value (£m)
Costs			
Capital	48·1		38·81
Operating costs	1·4	per annum	16·16
Benefits			
Diverted traffic	2·06	per annum	29·34
Non-diverted traffic	3·92	per annum	44·79
Generated traffic	0·82		11·74
Scrap value			0·29
Net present value of benefits and costs			31·19
Social rate of return			11·3%

Notes: The calculations assume a 5½-year construction period, a discount rate of 6 per cent, and a 50-year life for the capital. Various assumptions are also made concerning the trend rate of increase in the stream of benefits. For these and other details see C. D. Foster and M. E. Beesley, 'Estimating the social benefit of constructing an underground railway in London', *Journal of the Royal Statistical Society*, vol. 126 (1963).

On the costs side the data used was supplied by London Transport. The authors assumed a 50-year life for the capital. Given that the life of the capital covers a very long time span of this order, even if the actual life turned out to be somewhat shorter the results of the study would hardly be affected, since even large changes in the costs and benefits of such futurity would have a very small effect on the present value calculations.

The benefits are categorised under three main headings: the benefits to users who are expected to switch to the Victoria Line from other transport modes, including those switching from other underground lines (diverted traffic); the benefits to users of the network who do not switch to the Victoria Line (non-diverted traffic); and the benefits from additional use of the London Transport network (generated traffic).

The benefits to diverted traffic come in three forms: savings in time, increased comfort and convenience, and lower resource costs to suppliers. Estimates were made of the number of journeys by each of the existing modes between broad zones of the London area along the proposed route of the Victoria Line. The time taken to do each of these journeys was calculated and compared with the time taken if the Victoria Line were used. For all journeys where the time taken was less, passengers were assumed to switch to the new line. Where the time taken was the same, 50 per cent of passengers were assumed to switch to the new line. The number of journeys times the savings then gave a measure of the total time saved for each form of diverted traffic. Throughout the study an arbitrary measure of the value of time to travellers was used. The figures chosen were 25p per hour for leisure time and 36p per hour for working time. The proportion of leisure to work time was derived from existing survey material gathered by London Transport.

Increased comfort and convenience were measured by estimating and valuing the increased probability of finding an empty seat. Data on the ratio of sitting to standing passengers on existing routes along the Victoria Line were compared with the ratio predicted for passengers on the new line. The value of the benefits was measured by converting the increased probability of finding a seat into a time measure. Consumers' preferences in this respect were derived by estimating the additional journey times that users appeared prepared to accept in order to increase their seat probabilities by given amounts. The increased seat probability on the new line was then converted to a specific time measure and costed at the time rates referred to above.

Savings in resource costs for the suppliers of transport services were assumed to occur only when users switched from motor cars to the new line. Estimates were made of the car milage saved by diverted road users and the running costs of car use per mile. Otherwise it was assumed that resources released from other modes of transport after the opening of the Victoria Line would simply be used up in supplying the new service.

When traffic is diverted on to the Victoria Line, continuing users of alternative services benefit from reduced congestion in the form of time savings and increased comfort, and the suppliers of these services will save on resource costs. As can be seen from Table 9.3, the main benefit to non-diverted traffic is again in the form of time

Table 9.3 *The Benefits of the Proposed Victoria Line*

	Source of benefit	Form of benefit	Net present value (£m)
Diverted traffic			
from	(a) Other underground services	Time savings	4·32
		Increased comfort and convenience	3·96
	(b) British Rail services	Time savings	2·93
	(c) Buses	Time savings	6·58
	(d) Motor cars	Time savings	3·25
		Reduced vehicle-operating costs	8·02
	(e) Pedestrians	Time savings	0·28
			29·34
Non-diverted traffic			
users of	(a) Underground services	Cost savings	1·72
		Comfort and convenience	5·22
	(b) Buses	Cost savings	7·38
	(c) Road users	Time savings	21·54
		Reduced vehicle-operating costs	8·93
			44·79
Generated traffic			
	For central and outer London	Time savings	2·17
		Fare savings	1·31
		Other benefits	3·26
			11·74

Source: As for Table 9.2

savings. The VL study argued that time savings would be significant for undiverted traffic only in the case of road users. Estimating the savings to road users was done in three stages. First, estimates were made of the total annual mileage in the London area and the constitution of the traffic by vehicle type. Second, the number of journey miles likely to be diverted to the new line was subtracted, and the resulting measure was converted into an increase in vehicle speeds via established flow/speed tables and into time savings via established speed/journey time tables. Third, these speed increases and time savings were converted into money values using the predetermined time valuation and data on vehicle-operating costs.

The benefits to generated traffic were calculated by means of regression estimates using an equation relating the number of people travelling to the centre of London to work from each of a number of inner and outer borough zones, to the population of those zones, to social class (income), and to the time taken by existing modes to reach the centre. The time saved by using the Victoria Line when entered into this equation gave a measure of the increase in the number of travellers to be expected from each zone and therefore of the increase in total journey miles per year. The benefits to generated traffic can be represented by area ABC in Figure 9.5.

Figure 9.5

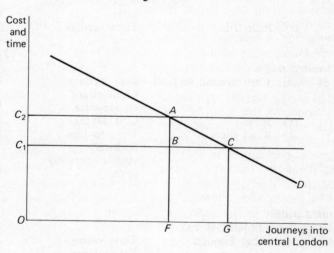

Journeys into central London

The demand curve here is a measure of the value of the journeys to central London to each individual. The marginal journey, F, will not be undertaken with costs at C_2. Nor will journey G. However, if costs fall to C_1 because of a reduction in journey times and/or costs, both journeys F and G will be undertaken. Costs are reduced in the sense that they are now lower than they would have been had the journeys been undertaken initially. Net benefits have increased from zero on journey F and from a negative figure on G. Savings, in this sense, are available. Clearly, however, the savings for journey F are greater than for G. We must in fact measure the benefit to generated traffic as the area of triangle ABC, that is $\frac{1}{2}$(the value of cost and time savings $\times$ the number of generated journeys). The total increase in journey miles estimated from the regression analysis was therefore multiplied by the average time savings per journey and by one-half the value of time used in the study.

There are several points in the VL study that are worth thinking about in the light of the analysis in earlier parts of this chapter.

First, because several important items in the calculation are very difficult to specify precisely, sensitivity analysis is invariably a useful part of any cost–benefit exercise. In the VL study the value of time used is introduced very arbitrarily. Clearly, more work in this area needs to be done. In the meantime, however, 'guesstimates' have to be made, and it pays to consider the implications of using different time valuations. Alternative values of leisure time of 15p and 50p (and corresponding values for work time) produced net present values of £13 million and £76 million respectively. As indicated earlier, sensitivity analysis was also used for the discount rate. There is a strong case for extending this approach to other difficult estimates, and for deriving final rates of return with different combinations of assumptions about the critical items.

Second, and again on the point of valuing time, it is apparent that time savings are a central element of the VL study. Benefits in time savings amount to something like 60 per cent of all benefits to diverted traffic and 50 per cent of all benefits to undiverted traffic. This emphasises the importance of the choice of the time valuation and the usefulness of sensitivity analysis. There are also question marks to be set against the likelihood of realising significant time savings. For instance, in relation to the benefits to non-diverted traffic, it may be that any gaps left by diverted traffic will be filled almost immediately by generated traffic, which is drawn on to the roads by the smallest increase in speeds. As a result, higher speeds will prevail only in the short run. The benefits to generated traffic will be realised, but the size of the benefit in time and cost savings to both generated and undiverted traffic will be small. There is also the more fundamental problem of the legitimacy of multiplying small individual time savings by the number of road users in order to arrive at an aggregate time saving. Any serious doubt about this aspect of cost–benefit analysis in the transport sector inevitably reduces our confidence in the results of investment appraisal.

Third, the demand predictions necessary to reach the final rate-of-return figures must be regarded as tentative, especially those for road use. Fourth, Table 9.3 makes no allowance for shadow prices. It is assumed that the present structure of relative prices in the transport sector will continue through the life of the capital. With important investments like the Victoria Line we should like to know what implications for the final rate of return follow if the prices of alternative transport modes reflected their full social costs. The VL study did in fact include estimates of the present value of the investment on the assumption that road prices reflecting congestion costs were introduced. These revealed that even moderate charges sufficient to push road speeds up from 10 to 13 mph would significantly improve the return on the Victoria Line. Fifth, the figures in Table 9.3 assume that the opening of the Victoria Line has no implications for transport prices. Clearly this is not appropriate if the new line makes losses. The way in which such losses are financed has to be taken into account, because if prices are increased this will no doubt influence the choice of transport mode. The VL study included estimates of the implications of three pricing strategies for the final return on the new line. With a general price increase across all London Transport services, 40–60 per cent of the net benefits would be lost. With a peak/off-peak differential, 10 per cent of the net benefits would be lost. With a differential on the Victoria Line to cover the losses 14–17 per cent of the net benefits would be lost. On the other hand, if road pricing were introduced, diverted traffic would produce more than enough extra revenue to cover all costs without necessitating price alterations inside London Transport.

Finally it should be noted that the VL study was conducted only after the project had been given government approval. It also only considered the VL proposal in isolation. There was no comparison of alternative forms of the underground extension, and no comparison with other possible investment projects to improve the London Transport system.

9.42   *The Third London Airport Study*
In 1970 a cost–benefit study was undertaken for the Roskill Commission, which was inquiring into the choice of site for the proposed third London airport (TLA). The study involved a detailed analysis of four alternative sites: Cublington, Thurleigh, Nuthampstead and Foulness. The benefits of siting the airport in each of the four locations were assumed to be the same. The question posed, therefore, was simply which of the four sites involved the lowest social costs. A cost–benefit approach was deemed to be the appropriate instrument for investment appraisal in this case, because some of the most controversial costs came into the category of externalities

both to the airlines and to the airport authorities and would therefore not enter into any financial calculation. Furthermore, the costs
to the users of the four sites would not be fully revealed using
observed prices as indicators, because this would ignore surplus
values.

Table 9.4 sets out the main findings of the airport study. Airspace
movement costs are the costs borne by the airlines in flying from
their point of entry to the London airspace to each of the four
proposed sites. Passenger user costs are the costs borne by air
travellers in getting from each of the four sites to their final desti-
nations. Other costs are primarily the capital costs of constructing
the airport. Noise costs measure the welfare losses due to noise
pollution suffered by residents in the neighbourhood of the proposed
sites.

Table 9.4   *The Cost and Benefits of the Proposed Third London Airport*

	Cublington (£m)	Foulness (£m)	Nuthamp-stead (£m)	Thurleigh (£m)
Airspace movement costs	1 685–1 899	1 690–1 906	1 716–1 934	1 711–1 929
Passenger user costs	1 743–2 883	1 910–3 090	1 778–2 924	1 765–2 922
Other costs, including capital costs	614–638	612–625	626–639	641–653
Noise costs	23	10	72	16
Total costs	4 065–5 433	4 222–5 631	4 192–5 569	4 133–5 520

Notes: All money values are in 1968 prices. The figures shown are present
values discounted to 1982 (the year of opening) using a discount rate
of 10 per cent. The range of figures reflects the high and low valuations for travelling time used in the study. For further details see
Commission on the Third London Airport, *Papers and Proceedings*,
vol. 2 (London: HMSO, 1970), pts 1 and 2.

The results show that Cublington emerges as the site imposing
the least social costs. The most satisfactory way to understand the
methodology employed is again to examine each of the items in the
summary table in turn.

The figures for airspace movement costs and passenger user costs
were arrived at by estimating these costs per passenger and multiplying them by a prediction of total passenger demand. Costs per
passenger were derived from surveys of the origin and destination of
passengers using the then available London airports, namely
Heathrow and Gatwick. The country was divided into geographical

zones, and the number of journeys from each zone was derived along with the distance travelled. Information on the distance of each of the four sites from each zone made it possible to predict the number of travellers likely to be diverted to a new airport and the distance saved. This information, together with data on aircraft, transport and time costs, was used to estimate the airspace movement costs and passenger user costs for different groups of passenger for each of the four TLA sites.

A prediction of the number of passengers likely to use each of the proposed sites over the planning period was derived in two stages: first an estimate was made of the likely growth in total passenger demand for the London airport network, including each of the four new airports in turn; then an estimate was made of the share of the calculated growth in demand that would go to the new airport.

A separate estimate of the growth in total demand for each of the possible future London airport networks was deemed necessary, because it was felt that the choice of the TLA site would itself influence demand, given that accessibility is a very relevant consideration for would-be passengers. Initially a growth factor was calculated on the basis of past experiences with existing facilities. This was then adjusted for the addition of each of the proposed TLA sites. The growth factor was calculated separately for each type of demand: working passengers, leisure passengers and cargo transport. A thirty-year planning horizon was used in each case. The growth factors were derived by relating travel propensities to the income of heads of households. Average air-travel propensities for passengers were measured for various groups of existing users defined in terms of income, these propensities being assumed to grow at the same rate as they had in the past. The number of people in each group through the thirty-year period was estimated on the basis of population growth figures extrapolated from past trends and on an assumption of a 3 per cent growth in real incomes. The total growth factor so derived was then adjusted to take account of the addition of each of the alternative TLA sites. This was done by employing a statistical analysis of the relationship between current passenger journeys and the cost of getting to existing airports from various parts of the country, so as to derive a quantitative relationship between demand and accessibility. This was then used to find the increase in demand that was likely to arise when the accessibility of the London airport network was improved by the addition of any one of the proposed airports.

The allocation of total demand between each airport was estimated with the use of a gravity model. The model related the current demand for each of the available airports from each zone of the country to the cost of getting to those airports, allowing for the choice of transport mode available and the possibility of full capacity use of the airports at certain times. Applying the cost figures for travel from each zone to each of the proposed TLA sites gave a prediction of the journeys likely to be undertaken, and from this the total demand for each of the proposed airports was calculated.

The estimates of passenger demand together with airline flight data enabled total airspace movement costs to be calculated. Passenger user costs include both transport and time costs, and were calculated separately for traffic generated by the new airport and for traffic diverted from existing airports. These calculations are too complicated to be easily summarised, and the interested reader is referred to the TLA study. However, something should be said about the estimation of time costs.

The value of time costs used in the TLA study was based on the principles set out earlier in this chapter. The average income of business people using existing facilities was found to be £3 100. To this was added a 50 per cent margin, to capture the capital under-utilisation that went with lost work time, giving an hourly cost figure for business time of £2·31. This was assumed to increase at a rate of 3·2 per cent per annum in real terms with increased productivity. Leisure time was measured at 25 per cent of business time, following the example of a number of other studies in the transport field. This gave an hourly time-cost figure of 55p, since the average income of leisure air travellers was found to be £1 820 per annum. The ratio of leisure costs to business costs was assumed to stay constant over the planning period.

In any cost–benefit study on an airport located near residential areas one would expect an analysis of noise costs to assume some importance. There are three types of people in a polluted area for whom noise costs have to be calculated: those who move away from the area as a direct consequence of the pollution, those who move away in the natural course of events, and those who stay where they are. The numbers of people involved in the TLA investigation were estimated very approximately from population figures in the zones close to the proposed sites with noise levels above an arbitrarily chosen level. The number of voluntary movers was calculated from known migration figures – about 4 per cent per annum. The number of people who would be forced to move includes those whose houses would have to be purchased for the building of the airport and those who would be pushed out because of noise. The number in the latter group was estimated as part of the calculation of noise costs.

The costs of noise to those who move in the natural course of events was assumed to be measured by the depreciation of their houses when they came to sell them. As described earlier in this chapter, this can be calculated by comparing the prices of houses in the polluted zones with those of similar houses in quiet areas. The airport study estimated the value of houses in each of the sites proposed for the new airport using a linear relationship between ratable values and prices calculated from observable data outside the polluted zones. A depreciation figure for house prices at different noise levels was then obtained from the advice of estate agents and valuers operating around Gatwick Airport. These depreciation rates were applied to the housing stock surrounding each of the proposed sites, allowing for noise levels and housing quality. The airport study assumed that all those suffering a higher-than-average depreciation in house prices (allowing for surplus loss and movement costs) would be people suffering a higher-than-median level of annoyance, and that they would therefore be likely to move.

For those not moving, noise costs were assumed to be measured by the depreciation rate of the group at the median level of annoyance. The costs to those who would be forced to move was measured by their depreciation loss plus the costs of movement and foregone surplus. The latter was derived from questionnaires, which asked house owners what level of compensation they would require on top of the sale price to give up their houses for a redevelopment programme without any loss of welfare. The answers produced an average surplus figure of 52 per cent of the sale price.

The TLA cost–benefit study was a very thorough and detailed piece of analysis, as befits a project that cost £1 million. Nevertheless it is possible to identify a number of methodological weaknesses in the study. First, to justify the cost minimisation approach it is necessary to demonstrate that all benefits are equal across the four sites. The TLA study simply assumed this to be the case. Second, with present techniques, making passenger predictions is a notoriously hazardous exercise. The extrapolation of past demand trends, the use of gravity models, and highly simplified accessibility indices do not constitute the tools necessary for accurate long-term predictions. Gravity models are too naive a view of the choice between different transport modes to predict the demand for a third London airport.

Third, valuations of time need to take into account the possibility that some work is actually undertaken in travelling time, that people substitute leisure time in flight for work time and work time for leisure time afterwards, and that some travel for leisure purposes actually gives significant benefits. Fourth, the questionnaire method of eliciting consumer surplus values is very unreliable, because, for one thing, the answers obtained depend very much upon the form of the question asked. The question asked in the TLA inquiry was as follows: 'Suppose that your house was wanted to form part of a large development scheme and the developer offered to buy it from you, what price would be just high enough to compensate you for leaving this house (flat) and moving to another area?' This question does not perhaps make it entirely clear that, in some cases at least, householders might have to move away from the area completely, with all the consequences in terms of changing jobs and schools and losing close contact with old friends. There is also the problem of ensuring that a householder's valuation should not be influenced by resignation to events and of convincing him that he does have a genuine chance of fair treatment. Then there is the problem of deciding on what constitutes a reasonable compensation for those householders who say that they would not be prepared to move at any price. The TLA inquiry settled on the arbitrary figure of £5 000. Fifth, and again on the noise issue, it is worth noting that any method of estimating noise costs using as a basis some comparison of noisy and quiet areas is likely to lead to an underestimate of the costs incurred. As noise levels increase all round it becomes increasingly difficult for individuals to attach a value to peace and quiet simply because it no longer appears in everyday life. As a result, over time one is likely to observe the paradox of steadily increasing noise levels and decreasing noise costs using accepted methods of calculation. All in all, the costs attributed to noise in the airport study seem remarkably low.

In addition to these specific points arising from the calculations in the TLA study there are more general issues worth pointing out. First, the study was intended as a basis for choice between alternative investment activities, that is, different TLA sites. The prior question that should have been asked was whether any third London airport is necessary. However, this was outside the terms of the reference of the inquiry. Second, it is not clear from the study how the important question of compensation was to be handled. Should, for instance, compensation be paid out of higher air fares or out of increased income tax? Considerations of equity are involved in deciding the method of compensation, but if air fares are increased this will affect demand and therefore the results of the cost–benefit study. This raises once again the crucial issue of what prices are to be assumed in any cost–benefit exercise, both for the activity in question and for the available substitute and complement activities. Should shadow prices be used reflecting the full social cost of the activity as economic theory would suggest? The answer is likely to be yes in any circumstance where price restructuring is a possibility in the future. Finally the airport study considered, but attached little importance to, the possible changes in the pattern of overall transport facilities in the planning period.

Clearly, however, changes in consumer tastes and, probably more important, changes in technology will have a significant impact on the outcome of any cost–benefit study. Anticipating these changes and predicting their impact is of course a most difficult task, but a necessary one nevertheless.

9.5   CONCLUSION

It should be clear from our discussion that cost–benefit analysis is not an exact science. It is as well to emphasise this, because reference to the technique of cost–benefit analysis may easily give a false impression of scientific precision. Politicians are also apt to brush aside awkward questions on items of public expenditure by reference to the fact that a cost–benefit study is to be undertaken and to give the impression very often that such a study has an exactness that it does not possess. In fact, as we have seen, a great deal of judgement is required in cost–benefit analysis – in deciding on the costs and benefits to be included and in the valuation of these items; in deciding on whether to use shadow rather than market prices; in the valuation of untraded items; in the treatment of uncertainty; and in the choice of discount rate. Cost–benefit analysis is the best tool we have for investment appraisal in the public sector, but it is important that it be used with care.

References

K. J. Arrow, *Social Choice and Individual Values*, 2nd edn (New York: Wiley, 1963).

A. B. Atkinson, *The Economics of Inequality* (London: Oxford University Press, 1975).

Lord Beveridge, *Social Insurance and Allied Services* (London: HMSO, 1942).

E. H. Chamberlin, *The Theory of Monopolistic Competition* (Cambridge, Mass.: Harvard University Press, 1933).

Commission on the Third London Airport, *Papers and Proceedings,* vol. 2 (London: HMSO, 1970), pts 1 and 2.

J. Downie, *The Competitive Process* (London: G. Duckworth & Co., 1958).

C. D. Foster and M. E. Beesley, 'Estimating the social benefit of constructing an underground railway in London', *Journal of the Royal Statistical Society*, vol. 126 (1963).

A. Harberger, 'Monopoly and resource allocation', *American Economic Review*, vol. 44 (May 1954).

C. D. Harbury and P. A. McMahon, 'Inheritance and the characteristics of top wealth leavers in Britain', *Economic Journal*, vol. 83 (1973).

C. D. Harbury and D. M. Hitchens, 'The inheritance of top wealth leavers', *Economic Journal*, vol. 86 (June 1976).

J. R. Hicks, 'The foundations of welfare economics', *Economic Journal*, vol. 48 (December 1939).

J. R. Hicks, 'The four consumers' surpluses', *Review of Economic Studies*, vol. 54 (1944).

N. Kaldor, 'Welfare propositions of economics and interpersonal comparisons of utility', *Economic Journal*, vol. 48 (September 1939).

H. Leibenstein, 'Allocative efficiency *v.* "X" efficiency', *American Economic Review*, vol. 56 (1966).

A. H. Marshall, *Principles of Economics*, 3rd edn (London: Macmillan, 1920).

K. Marx and F. Engels, *The Communist Manifesto*, English edn (London: William Reeves, 1888).

J. E. Meade, *The Theory of Economic Externalities* (Leiden: A. W. Sijthoff, 1973).

OECD, *Income Distribution in OECD Countries*, Occasional Paper (July 1976).

G. B. Richardson, 'The pricing of heavy electrical equipment: competition or agreement?', *Bulletin of the Oxford Institute of Statistics*, vol. 28 (1966).

Joan Robinson, *The Accumulation of Capital* (London: Macmillan, 1956).

Royal Commission on the Distribution of Income and Wealth, *Report No. 4* (London: HMSO, October 1976).

T. Scitovsky, 'A note on welfare propositions in economics', *Review of Economic Studies*, vol. 9 (November 1941).

T. Scitovsky, *Welfare and Competition*, revised by Richard D. Irwin (London: Allen & Unwin, 1971).

A. Silberston, 'Economies of scale in theory and practice', *Economic Journal*, Supplement (March 1972).

A. Smith, *An Inquiry into the Nature and Causes of the Wealth of Nations*, Cannon edn (London: Methuen, 1961).

O. E. Williamson, 'Economies as an anti-trust defense', *American Economic Review*, vol. 58 (March 1968).

Further Reading

CHAPTERS 2 AND 3: THE THEORY OF WELFARE ECONOMICS

F. M. Bator, 'The simple analytics of welfare maximisation', *American Economic Review*, vol. 57 (March 1957); reprinted in W. Breit and H. M. Hochman (eds), *Readings in Microeconomics* (London: Holt, Reinhart & Winston, 1969).

W. J. Baumol, *Welfare Economics and the Theory of the State* (London: Bell, 1965).

W. J. Baumol, *Economic Theory and Operations Analysis* (Englewood Cliffs, NJ: Prentice-Hall, 1967).

E. J. Mishan, 'A survey of welfare economics', *Economic Journal*, vol. 70 (June 1960); reprinted in Royal Economic Society, *Surveys of Economic Theory*, vol. 1 (London: Macmillan, 1965).

S. K. Nath, *A Reappraisal of Welfare Economics* (London: Routledge & Kegan Paul, 1969).

CHAPTER 4: THE DISTRIBUTION OF INCOME AND WEALTH

A. B. Atkinson, *The Economics of Inequality* (London: Oxford University Press, 1975).

J. C. Kincaid, *Poverty and Equality in Britain* (London: Penguin, 1975).

J. E. Meade, *The Intelligent Radical's Guide to Economic Policy* (London: Allen & Unwin, 1975).

Royal Commission on the Distribution of Income and Wealth, *Report Nos 1–4* (London: HMSO, 1975 and 1976).

CHAPTER 5: PUBLIC UTILITY PRICING AND INVESTMENT

R. L. Meek, 'An application of marginal cost pricing: the green tariff in theory and practice', *Journal of Industrial Economics*, vols 11 and 12 (July and November 1963).

R. Millward, *Public Expenditure Economics* (London: McGraw-Hill, 1971).

E. J. Mishan, 'Second thoughts on second best', *Oxford Economic Papers*, vol. 14 (October 1962).

R. Rees, *Public Enterprise Economics* (London: Weidenfeld & Nicolson, 1976).

R. Turvey, 'Marginal cost pricing in practice', *Economica*, vol. 31 (November 1964).

M. Webb, *The Economics of Nationalised Industries* (London: Nelson, 1973).

O. E. Williamson, 'Peak load pricing and optimal capacity under indivisibility constraints', *American Economic Review*, vol. 56 (September 1966).

CHAPTER 6: FACTOR INDIVISIBILITIES, SIZE AND EFFICIENCY
IN THE PRIVATE SECTOR

P. Doyle, 'Economic aspects of advertising: a survey', *Economic Journal*,
vol. 78 (September 1968).

J. H. Dunning (ed.), *Economic Analysis and the Multinational Enterprise*
(London: Allen & Unwin, 1974).

K. D. George and C. Joll (eds), *Competition Policy in the UK and EEC*
(Cambridge: Cambridge University Press, 1975).

K. D. George, 'Big business, competition and the state', in G. Yarrow
(ed.), *Industrial Policy and Economic Performance in the UK* (Farn-
borough: Teakfield, Saxon House Series, 1977).

S. J. Prais, *The Evolution of Giant Firms in Britain* (Cambridge: Cambridge University Press, 1976).

G. B. Richardson, 'The pricing of heavy electrical equipment: competition or agreement?', *Bulletin of the Oxford Institute of Statistics*, vol.
28 (1966).

F. M. Scherer, *Industrial Pricing: Theory and Evidence* (Chicago: Rand
McNally, 1970).

Z. A. Silberston, 'Economies of scale in theory and practice', *Economic
Journal Supplement* (March 1972).

CHAPTER 7: PROBLEMS OF ADJUSTMENT

J. Downie, *The Competitive Process* (London: G. Duckworth & Co.,
1958).

K. D. George and Z. A. Silberston, 'The causes and effects of mergers',
Scottish Journal of Political Economy, vol. 42 (June 1975).

H. G. Johnson and J. E. Nash, 'UK and floating exchanges', IEA Hobart
Paper No. 46 (1969).

N. Kaldor, 'The case for regional policies', *Scottish Journal of Political
Economy*, vol. 17 (November 1970).

M. I. Kamien and N. L. Schwartz, 'Market structure and innovation',
Journal of Economic Literature, vol. 13 (March 1975).

G. McCrone, *Regional Policy in Britain* (London: Allen & Unwin, 1969).

G. B. Richardson, *Information and Investment* (London: Oxford University Press, 1960).

W. E. G. Salter, *Productivity and Technical Change*, 2nd edn (Cambridge:
Cambridge University Press, 1966).

A. Singh, 'Take-overs, "natural selection" and the theory of the firm',
Economic Journal, vol. 85 (September 1975).

O. E. Williamson, 'Economies as an anti-trust defense', *American Economic Review*, vol. 58 (March 1968).

CHAPTER 8: EXTERNALITIES AND PUBLIC GOODS

F. M. Bator, 'Anatomy of market failure', *Quarterly Journal of Economics*, vol. 47 (1958); reprinted in W. Breit and H. M. Hochman (eds),
Readings in Microeconomics (London: Holt, Reinhart & Winston,
1969).

W. J. Baumol and W. E. Oates, 'The use of standards and prices for the protection of the environment', in P. Bohm and V. Kneese (eds), *The Economics of the Environment* (London: Macmillan, 1971).

R. M. Coase, 'The problem of social cost', *Journal of Law and Economics*, vol. 3 (1960).

J. G. Head, 'Public goods and public policy', *Public Finance*, No. 4 (1962).

J. E. Meade, *The Theory of Economic Externalities* (Leiden: A. W. Sijthoff, 1973).

Ministry of Transport, *Road Pricing: The Economic and Technical Possibilities* (London: HMSO, 1964).

R. Turvey, 'On divergencies between social cost and private cost', *Economica*, vol. 30 (August 1963).

CHAPTER 9: COST–BENEFIT ANALYSIS

M. S. Feldstein, 'The social time preference discount rate in cost benefit analysis', *Economic Journal*, vol. 74 (1964).

J. Hirshleifer, 'On the theory of the optimal investment decision', *Journal of Political Economy*, vol. 66 (1958).

R. Layard (ed.), *Cost Benefit Analysis* (London: Penguin, 1972).

R. N. McKean, 'The use of shadow prices', in S. B. Chase (ed.), *Problems in Public Expenditure Analysis* (Washington DC: Brookings Institution, 1968).

A. J. Merrett and A. Sykes, *The Finance and Analysis of Investment Projects* (London: Longmans, Green, 1967).

E. J. Mishan, *Cost Benefit Analysis*, 2nd edn (London: Allen & Unwin, 1975).

Index